SPIRIT
OF THE LIVING GOD

What the Bible Says
About the Spirit

by
DALE MOODY

BROADMAN PRESS
Nashville, Tennessee

Dewey Decimal Classification: 231.3
Subject Heading: HOLY SPIRIT

Library of Congress Catalog Card Number: 76-29147
Printed in the United States of America

TO
MY STUDENTS
PAST   PRESENT   FUTURE

You show that you are a letter from Christ
    delivered by us,
written not with ink
    but with the Spirit of the living God,
not on tablets of stone
    but on tablets of human hearts.

                                    (II Cor. 3:3.)

CONTENTS

PREFACE   9

1. THE SPIRIT OF THE LORD IN THE OLD TESTAMENT   11

   The Ecstatic Spirit (Primitive)   14
   The Messianic Spirit (Prophetic)   19
   The Creator Spirit (Postexilic)   27

2. THE DESCENT OF THE DOVE IN THE SYNOPTIC GOSPELS   33

   The Strong Man's House (Mark)   34
   God with Us (Matthew)   42
   The Power of the Most High (Luke)   49

3. THE GIFT OF THE HOLY SPIRIT IN ACTS   58

   "Witnesses in Jerusalem" (Acts 1:1 to 6:7)   59
   "And in All Judea and Samaria"
      (Acts 6:8 to 12:24)   69
   "And to the End of the Earth"
      (Acts 12:25 to 28:31)   74

4. THE SPIRIT OF LIFE IN EARLY PAULINE WRITINGS (I)   82

   The Holy Spirit and Proclamation
      (I, II Thessalonians)   82
   The Holy Spirit and Edification
      (I, II Corinthians)   87

5. THE SPIRIT OF LIFE
   IN EARLY PAULINE WRITINGS (II)   107

   The Holy Spirit and Justification (Galatians)   108
   The Holy Spirit and Salvation (Romans)   116

6. THE SPIRIT OF UNITY
   IN THE LATER PAULINE WRITINGS   128

   Introduction (Philippians, Colossians)   129
   The Holy Spirit and Recapitulation (Ephesians)   131
   The Holy Spirit and Organization
      (Pastoral Letters)   139

7. THE SPIRIT OF TRUTH
   IN THE JOHANNINE GOSPEL AND FIRST LETTER   150

   The Spirit (John, Chs. 1 to 7)   150
   The Paraclete (John, Chs. 14 to 16; 20)   164
   The *Koinōnia* (First John)   175

8. THE SPIRIT OF CHRIST
   IN OTHER NEW TESTAMENT WRITINGS   182

   The Spirit of Wisdom (James)   182
   The Spirit of Grace (Hebrews)   185
   The Spirit of Glory (I, II Peter, Jude)   192
   The Spirit of Prophecy (Revelation)   200

NOTES   209

INDEX OF SCRIPTURE REFERENCES   223

INDEX OF NAMES   235

INDEX OF SUBJECTS   239

PREFACE

RECENT DISCUSSIONS on the reality of the living God raise the question of God's action and presence in a new way, and this often precipitates debate on the meaning of the Holy Spirit. Any approach to this question sooner or later must get around to the Biblical concepts understood in their context. That is the purpose behind these pages. The result has been a theology of the Holy Spirit, for many of the major concerns of Biblical thought are vitally related to this concept.

As far as I am aware, no recent effort has been made to interpret the Biblical concepts in their historical and literary context. This was done in English by H. B. Swete in 1909 and in German by Friedrich Büchsel in 1926, but the situation in New Testament studies has changed at many points since these valuable volumes.

This modest survey is not so detailed as either Swete or Büchsel, but this is not necessary in the light of the many monographs on separate items now available. Footnotes have usually been limited to those writings which are of most value for further study, but there are exceptions. Special mention should be made of the article by Eduard Schweizer and others in Kittel's *Theological Dictionary of the New Testament*, but there are points where I depart from their conclusions.

The work is dedicated to my students. Over a period of years I have offered lectures on the subject, but recent interest in the so-called charismatic revival has prompted their pub-

9

lication. I have tried to avoid extremes in both directions at this point, but I'm sure my sympathies are more with those who long for renewal and a deeper awareness of the living God in daily life. Careful scholarship and the charismatic community can be united, and this is a great need of our time.

I must again thank Dr. and Mrs. E. Glenn Hinson for transforming my chaotic original into a typed copy. Several other colleagues and students have read parts of the manuscript. Dr. Wayne E. Oates read all of the manuscript. Dr. J. J. Owens read the Old Testament part, and Dr. James Blevins read all of the New Testament material. James R. Bruton, William G. MacDonald, Salvador T. Martinez, and Manfred Grellert, all graduate students in Southern Seminary, with different backgrounds, have read the whole manuscript and given me help in many other ways. To all of them I am grateful. Martinez, as usual, has gone the second mile by reading the final copy and making the indexes.

D. M.

Preface to the Second Edition

Since 1968 when the first edition of this study was published there has been an increase of interest in the subject. Many books have been written on some of the topics, but none covers all the passages of the Bible as this book attempts to do. Some of the books of special value have been mentioned, but all changes in substance are the results of my own reflection.

DALE MOODY

August 12, 1975

1

THE SPIRIT OF THE LORD
IN THE OLD TESTAMENT

BREATH and WIND belong to the most basic metaphors for that awareness of Presence which Biblical thought came to call the Spirit of God or the Holy Spirit. Both metaphors are abundantly illustrated in the Old Testament, and it is to this source that one turns for the first reflections on this mysterious power which gives life and unity to all.

Neshamah, the usual word for "breath" in the Old Testament, expresses life in both God and man, and it is not easy to know which comes first. Man seems to be aware of the living God from the time he is aware of his own life. This may be disputed in this secular age, but Biblical faith thinks always of man in relation to God. Awareness of God and awareness of man are born as twins.

The *neshamah* of the living God is described in both creative and destructive terms. The Paradise story, one of the oldest sources in Hebrew faith, accounts for the origin of man by the breath of God (Gen. 2:7 JE):

The LORD God formed man of dust from the ground,
    and breathed into his nostrils the breath of life;
        and man became a living soul. (Cf. Job 27:3; 33:4.)

God's creative activity unites dust and breath to bring into being the living soul that man is. Dust plus breath in relation to God is man. The living soul is the whole man in all his relations.

The *neshamah* of living creatures is found also in the Para-

11

dise story. English translations often obscure the fact that animals are also said to be created by the living God as living souls.

> So out of the ground the LORD God formed every beast of the field and every bird of the air, and brought them to the man to see what he would call them; and whatever the man called every living soul [*nephesh hayyah*], that was its name. (Gen. 2:19 JE)

Unless one resorts to the claim that this verse is an interpolation from a later time, the Paradise story attributes the living souls of both man and animals to the *neshamah* of God. The *neshamah* of animals is implied from the *nephesh hayyah*.

The Flood story also describes "the breath of life" of all living things as that which gives them their historical existence. (Gen. 7:22 J.) God gives them breath, and they are alive; God takes away their breath, and they are dead. Giving breath is creative; taking breath is destructive.

Destructive *neshamah* expresses the wrath of God. It is God's judgment on man in action. In two places it is described as follows (II Sam. 22:16; Ps. 18:15):

> The channels of the sea were seen,
>   the foundations of the world were laid bare,
>   at the rebuke of the LORD,
>   at the blast of the breath of his nostrils.

An oracle against Assyria sees the breath of God as "a stream of brimstone" that kindles a fire (Isa. 30:33). The Old Testament does not seem to depart from this picture of God's breath as both creative and destructive, as redemption and judgment.

Ruach ("wind" or "spirit") is the more usual way to represent God's presence among men and in his creation as a whole. The Paradise story again is a rich source. God's presence is represented as a voice (*qol*) heard or resounding in the cool breeze (*leruach*) at the end of the day. The refreshing wind blowing into the land from the sea, as the hot desert wind recedes at the close of day, illustrates man's awareness

12

of that spiritual environment which penetrates as a Presence into man's physical environment.

At a later time the "still small voice" is separated from the violence of wind, fire, and earthquake (I Kings 19:11 f.), but the Paradise story has it related to the gentle breeze. This metaphor is not discarded in John's Gospel, "the spiritual Gospel," for the dialogue of Jesus with Nicodemus employs it (John 3:8). Indeed, John's Gospel also retains the metaphor of breath (ch. 20:22), so dismissal of the picture as primitive thinking is difficult to justify.

Ruach is Hebrew language for the Presence proclaimed by the highest poetic and philosophical mysticism. William Wordsworth wrote while not far from Tintern Abbey:

> And I have felt
> A presence that disturbs me with the joy
> Of elevated thoughts; a sense sublime
> Of something far more deeply interfused,
> Whose dwelling is the light of setting suns,
> And the round ocean and the living air,
> And the blue sky, and in the mind of man:
> A motion and a spirit, that impels
> All thinking things, all objects of all thought,
> And rolls through all things.

John Baillie's *The Sense of the Presence of God* gathers up this awareness and undergirds it with a structure of thought seldom seen. It is the type of Christian mysticism crying to be reborn after the scorching winds of secularism.

Ruach has reference also to God's power. This may be illustrated by two events in which *ruach* still means wind, although it is a wind through which God works directly. At the time of the exodus, God uses an east *ruach* to bring the locusts as a plague and a west *ruach* to drive them into the Red Sea (Ex. 10:13, 19). It was also the east *ruach* that the Lord used to divide the waters when Israel passed over on dry ground (Ex. 14:21). The primacy of the exodus in Israel's faith promoted *ruach* as the metaphor for God's direct action in nature and history. As late as the time of Jonah, *ruach* is used in this vivid way (Jonah 1:4; 4:8).

Ruach as the vital force in man is both physical and psychological. The *nephilim* story in Gen. 6:1-4 preserves the primitive picture of man as dependent on God for his physical existence. God limits man's life by his *ruach*, and the removal of the *ruach* is the death of man. As the Lord says, "My *ruach* shall not abide in man for ever, for he is flesh, but his days shall be a hundred and twenty years." (Gen. 6:3.) It is possible, by a change of the Hebrew text, that the original reading was "Noah" rather than *ruach*, but this is conjecture.

Elihu says (Job 34:14):

> If he should take back his *ruach* to himself,
> and gather to himself his *neshamah*,
> all flesh would perish together,
> and man would return to dust.

It will be seen later that this type of thought led to belief in *ruach* as creator.

Ruach as a psychological function in man is clearly indicated in the Joseph story. Pharaoh's *ruach* was troubled (Gen. 41:8), and it was the *ruach* of God in Joseph that enabled him to interpret Pharaoh's dreams. Rebekah's *ruach* was bitter (Gen. 26:35 P; cf. Ps. 106: 33), and Jacob's *ruach* revived (Gen. 45:27).[1]

A survey of the Old Testament concepts of *ruach* allows for at least three major stages of development — the ecstatic Spirit, the messianic Spirit, and the Creator Spirit. However, these phases cannot always be arranged in chronological order, for there is overlapping.

The Ecstatic Spirit (Primitive)

"Ecstasy" is a Greek word used to describe the experience of feeling outside oneself, but there is no technical term in Hebrew to designate the phenomenon. This is not due to the fact that this is unknown in the Bible. One of the classic examples is an experience of the apostle Paul (II Cor. 12:1-4),

14

and there is an abundance of Old Testament material on ecstasy.[2] The experience is not confined to one people, ancient or modern.[3]

Ecstasy is manifested in the Old Testament primarily as ecstatic power in the *shophetim* ("judges") and as ecstatic prophecy in the *n^{e}bhi'im* ("prophets"). Four ecstatic personalities among the *shophetim* are well known. Othniel accomplished his military exploits by the *ruach* of the Lord (Judg. 3:10). This is described in terms of "possession," rather than prophetic inspiration, in the case of Gideon (Judg. 6:34). The Hebrew says the *ruach* of the Lord "clothed itself with Gideon." The ordinary ego of Gideon dropped into the background and the extraordinary inflow of *ruach* constituted a new ego that made Gideon irresistible. This idea of possession is retained in the later history known as Chronicles, both in the case of Amasai (I Chron. 12:18) and Zechariah (II Chron. 24:20). The metaphor appears in the New Testament, but the ordinary ego is apparently not displaced: "until you are clothed with power from on high" (Luke 24:49). Lindblom thinks this distinction between possession and inspiration is basic.[4]

The *ruach* of the Lord "came upon" even the ruffian Jephthah, "the son of a harlot," the Robin Hood of the Old Testament. The chief example of *shophetim* "possessed" with the ecstatic power of the Lord's *ruach* was Samson. This hero of the tribe of Dan was conceived and born in wonder and lived the ascetic life of a Nazirite. The *ruach* of the Lord "began to stir him in Mahaneh-dan" (Judg. 13:25). When "the Spirit of the LORD came mightily upon him," he was able to tear a lion asunder, take the life of thirty men at a time, and break ropes on his arms as if they were flax (Judg. 14:6, 19; 15:14). There is some connection between his power and his obedience, but not on the high ethical level of Acts 5:32 ("God has given the Holy Spirit to those who obey him").

Ecstatic power is elevated to prophetic inspiration in the *n^{e}bhi'im*, the cultic prophets from the time of Samuel. Three cycles of stories are focused around three pairs of ecstatic personalities: Saul and David, Zedekiah and Micaiah, Elijah and Elisha. Possession is still present with their inspiration. Saul was thought to be among the $n^ebhi'im$ as the *ruach* of the Lord came mightily upon him and turned him "into another man" or "gave him another heart" (I Sam. 10:6, 9). This possession was collective and contagious, for those who followed Saul were "men of valor whose hearts God had touched" (v. 26).

The description of "touched" men has been preserved in I Sam. 19:18-24, and it may be quoted in detail.

> Now David fled and escaped, and he came to Samuel at Ramah, and told him all that Saul had done to him. And he and Samuel went and dwelt at Naioth. And it was told Saul, "Behold, David is at Naioth in Ramah." Then Saul sent messengers to take David; and when they saw the company of the prophets prophesying, and Samuel standing as head over them, the Spirit of God came upon the messengers of Saul, and they also prophesied. When it was told Saul, he sent other messengers, and they also prophesied. And Saul sent messengers again the third time, and they also prophesied. Then he himself went to Ramah, and came to the great well that is in Secu; and he asked, "Where are Samuel and David?" And one said, "Behold, they are at Naioth in Ramah." And he went from there to Naioth in Ramah; and the Spirit of God came upon him also, and as he went he prophesied, until he came to Naioth in Ramah. And he too stripped off his clothes, and he too prophesied before Samuel, and lay naked all that day and all that night. Hence it is said, "Is Saul also among the prophets?"

David behaved much in the same way when he danced before the Ark being brought to Jerusalem (II Sam. 6:16-23).

The cycle of stories about Saul and David has a demonic and tragic element. The ecstatic *ruach* of the Lord that displaced the normal ego may depart and leave place for an evil *ruach* from the Lord. It was said that in the time of the *shophetim* "God sent an evil spirit between Abimelech and the men of Shechem" (Judg. 9:23), but this is only a suggestion of what happened to Saul. "Now the Spirit of the LORD departed from Saul, and an evil spirit from the LORD tormented him." (I Sam. 16:14.) By the use of music David was able to calm Saul's raving (vs. 14-23), but one day his raving was so deranged that he cast his spear twice at David (ch. 18:10 f.). He who first appears on the scene as an ecstatic prophet disappears as a tragic madman consulting a medium at Endor (ch. 28). He was the Hamlet of the Old Testament.

The conflict between Zedekiah, the leader of the cultic prophets, and Micaiah, the first of the classical prophets, contained this same belief in the demonic. After the imitative magic of Zedekiah in the midst of the ecstatic prophets, Micaiah related two visions. In the "word of the LORD" he said:

I saw the LORD sitting on his throne, and all the host of heaven standing beside him on his right hand and on his left; and the LORD said, "Who will entice Ahab, that he may go up and fall at Ramoth-gilead?" And one said one thing, and another said another. Then a spirit came forward and stood before the LORD, saying, . . . "I will go forth, and will be a lying spirit in the mouth of all his prophets." And he said, "You are to entice him, and you shall succeed; go forth and do so." Now therefore behold, the LORD has put a lying spirit in the mouth of all these your prophets; the LORD has spoken evil concerning you. (I Kings 22:19-23.)

As Zedekiah struck Micaiah on the cheek and asked, "How did the Spirit of the LORD go from me to you?" the Hebrew distinction between the true prophet and the lying prophet is evident. True prophets are inspired by the ecstatic *ruach;* lying prophets are inspired by an evil *ruach.*

The cycle of stories about Elijah and Elisha has three ideas that may well serve as a summary of ecstasy among the *n^ebhi'im.* The first is the rapture of *ruach.* In ecstasy a *nabi* would at times suddenly disappear and be taken to another place. Two different instances in the life of Elijah indicate that he was bodily transported. The prophet Obadiah hesitated to report the presence of Elijah to Ahab lest the *ruach*

17

of the Lord snatch Elijah away and Obadiah be killed by Ahab in revenge (I Kings 18:12). Later, Elisha followed him closely lest the great father of the prophetic band disappear in precisely this manner (II Kings 2:16). Acts 8:39 says Philip disappeared from the eunuch by the rapture of the Spirit.

The inheritance of the *ruach* was a second idea in the relationship between Elijah and Elisha. It is clear from I Sam., ch. 10, that the *n^ebhi'im* went about in bands much as medieval monks later did. In the Naioth of I Sam., ch. 19, Samuel was perhaps the abbot of a type of abbey where the *n^ebhi'im* lived, and the prophets in I Kings, ch. 22, numbered four hundred. It is certain from the stories of Elijah and Elisha that sons of the prophets lived in groups with an abbot at their head. That is why Elisha cried, " My father, my father! " (*abi, abi,* II Kings 2:12) when Elijah ascended into heaven.

Elisha succeeded Elijah as the new abbot when he received a double share of the *ruach* of Elijah (II Kings 2:9). Lindblom points out that the double share has reference to the regulation that gave the firstborn a double share of the inheritance (Deut. 21:17).[5] Imparting power by a mantle or some other physical means appears in the New Testament times also (Luke 8:46; Acts 19:12).

Imparting the *ruach* of an ecstatic and charismatic leader to a group is seen in the story of the seventy elders in Num. 11:24 f. When the Lord took some of the *ruach* from Moses and put it upon the seventy elders they raved in prophecy, and the example of Eldad and Medad suggests that it would be well if this would happen to all the Lord's people (vs. 26-30).

The third characteristic of the ecstatic *n^ebhi'im* appears also in the classic reference (I Sam., ch. 10). Music and wine were aids to prophetic ecstasy from the beginning, and this may suggest Canaanite influence on the movement, but music increased in importance. It has already been seen that David used music to stimulate spiritual ecstasy in Saul, and the music of a minstrel was used by Elisha to induce a trance

18

out of which he would utter his oracle (II Kings 3:15): "When the minstrel played, the power of the Lord came upon him."

Perhaps the most descriptive term to designate these ecstatic prophets is that which appears frequently in the Deuteronomic history: man of God. It is used of both angels and men. The heavenly messenger, the angel of the Lord, sent to announce the birth of Samson, was called "a man of God" (Judg. 13:6), but it is used more frequently of men recognized as inspired oracles and messengers of God (I Sam. 9:6-10; I Kings, ch. 13; II Kings, chs. 4 to 6; etc.).

The Messianic Spirit (Prophetic)

This transition from the ecstatic Spirit of the cultic prophets to the messianic Spirit in the classical or literary prophets confronts two preliminary problems. The term "messianic" may be challenged if interpreted in a restricted sense, but it is here used not to exclude ecstasy altogether but to focus attention on a people and the representative of the people through whom the Lord works by anointment with his *ruach*. The second problem has been vigorously debated in recent research. It has been the custom in much discussion of the prophets to deny all cultic function to the classical or literary prophets, but this has been brought into question.[6]

The controversy often centers on the famous conflict between Amaziah and Amos (Amos 7:12-14). Amaziah has been interpreted to be derogatory by the very use of the noun *chozeh* ("seer," v. 12) and the verb *nataph* ("to drop," v. 6), and Amos has been pictured as resenting the suggestion that he belongs to the ecstatic bands of cultic prophets. A *chozeh* prophesied for a fee.[7] H. H. Rowley has put the passage in a different light when he says: "When Amaziah scornfully told him to go and prophesy in Judah, where he could make a living out of it, he indignantly replied that he was not a prophet because he wanted to get a living by it, but because he had to be."[8]

This is a point often overlooked, but there is still a strange shyness in Amos to assign his inspiration to the *ruach* of the Lord, the source of cultic inspiration. His inspiration by which he heard voices and saw visions was attributed to the *dabar* ("word") of the Lord, a word untainted with cultic associations now decadent. He "saw" the "words" (Amos 1:1), yet he still identified himself with "his servants the prophets" (ch. 3:7 f.).

References to *ruach* that are definitely derogatory appear in some classical prophets. Hosea speaks of *ruach* only in a popular taunt (Hos. 9:7):

> The prophet is a fool,
> the man of the *ruach* is mad.
> (Cf. II Kings 9:11.)

The taunt may be Hosea's opinion of false prophets, but it is more likely the people's remark about him. A similar reproach was hurled at Micah, and he defends himself with the question: "Is the Spirit of the Lord to be restricted?" (Micah 2:7),[9] but H. H. Rowley rules out the strong and favorable words "with the Spirit of the LORD" in ch. 3:8 on grounds of "syntax and rhythm."[10]

Ruach and lies are related in Micah 2:11, and this may be a reference to false prophets. This is even more likely in Isa. 28:7, where prophets and priests use wine and strong drink rather than *ruach* to induce ecstasy. Yet even these degenerate practices did not exclude all ecstatic and cultic features from the classical prophets. Some scholars have used Isa. 28:10 as evidence for glossolalia, the gift of tongues, in classical prophets.[11] The least that can be said is that I Cor. 14:21 so interprets the following verse.

The lowest level of the cultic prophets was reached at the time of Jeremiah, who declares (Jer. 5:13):

> The prophets will become wind [*ruach*];
> the word [*dabar*] is not in them.

And again, the Lord says (ch. 23:21):

> I did not send the prophets,
>   yet they ran;
> I did not speak to them,
>   yet they prophesied.

The real return of *ruach* as a term to explain prophetic ecstasy came with Ezekiel, the beginning of the so-called second age of prophecy. At the very beginning of Ezekiel, *ruach* as a stormy wind comes out of the north (Ezek. 1:4), the locality of deity in Canaanite thought, and *ruach* is the directive power of the Lord's throne-chariot that takes him from place to place (vs. 12, 20 f.). *Ruach* as a strong force, as both wind and spirit, is always in the hand of God.

Ecstatic prophecy is again associated with *ruach*. *Ruach* enters into (Ezek. 2:2), takes up (ch. 3:12), carries away (v. 14), and falls upon (ch. 11:5). *Ruach* is the "hand" of God, Ezekiel's favorite term, and the ecstatic state ascribed to *ruach* is equal to any mystical experience to be found.

> He put forth the form of a hand, and took me by a lock of my head; and the Spirit lifted me up between earth and heaven, and brought me in visions of God to Jerusalem. . . . And behold, the glory of the God of Israel was there, like the vision that I saw in the plain. (Ezek. 8:3 f.; cf. 11:1, 24; 43:5.)

Spiritual renewal in the prophecy of Ezekiel includes both a new heart and a new Israel. At the beginning of the prophetic movement in Israel it was noted that the coming of the *ruach* of the Lord upon Saul "gave him another heart" (I Sam. 10:9). Jeremiah prophesied that the new covenant would be written upon the hearts of God's people (Jer. 31:33), but it was Ezekiel who revived the idea that reception of God's *ruach* would result in a new heart.

At one place Ezekiel speaks of the new heart and the new *ruach* as that which is *given* (Ezek. 11:19), an act of God upon his people; but another time this spiritual renewal is that which *is gotten* through repentance from transgression (ch.

18:31). There is really no contradiction here, for both renewal and repentance belong to the covenant relation between God and his people. God does not *give* to those who do not *get* (ch. 11:21). Renewal and repentance come through reception of God's *ruach*. The three passages on the new heart and the new spirit are very much the same in content, but the last is most complete. In it God says through the prophet (ch. 36:26-28):

> A new heart I will give you, and a new spirit I will put within you; and I will take out of your flesh the heart of stone and give you a heart of flesh. And I will put my spirit within you, and cause you to walk in my statutes and be careful to observe my ordinances. You shall dwell in the land which I gave to your fathers; and you shall be my people, and I will be your God.

A new Israel will arise when God puts his *ruach* within his people. This will be a renewal that is nothing less than a resurrection of the nation, as the vision of the valley of dry bones so vividly predicts.

The role of *ruach* is seen in both the revelation to the prophet and the resurrection of the people (ch. 37:1-14).

> The hand of the LORD was upon me, and he brought me out by the *ruach* of the LORD, and set me down in the midst of the valley. . . . Thus says the Lord GOD to these bones: Behold, I will cause *ruach* to enter you, and you shall live. And I will lay sinews upon you, and will cause flesh to come upon you, and cover you with skin, and put *ruach* in you, and you shall live. . . . Then he said to me, " Prophesy to the *ruach*, . . . and say to the *ruach*, Thus says the Lord GOD: Come from the four winds, O *ruach*, and breathe upon these slain, that they may live." . . . And the *ruach* came into them, and they lived. . . . " Prophesy, and say to them, . . . I will put my *ruach* within you, and you shall live."

Ruach in The Book of Ezekiel was related most closely to a messianic people, a people renewed by the Spirit to fulfill the purpose of God in history, but The Book of Isaiah is primarily concerned in this regard with a messianic person, the per-

22

sonification or representative of God's people. The Book of Isaiah does have the idea of a faithful remnant made clean by "a *ruach* of judgment and by a *ruach* of burning" (Isa. 4:4), and the prophet is sent with the *ruach* as the messenger of the Lord (ch. 48:16).

Some oracles in Isaiah are near to the view in Ezekiel. An oracle on salvation in Isa. 44:3 sees the renewal of the seed, the descendants, together with the land, by the outpouring of *ruach*. The Lord says through his prophet:

> For I will pour water on the thirsty land,
>   and streams on the dry ground;
> I will pour my *ruach* upon your descendants,
>   and my blessing on your offspring.

This kinship between the people and the land becomes a basic assumption in Biblical eschatology. Desolation reigns (ch. 32:15):

> Until the *ruach* is poured upon us from on high,
>   and the wilderness becomes a fruitful field,
>   and the fruitful field is deemed a forest.

Renewal in the consummation is the restoration of the powers of creation.

God's covenant with Israel assures the presence of his *ruach* and his *dabar* in Judah (Isa. 59:21), and this also belongs to the picture of a messianic people. This union of *ruach* and *dabar* has overcome the earlier tension between the cultic and classical prophets.

Three other figures appear: the branch, the servant, and the prophet. These are a step beyond Ezekiel. The long rule of the house of David in Jerusalem anchored the hope of Israel to leaders from this lineage. The Last Words of David, a hymn of praise in II Sam. 23:1-7, summarized and memorialized this ideal, and it is there that the inspiration of the Spirit is prominent (v. 2):

> The Spirit of the LORD speaks by me,
>   his word is upon my tongue.

23

The details of this development, however, are found in the oracles of The Book of Isaiah.

Visions of an ideal king were not at first specifically stated in terms of a Davidic monarch, if the Immanuel oracle of Isa. 7:14 is considered in this conection, but phrases from the Davidic monarchy fill the prediction of a Prince of the Four Names in ch. 9:2-7. It is not until ch. 11:2 that this ideal king is described in messianic terms, in terms of one who shall reign as an instrument of God's *ruach*.

The rule of the ideal king in his ideal kingdom is to be a restoration of the conditions of Eden, a "paradise regained" through the renewing power of the Lord's *ruach* in a glorious age of peace. This is ushered in by the branch (Isa. 11:2):

> And the Spirit of the LORD shall rest upon him,
>   the spirit of wisdom and understanding,
>   the spirit of counsel and might,
>   the spirit of knowledge and the fear of the LORD.

The Septuagint adds to these six "gifts of the Spirit" a seventh, piety, and this is followed by the Latin Vulgate.

If the Septuagint reading is not behind the references to "the seven spirits of God" in the book of Revelation (Rev. 1:4; 3:1; 4:5; 5:6), it is very soon so interpreted in church history.[12] In general the three pairs in Hebrew represent gifts that are intellectual ("wisdom and understanding"), administrative ("counsel and might"), and religious ("knowledge and the fear of the LORD").

One of the most influential Old Testament passages in the history of Christianity, the so-called "seven gifts of the Spirit" have been variously applied. At first the gifts were closely related to baptism, then to confirmation by the laying on of the hands of the bishop when baptism and confirmation come to be viewed as separate sacraments, a separation that wrought havoc in baptismal theology and practice.[13]

In the Frankish Empire the gifts became associated with the coronation of Christian rulers, a connection easily made with the kingly functions that follow in the text of Isa., ch. 11.

24

In the ninth century a majestic hymn, *Veni, Creator Spiritus* ("Come, Holy Spirit"), increased the use of the idea. The hymn, at times attributed to Charlemagne or his grandson Charles the Bald, was probably the work of Rabanus Maurus, the greatest theologian of his age. The first stanza of the hymn is translated:

Come, Holy Spirit, our souls inspire,
And lighten with celestial fire;
Thou the anointing Spirit art,
Who dost thy sevenfold gifts impart.

Since 1662 the hymn has been a part of the Anglican ordinal for the ordination of priests and bishops, and there are many other occasions when both the text and the hymn express the promise and the prayer that God will bestow the fullness of the Spirit upon his servants.[14]

The servant figure is found in four songs known as the Servant Songs (Isa. 42:1-4; 49:1-6; 50:4-11; 52:13 to 53:12). The first Servant Song assigns a messianic mission to the Servant of the Lord. Speaking through the prophet, the Lord says (ch. 42:1):

Behold my servant, whom I uphold,
my chosen, in whom my soul delights;
I have put my Spirit upon him,
he will bring forth justice to the nations.

This messianic mission is to establish *mishpat* ("justice"), social relations according to the righteous standard of God. This he will do through patience (vs. 2 f.) and perseverance (v. 4).

The servant has been variously interpreted, some seeing him as Israel and others as an individual. If a fluid interpretation is accepted, it is possible to follow both, and this is in harmony with the application of the song to the mission of Jesus himself (Matt. 12:18-21). The mission of Jesus in the world corresponds in a striking way to the stages of development in the Servant Songs.[15] Israel first, anointed with *ruach*,

25

was the *imperfect* instrument of the Lord in history, but in a true fulfillment that lacked nothing Jesus came to establish justice in the earth. The threefold repetition of justice and the sevenfold negative present this mission in a powerful way.

The herald of Isa. 61:1-3 is both a prophet and a messianic person, much like the Servant of the Lord in the Servant Songs. It is the prophet himself who speaks when he says:

> The Spirit of the Lord GOD is upon me,
>   because the LORD has anointed me
> to bring good tidings to the afflicted;
>   he has sent me to bind up the brokenhearted,
> to proclaim liberty to the captives,
>   and the opening of the prison to those who are bound;
> to proclaim the year of the LORD's favor,
>   and the day of vengeance of our God;
> to comfort all who mourn;
> to grant to those who mourn in Zion —
>   to give them a garland instead of ashes,
> the oil of gladness instead of mourning,
>   the mantle of praise instead of a faint spirit;
> that they may be called oaks of righteousness,
>   the planting of the LORD, that he may be glorified.

Here again the call of the prophet is attributed to God's *ruach* resting upon him. Anointing was usually associated with a kingly figure, as in the case of David (I Sam. 16:14-23; II Sam. 23:1-7), but the anointment of a prophet as a sign of his commission and as the source of his inspiration was not unknown (I Kings 19:16). This call of a prophet through the coming of the *ruach* may be the case even outside of Israel. At least Balaam is so described (Num. 24:2).

The mission of the anointed prophet and the liberation that he is to announce is stated in the threefold proclamation and the seven infinitives. There is to be an age of jubilee as each half century brought a year of jubilee that set the slaves free. (Lev. 25:10.) It was the first seven lines of the above quotation that Jesus read in the synagogue of Nazareth (Luke 4:18 f.), and the fulfillment of this mission in the life of

Jesus, "full of the Holy Spirit" (Luke 4:1), is one of the central themes of Luke-Acts. What God began to accomplish in the Christ he continued to accomplish in the church.

THE CREATOR SPIRIT (POSTEXILIC)

As long as the nation stood, the ruach relation was conceived primarily in terms of the covenant between the Lord and his people. During the Babylonian exile, when contact with the creation stories of that culture was frequent and influential, reflection on the ruach relation between God and creation became dominant in most postexilic writings.

The movements of postexilic thought were not always uniform, but at least four developments may be discovered: the cosmological, the anthropological, the theological, and the eschatological. The cosmological development reflects the Old Testament view of creation, at points similar but at important other points profoundly different from the Babylonian creation story that has been preserved in the so-called Babylonian Genesis.[16]

The Babylonian Genesis tells the story of how Marduk, one of the gods in the Babylonian religion, began the creative process by slaying Tiamat, the dragon that ruled the deep. Several times the Old Testament corrects this creation story by showing how the Lord, the one God sovereign in all creation, brought order out of the primordial chaos by his creative action, often assigned to his spirit (ruach) or his word (dabar).

The ruler of the primordial chaos in the Old Testament is variously symbolized. One of the symbols is called Leviathan, in the form of a crocodile in some passages (Job 41:1; Ps. 74:14), then a sea monster like a whale (Ps. 104:26), and finally the name for a Satan (Isa. 27:1). Much of the primordial symbolism is preserved in Ps. 74:14.

> Thou didst crush the heads of Leviathan,
> thou didst give him as food for
> the creatures of the wilderness.

Ruach as the Lord's creative action is described as casual in the Priestly story of creation, where God creates the heavens and the earth out of a formless void (Gen. 1:2):

The earth was without form and void,
and darkness was upon the face of the deep [*tehom*];
and the *ruach* of God was moving over the face of
the waters.

Some would translate *ruach* as "wind," but this is doubtful in the light of the high monotheism of the whole chapter. The word for "deep" (*tehom*) is kin to the Babylonian Tiamat, but there is no evidence that it is here viewed as a deity. Polytheism has been profoundly purged, and the lofty faith in one sovereign God, who brings order out of chaos by his *ruach*, reigns supreme. Word and spirit are parallels in Ps. 33:6. (Cf. Job 26:13.)

By the *dabar* of the LORD the heavens were made,
and all their host by the *ruach* of his mouth.

Creation through the *ruach* relation is continuous as well as causal. God is active through his *ruach* in the whole cycle of the creative process. The great psalm of creation that is Ps. 104 says (v. 30):

When thou sendest forth thy *ruach*, they are created;
and thou renewest the face of the ground.

All things depend upon God's *ruach* for their existence, and God creates all life both in the cycle of the seasons and in the successive generations of mankind.

Western theology has tended to confine the activity of the Creator Spirit to the redemptive realm of the church, but Eastern Orthodoxy, which employs Ps. 104 in daily worship, has vigorously challenged this confinement and contended for both a creative and a redemptive work of the Spirit. At least on this point the West can learn from the East, for creation cannot be excluded as a realm in which the Spirit works.

The anthropological development has already been noted

in reference to the *ruach* in man, but writings after the exile bring the spirit of man into full focus. At times *neshamah* is also used to denote the human spirit as a self-conscious person. Indeed (Prov. 20:27):

> The *neshamah* of man is the lamp of the LORD,
> searching all his innermost parts.

The development of God's Spirit in man parallels this concept of man's spirit.

Military exploits are attributed to God's Spirit working in man. All of these are echoes of the ecstatic Spirit noted already among the *shophetim*. Amasai offered himself and his thirty men as officers of David's troops when the *ruach* came upon Amasai (I Chron. 12:18). "The *ruach* of God" came upon Azariah and he went out to meet Asa (II Chron. 15:1). When Judah assembled to pray for deliverance from Moab and Ammon, "the *ruach* of the LORD came upon Jahaziel" (II Chron. 20:14). It has already been noted that Zechariah was a "possessed" man, since "the *ruach* of the LORD clothed itself with" him (II Chron. 24:20, margin).

Mental insights are also attributed to the *ruach* of God in man, but this is described more often in terms of an indwelling than a seizure or possession. Joseph was able to discern the meaning of dreams because he was a man "in whom is the *ruach* of God" (Gen. 41:38). Daniel was a man with a *yattir ruach*, "an excellent spirit," a superspirit, that enabled him to interpret dreams (Dan. 5:12; 6:3), and this is recognized as "the spirit of the holy gods" (chs. 4:8, 9, 18; 5:11, 14). Ability, knowledge, and understanding are viewed as gifts of God. Bezalel possessed skill as a craftsman because God filled him with his *ruach* (Ex. 31:3; 35:31).

The most unusual instance in the Old Testament of mental insights growing out of *ruach* seizure was the Mesopotamian diviner Balaam. Oracles poured from his mouth when "the *ruach* of God" came upon him (Num. 24:2). One of the best examples of ecstasy describes him under compulsion to bless Israel and unable to curse (vs. 3 f.):

The oracle of Balaam the son of Beor,
    the oracle of the man whose eye is opened,
    the oracle of him who hears the words of God,
    who sees the vision of the Almighty,
    falling down, but having his eyes uncovered.

This is clear indication that the *ruach* of God is not confined to the covenant people. Inside and outside the covenant, in redemption and creation, the *ruach* of God may be manifested.

The theological development of *ruach* after the exile was also in different directions. Ethical qualities begin to appear. God's *ruach* is now called "the holy *ruach*." Men may rebel and so grieve this holy *ruach* that God becomes their enemy and fights against them (Isa. 63:10 f.; cf. Eph. 4:30). The rebellion of Israel stands in sharp contrast to the previous presence of God, through his *ruach*, between the Red Sea and the rebellion in the wilderness (Isa. 63:11-14). Even after "the Spirit of the LORD gave them rest" (v. 14) there was rebellion.

Psalm 51:11 indicates that the presence of God is one with possession of *ruach*. To be cast from the presence of God is to lose this holy *ruach*. Therefore, the prayer (vs. 10 f.):

Create in me a clean heart, O God,
    and put a new and right *ruach* within me.
Cast me not away from thy presence,
    and take not thy holy *ruach* from me.

The holy *ruach* is the *ruach* that belongs to the holy God. The restoration of "a new and right *ruach*" comes by "a broken *ruach*" (vs. 10, 17). Repentance renews and restores.

The holy *ruach* is also the good *ruach*. Nehemiah, ch. 9, expands the pattern of deliverance and rebellion in Israel's history from the exodus down to his time. He remembers how the Lord gave his "good *ruach* to instruct them," how he gave them manna and water in the wilderness (v. 20), but they then "were disobedient and rebelled" (v. 26). The pattern continued as the Lord in his great patience warned them by his *ruach* through his prophets (v. 30). Psalm 95:7b-11; I Cor. 10:1-13; and Heb. 3:1 to 4:13 show how dreadful was

30

the remembrance of this rebellion in Biblical faith.

The universal activity of *ruach* is pronounced in the post-exilic period. The God who abode with his people when they came out of Egypt promises to be present through his *ruach* even in the time of cosmic catastrophe and judgment (Hag. 2:5). The Lord will not only be present in his glory when the house of the Lord is restored, but he is already with them in the *ruach*. The glory is his visible and particular presence, but the *ruach* is his invisible and universal presence.

God's presence in the whole earth is attended by the promise: "Not by might, nor by power, but by my *ruach*, says the LORD of hosts" (Zech. 4:6). This warning to wait for God to work through his *ruach* rather than to depend upon the force of arms is at once a résumé of the Old Testament development and most relevant to present realities. J. E. Fison has well said that this passage "expresses tersely the secret of all manifestations of God's kingdom upon earth." [17] God acts by his *ruach* to change the course of history. Some see this universal activity in the restless *ruach* in the north country, but others interpret *ruach* here as wrath (Zech. 6:8).

God's universal presence through his *ruach* finds classic expression in the magnificent reflections of Ps. 139:7 f.:

> Whither shall I go from thy *ruach*?
> Or whither shall I flee from thy presence?
> If I ascend to heaven, thou art there!
> If I make my bed in Sheol, thou art there!

Here the parallelism between the possession of *ruach* and the presence of the Lord is positive, in contrast to the negative cry in Ps. 51:11, but the omnipresence of God is the central thrust.

The eschatological development in the Priestly concept of the Spirit is a return to the beginning at the end. In some future time prophetic inspiration through *ruach* is expected for all people. The connection between the elders of Israel and prophecy has already been noted in Num. 11:29 f. Much has been said in Christian history about universal priesthood,

31

the approach to God of all who believe, but Moses' wish in Num. 11:29 points to a universal prophethood among God's people:

Would that all the LORD's people were prophets,
that the LORD would put his *ruach* upon them!

An oracle in Zechariah looks forward to the time when a "*ruach* of compassion and supplication" will be poured out on the house of David (Zech. 12:10). This will be manifest in the mourning that comes upon the people when they look upon the pierced Messiah, a figure like unto the Suffering Servant in Isa., ch. 53. The fulfillment is related to the first coming of Christ in John 19:37 and to the second coming in Rev. 1:7.

A future age of universal prophetism is promised in Joel 2:28 f. The Lord says:

And it shall come to pass afterward,
that I will pour out my *ruach* on all flesh;
your sons and your daughters shall prophesy,
your old men shall dream dreams,
and your young men shall see visions.
Even upon the menservants and maidservants in those days,
I will pour out my *ruach*.

All these spiritual gifts are to be added to the material blessings of God before the great day that is the final judgment of the nations. On the day of Pentecost, that new beginning when God's Spirit was poured out on the disciples of Jesus, Peter proclaimed: "This is what was spoken by the prophet Joel" (Acts 2:16).

This concludes the brief survey of the Spirit of the Lord in the Old Testament, but the fulfillment of the promise is found in the new covenant of our Lord Jesus Christ for whom the old covenant and the various manifestations of the Spirit were background and preparation. There is a development in extracanonical literature, but there is more direct connection with the Old Testament.

2

THE DESCENT OF THE DOVE
IN THE SYNOPTIC GOSPELS

THE BACKGROUND of noncanonical literature is of some help for the understanding of the New Testament teachings on the Holy Spirit, but these writings are never quoted in the New Testament teachings on the Spirit. Background materials to the Gospels have been surveyed in a more detailed study by C. K. Barrett.[1] This is kept in mind in the following discussion, but the religious-historical approach does not produce the help that it once promised. The Gospel writers had distinctive views of the Spirit, and the study of their teachings in context is more fruitful.

They go back to Old Testament prophecy as the point of beginning. Prophetic inspiration was not frequent much of the time in the years immediately before the appearance of John the Baptist and Jesus. At the time Ps. 74:9 was composed, there was the complaint:

> We do not see our signs;
> there is no longer any prophet,
> and there is none among us who knows how long.

An oracle in Zechariah spoke of times when the prophet would be ashamed of his vision and deny that he was a prophet (Zech. 13:4 f.). This silence was broken by the message of the Synoptic Gospels.

The teachings in the Gospel of Mark on the Holy Spirit may be grouped around two topics: the Holy Spirit and the Christ, and the Holy Spirit and the Twelve. The Holy Spirit in special relation to Jesus as the Christ includes the baptism with the Holy Spirit in Mark 1:1-13 and the blasphemy against the Holy Spirit in Mark 3:20-30.

The Prologue of the Gospel of Mark (ch. 1:1-13) is a recessional from "the beginning of the gospel of Jesus Christ" (v. 1) to the beginning in Genesis (Gen. 1:1). The domination of man by the demonic which began with the temptation of the First Adam is defeated in the temptation of the Second Adam. Satan starts on the way to destruction. It is indeed a new beginning (*archē*) that is proclaimed as John is arrested and the ministry of Jesus begins.

Interpreting John the Baptist as the "messenger" of Mal. 3:1 and the "voice" of Isa. 40:3, the Holy Spirit is seen as the agent of this new beginning as he was the agent of the beginning in Genesis when "the Spirit of God was moving over the face of the waters" (Gen. 1:2). C. K. Barrett says: "A new thing was wrought in the waters of baptism comparable with the creation of heaven and earth out of primaeval chaos." [2] And the comment of Vincent Taylor is very much the same. [3]

Water imagery is in the background of the three pericopes that follow this beginning. In the first pericope (Mark 1:4-8) John the Baptist appears in the role of Elijah who smote the Jordan with his mantle to cross over before imparting a double portion of his spirit to Elisha (II Kings 2:6-18). Now in the preaching of John the purification of the people of God is promised. John's water baptism was "a baptism of repentance for the forgiveness of sins" offered to the throngs who came "confessing their sins" (Mark 1:5).

John's purification may have been influenced to some degree by the baptism for proselytes described so vividly in the Talmud. After circumcision, the proselyte stands in the water as the more important commandments are read to him. If he accepts this way of life " he immerses himself and when he comes up he is in all respects an Israelite" (*Yebamoth* 46b). Immersion in water cleanses him from Gentile uncleanness. Even more likely is the influence of the desert tradition in the Rule of Qumran in which the postulant becomes professed by "the purification of the Great" (VI:14-21). Evidence is strong that John the Baptist came from this so-called sectarian Judaism.[4]

The Rule of Qumran spoke of a baptism of the Spirit for the righteous and a baptism of fire for the wicked (IV:19-22). The preaching of John was apparently a messianic application of this eschatological hope (Mark 1:8):

> I have baptized you with water;
> but he will baptize you with the Holy Spirit.

The claim that preaching of this type was post-Pentecostal is without foundation, for the Qumran teaching is unmistakable. The Q source in Matt. 3:11||Luke 3:16 that adds the phrase "and with fire" and adds the terrible picture of judgment as a threshing floor is no distortion of Mark, for both Spirit and fire belong to the beginning of the messianic age.

The contrast between a purification "with water" (*hydati*) and a purification "with the Holy Spirit" (*pneumati*) has raised the question of when and how this baptism with the Holy Spirit took place. A radical form of "realized eschatology" has challenged the traditional association with Pentecost. It is true, as later discussion will develop, that Luke clearly conceived this to be beyond the crucifixion and resurrection of Jesus, and John bluntly says the Spirit was not "given" before the crucifixion (John 7:39). J. E. Yates thinks this is all wrong.[5] He claims that Mark has preserved an older view in which the people of God would be purified between the arrest of John and the arrest of Jesus.

This is clearly based on C. H. Dodd's view of the Kingdom of God as a present process. The Hebrew *ruach* and the Greek *pneuma* mean "wind" or "Spirit," and Yates argues that this baptism with the Spirit has reference to a process of purification rather than a future endowment of power as in Luke and John. The time of purification is indeed indefinite in Mark and Matthew, but it is not necessary to bring them into conflict with Luke and John, as Yates does. Against the background of Qumran it would seem that Mark and Matthew have preserved the apocalyptic hope of God's direct intervention in human history to usher in the messianic age by pouring out his Spirit on the righteous and his wrath upon the wicked. The cry of Qumran is still heard in John's preaching.

The Spirit came to Jesus (*eis auton*, Mark 1:10) at his baptism to enable him to invade the demon-infested dominion of Satan and deliver those in bondage, but the baptism of his disciples with the Spirit remains in the indefinite future. Jesus was anointed with the Spirit at his baptism, but he will baptize his disciples with the Spirit before the Day of Judgment dawns. This does not contradict Luke and John.

Mark's pericope on the baptism of Jesus (ch. 1:9-11) brings more water imagery into focus. David Daube thinks that John chose to baptize in the Jordan as a remembrance of Joshua's crossing the Jordan into the Promised Land. In the "coming up" of Jesus out of the water he finds an echo of the Old Testament narrative in Josh. 4:14 ff.⁶ This may well be, but the descent of the dove would suggest the brooding of the Spirit over the water chaos and perhaps the dove that was sent in search of dry land after Noah's flood (Gen. 8:8-12). The meaning of such symbolism may be lost, but it would suggest the new creation after passing through the water chaos (cf. I Peter 3:18-22).

The descent of the dove was accompanied by the voice of God that designated Jesus as both the Son of God in Ps. 2:7 and the Servant of the Lord in Isa. 42:1, for the new age of the Spirit is to be inaugurated through him who came to be baptized by John in the Jordan. Some have interpreted the Spirit's descent as God's act by which Jesus became the Son of God, but the primitive kerygma interprets it as an anointment of Jesus "with the Holy Spirit and with power" (Acts

36

10:38). This anointment enabled him to go "about doing good and healing all that were oppressed by the devil" (v. 38).

The temptation pericope in Mark 1:12 f. is in harmony with the primitive kerygma. Under the compulsion of the Holy Spirit, Jesus is driven into the desert, the traditional abode of demonic powers, to do battle against Satan against whom the First Adam was helpless. The forty days suggest the fasting of Moses and Elijah (Ex. 24:18; 34:28; Deut. 9:9; 10:10; I Kings 19:8), but other details go back to Adam. It recalls the Paradise story in which Adam lived alone with the birds and the beasts. All was innocence and harmony. Joachim Jeremias observes:

> The account of the temptation in Mark (ch. 1:13) shows how Jesus as the new man overcame the temptation which overthrew the first man. Jesus, like Adam, is tempted by Satan. Again, as Adam was once honoured by the beasts in Paradise according to the Midrash, so Christ is with the wild beasts after overcoming temptation. He thus ushers in the paradisial state of the last days when there will be peace between man and the animals (Isa. 11:6-8; 65:15). As Adam enjoyed angels' food according to the Midrash, so angels give the heavenly food to the new man. Jesus reopens the Paradise closed by the first man.[7]

This is the type of allegorical interpretation that was developed almost to the point of fancy in the church fathers.[8]

Parallels in Matthew (ch. 4:1-11) and Luke (ch. 4:1-13) give details of the temptations. The three temptations of Jesus are the three points at which Adam failed, but Jesus was victorious. He was "in every respect . . . tempted as we are, yet without sinning" (Heb. 4:15). Matthew in particular has merged the Second Adam typology in Mark with his own peculiar interest in the Second Moses.

The constant concern of the Prologue of Mark with the wilderness typology (Mark 1:3, 4, 12) has led Ulrich W. Mauser to magnify the exodus as the dominant Old Testament type. The typology of the new creation, traced by Taylor and Jeremias, is passed over lightly as if a choice between the two must be made, but this is unnecessary. The typologies of the new creation and the second exodus were thoroughly blended even in the Old Testament (Isa. 11:6-11; 51:9-11; chs. 63 to 66). Paradise is regained in the redemption of the second exodus. This is to supplement, not to discount, Mauser's magnificent study.[9]

The current trend in the study of Mark views the whole narrative as a dramatic struggle between Jesus in whom the Spirit works and the demonic powers over whom Satan reigns. The standard statement of this continuous cosmic struggle is an important work by J. M. Robinson, who follows many clues by Oscar Cullmann and who has been followed by most recent writers.[10] This view has been challenged by Ernest Best, who sees the real defeat of Satan in the temptation and that which follows as the plundering of the defeated strong man's house.[11] In the passion, Jesus dies for the sins of men. If Best is correct, the Spirit in Mark has more kinship with the Spirit in Luke than is commonly recognized. There is no "return" of Satan in Mark, as Best observes, between the temptation and the passion. Satan is helpless before him upon whom the Spirit has descended.

The pericope on the blasphemy against the Holy Spirit (Mark 3:20-30) tends to support Best's view of the temptation. Satan is bound and the demons are powerless before Jesus. This charismatic and spiritual power is so compulsive that the friends of Jesus thought he was beside himself (*exestē*, v. 21). Some supernatural power had come over Jesus, but they were not sure whether this power was due to the Spirit or to Satan. Does Beelzebul, the lord of the house, destroy his own house? That was the question.

The three parables that follow interpret this power to be the work of God. The first parable (vs. 24-26) points out the absurdity of saying Satan is casting out Satan. This would be civil war, and that would be self-destruction. Not even Satan is that foolish, for this would be the end of his Satanic kingdom. Another answer must be found to explain the source of this supernatural power.

38

The second parable (v. 27) takes a step forward by interpreting Jesus as the Stronger One who is able to cast out the Strong One, Satan. The first stage in the defeat of Satan took place at the temptation when he was decisively defeated, but now his house, his demonic realm, is being plundered by the Stronger One, Jesus. The Stronger One is the eschatological deliverer who sets the captives free (Isa. 49:25).

The third parable (Mark 3:28-30) makes clear that the source of Jesus' supernatural power is the Holy Spirit. He who attributes these exorcisms to Satan has committed blasphemy against the Holy Spirit, and this sin can never be forgiven. It is a spiritual blindness for which there is no cure.

The Holy Spirit was the source of authority in the ministry of the Twelve. This is most evident in both their call and the charge that Jesus gives to them. When Jesus called and appointed the twelve disciples to be with him and to preach, he gave them "authority to cast out demons" (v. 15). Authority (*exousia*), in both Jewish and Christian thought, comes from God, but it may be imparted to men.

Authority was a special quality in the teaching of Jesus. The people "were astonished at his teaching, for he taught them as one who had authority, and not as the scribes" (Mark 1:22). His hearers said in amazement: "With authority he commands even the unclean spirits, and they obey him" (v. 27). The question of his authority was one of the issues that precipitated violent opposition (ch. 11:28 f., 33). This numinous quality about him is at times called power (*dynamis*). This power goes forth to heal (ch. 5:30). Herod feared that Jesus was John the Baptist raised from the dead because of the strange "powers" at work in him (ch. 6:14).

When this authority or power is imparted to the Twelve, they are able to command the demons (*daimonia*). Demons are evil spirits subordinate to Satan or Belial or Beelzebul. Originally they were looked upon as gods whose names were unknown, and from this the New Testament idea of malign powers developed.[12]

Diseases and demons were closely associated in the thought

of New Testament times, and Jesus had power over both (Mark 1:34). After the Holy Spirit "drove" Jesus into the wilderness, Jesus was able to "cast out" demons (v. 34, *exebalen*. Cf. chs. 1:39, 43; 3:15, 22; 6:13; 7:26; 9:18, 28). This was the authority imparted to the disciples, when "he appointed twelve, to be with him, and to be sent out to preach and have authority to cast out demons" (ch. 3:14 f.).

This imparting of authority and power to the twelve disciples is even more evident in the charge Jesus gives to them. Jesus "called to him the twelve, and began to send them out two by two, and gave them authority over the unclean spirits" (Mark 6:7). The demons are here called "unclean spirits." These "unclean spirits" are first mentioned as victims helpless before Jesus, whom they call "the Holy One of God" (ch. 1:23 f.).

This contrast between the unclean and the holy is a further description of the demons as those under the rule of Satan. They have supernatural knowledge and power, but the authority and power of Jesus, derived from the anointment with the Holy Spirit, is greater. By the power of the Holy Spirit poured out on him after his baptism, Jesus bound the Strong One, Satan, so now his underlings are unable to stand before the Stronger One, Jesus.

It is not so much a "struggle," as J. M. Robinson has argued, but a "surrender" of those whose leader is already bound. The unclean spirits "fall down" (Mark 3:11) before the strong Jesus, so it is blasphemy to say, "He has an unclean spirit" (v. 30). They beg Jesus to let them enter the swine rather than to be tormented by the Son of the Most High God (ch. 5:2, 7 f., 13).

This authority and power is transmitted to the twelve disciples, so that they "cast out many demons, and anointed with oil many that were sick and healed them" (Mark 6:13). It is so related to the name of Jesus that a man other than the twelve disciples is able to use it to cast out demons (ch. 9:38-41).

Outside the passion narrative the Gospel of Mark seems

clearly to describe how the Holy Spirit working in Jesus especially, but also in the twelve disciples and others, broke the power of Satan and demons in two stages: first Satan is bound by Jesus in the wilderness temptation, then the demons or unclean spirits are unable to stand before such superior power. "No one can enter a strong man's house and plunder his goods, unless he first binds the strong man; then indeed he may plunder his house." (Mark 3:27.)

Apart from this theme of the conquest of Christ over Satan the teachings on the Holy Spirit in the Gospel of Mark are few. The inspiration of David by the Holy Spirit (ch. 12:36) and the promise of inspiration to the disciples in times of trials and testings (ch. 13:11) look backward and forward, but the decisive battle in the days of the Son of God on earth was the Spirit versus Satan. And Satan lost.

The persecution saying (Mark 13:11) reaches back beyond Mark, for it is found in other settings in both Matthew (ch. 10:20), where it is found with the charge to the Twelve, and in Luke (ch. 12:11 f.), in the travel narrative linked to the saying on the blasphemy of the Spirit. Mark has it in the so-called Synoptic Apocalypse.

And when they bring you to trial and deliver you up,
do not be anxious beforehand what you are to say;
but say whatever is given you in that hour,
for it is not you who speak,
but the Holy Spirit.

This has been related to three different theological traditions.

The first is the theology of martyrdom. Several have followed the interpretation of Ernst Lohmeyer, who claimed that only the martyr was the bearer of the Spirit. Martyrs obedient unto death no doubt knew the help of the Spirit in their confessions, but there is no evidence that other disciples were devoid of the Spirit in the interim between the sufferings of Christ and his return in glory.

The second is the theology of wisdom. C. K. Barrett argues

41

that the original saying is found in Luke 21:15 ("For I will give you a mouth and wisdom, which none of your adversaries will be able to withstand or contradict").[13] This saying is very much the same as the one found on the lips of the first Christian martyr, Stephen, where it is related to the Spirit ("But they could not withstand the wisdom and the Spirit with which he spoke," Acts 6:10), and these in turn were based on the promise to Moses and Aaron ("and I will be with your mouth and with his mouth, and will teach you what you shall do," Ex. 4:15). These, however, seemed rooted in Luke's second exodus theology.

The third theology belongs to the Abba tradition preserved in Matthew (ch. 10:20), where "the Spirit of your Father" is promised.[14] This would go back to the Jewish Christian community. If this is a sound judgment, then there is strong evidence that Jesus spoke of a time of persecution between his sufferings and the coming of the Son of Man in glory when the disciples would be helped by the Holy Spirit. This would also be the presence of Christ with them.

Most of Mark's teachings on the Holy Spirit gather around the temptation of Jesus and the consequences of his victory, but the focus of this final reference is on the passion.[15]

GOD WITH US (MATTHEW)

In Mark, the Holy Spirit is *power*, the power by which Jesus the Stronger One defeats Satan the Strong One, but Matthew's Gospel portrays the Spirit as *presence*, "God with us." There is less emphasis on the Holy Spirit in Matthew than in either Mark or Luke, but two matters call for consideration: the modifications made in the use of Mark, and the miraculous conception or virgin birth of Jesus.

The modifications of Mark are at four points. It has already been noted how the preaching of John in Q has added (or preserved!) the idea of a baptism "with fire" (Matthew 3:11||Luke 3:16). The previous references were to the Rule of Qumran, but an Essene hymn composed by the Teacher of

42

Righteousness is more than adequate to explain why a baptism of the wicked with a fiery judgment is nothing new (The Hymns III:28b-30):

And the bonds of death tightened leaving no escape,
and the torrents of Belial overflowed all the high banks
like a fire consuming all their shores,
destroying from their channels every tree green and dry
and whipping with whirlwinds of flame
until the vanishing of all that drinks there.[16]

This idea of a fire of judgment goes back to the Old Testament (Isa. 66:14 f.; Mal. 3:1 f.), so it may well be older than the baptism with the Holy Spirit.

Matthew's view of the Holy Spirit in the temptation of Jesus toned down the strong idea of the Holy Spirit driving Jesus into the wilderness to do battle with Satan to the idea that he was "led up by the Spirit into the wilderness" (Matt. 4:1), but the idea of Satan's defeat is increased by the details of the three temptations and the triumphant rebuke: "Begone, Satan!" (v. 10). This agrees with Mark and Luke, in their teaching that Satan was bound in the ministry of Jesus, for "the devil left him, and behold, angels came and ministered to him" (Matt. 4:11; cf. Ps. 91:11-14).

The role of the Holy Spirit in the Beelzebul controversy is made explicit in Matthew. The "finger of God" (Luke 11:20) in Q based on Pharaoh's metaphor in Ex. 8:19, has been interpreted as the "Spirit of God" in Matt. 12:28. By the Spirit of God, Jesus casts out the demons, and so the Kingdom of God has come in this manifestation of the spiritual power that belongs to the coming age of glory. He attributes this manifestation to Beelzebul who "speaks against the Holy Spirit," and he "will not be forgiven, either in this age or in the age to come" (v. 32). To speak against the Holy Spirit is not as strong as blasphemy, but it means the same in this context.

Mark's idea of David's inspiration is repeated by Matthew (ch. 22:43) as it is not in Luke (ch. 20:41), but this is of no great significance. It is a traditional formula for inspiration.

43

The problem of the Holy Spirit in the Great Commission (Matt. 28:16-20) departs even more from Mark. The longer ending of Mark (ch. 16:9-20), about which there is still some dispute, has reference to "signs" following the apostolic mission, but there is no triune baptismal formula.

There are two forms of the Great Commission. The short one, found at times in Eusebius, has "in my name" in the place of "baptizing them in the name of the Father and of the Son and of the Holy Spirit." This would balance the lines as follows:

> All authority has been given to me
> in heaven and on earth
> Go therefore and make disciples of all nations,
> in my name
> Teaching them to observe all
> that I have commanded you;
> And lo, I am with you always,
> to the close of the age.

This is more in line with Aramaic poetry and agrees with baptizing "in the name of Jesus Christ" in Acts (chs. 2:38; 8:16; 10:48; 19:5; 22:16). If the triune name is original, this difference would be difficult to explain.

The long form could take place in at least two ways. First, the short form was expanded into the triune formula before the Gospel of Matthew was written. This would explain why the short form is rare. The second possibility takes the question into the second century when baptism in the triune name and by triune immersion became primary. The names and the forms were so closely linked that one immersion and one name, as in the first century, and three immersions in the triune name, as in the second century, would be most reasonable. The question, however, is one that could best remain open for further light.[17]

The triune formula, however it arose, had great influence in the development of the doctrine of the Holy Trinity and

44

the belief in the deity of the Holy Spirit, for this became a part of the entrance rite into the Christian community of faith.

The miraculous conception and virgin birth of Jesus is attributed to the Holy Spirit in Matt. 1:18, 20. Accepted by most Christians as literally true until the nineteenth century, the subject has become more controversial for over a century.

The church fathers, seeing at first the virgin birth as the means of redemption and then the means by which the Word of God became incarnate in human flesh, used the belief in the miraculous conception to defend the humanity of Jesus against Gnostic attacks. They made it impossible for Gnostics to receive baptism by requiring the confession that Jesus was "conceived by the Holy Spirit, born of the Virgin Mary."

The later emphasis on monasticism and virginity shifted attention from the humanity of Jesus to the perpetual virginity of the Virgin Mary. After Jerome's conflict with Helvidius, who rejected Mary's perpetual virginity, the belief that the infant Jesus passed through the virgin's womb as the crucified and risen Lord passed through the wall of Joseph's tomb became orthodoxy.

The writings called pseudepigrapha, written under false names, and apocrypha, meaning "hidden," ran riot on the wonders of the birth of Jesus and the glories of the Virgin Mary. It is ironic to note that a belief once used to defend the humanity of Jesus becomes the occasion for losing the humanity of even the Virgin Mary.

The Reformation did little to correct this condition. Luther steadfastly defended Mary's perpetual virginity. It was almost inevitable that historical and critical study of the New Testament and church history would lead to attacks on the virgin birth. The conflict between naturalistic philosophy, which viewed the virgin birth as mythology, and supernaturalistic theology, which took it as literal truth, was violent in the nineteenth century.

Comparative religion claimed pagan analogies to the virgin birth. It was pointed out that Philo Judaeus (*On the Cherubim,* 40-52) used the idea, but he was speaking of the begetting of the soul or the virtues of the soul. Stories about how Zeus begat such persons as Hercules, Perseus, and Alexander were advanced, but these turn out to be mythological fornication. The same may be said of the myths that speak of Apollo begetting Ion, Asclepius, Pythagoras, Plato, and Augustus.

The most interesting " parallel " is found in Plutarch (4.4). He suggests that a woman may be approached by a divine *pneuma* (" spirit ") and made pregnant. The legend of Numa Pompilius claimed that, after the death of his wife, he withdrew into solitude to have intercourse with a divine being named Egeria. Careful examination indicates that Plutarch was speaking of real sexual intercourse and the *pneuma* was none other than the Egyptian designation for Zeus (Amen. Cf. *On Isis and Osiris*, 36).

Literary analysis of the Scriptures has led to different results. Some have concluded that the infancy narratives are legends to enhance reverence for Jesus, but others have found theological truth. Karl Barth, trained in critical scholarship, caught many of his colleagues by surprise by coming to the defense of the belief that Jesus was truly conceived by the Holy Spirit. At the beginning of a chapter on " The Mystery and the Miracle of Christmas " he says:

> The truth of the conception of Jesus Christ by the Holy Spirit and His birth of the Virgin Mary points to the true Incarnation of the true God achieved in His historical manifestation, and recalls the special form through which this beginning of the divine act of grace and revelation, that occurred in Jesus Christ, was distinguished.[18]

The most likely background to belief in the virgin birth is found in the wonder births of the Old Testament.[19]

The literary questions, rooted in the quotation of the annunciation formula of Isa. 7:14 in Matt. 1:23, are complicated by the parallels in the Ugaritic literature, as well as in the Old Testament. Since the excavation of the Nikkal poem at Ras Shamra (Ugarit) in 1933, the following lines have been debated: (*a*) 77:5. " a virgin [*bethulah*] will give birth ";

(b) 77:7. "Lo, a young woman ['almah] bears a son."

Similar wonder births are found in Gen. 16:11 (Ishmael); 17:19 (Isaac); Ex. 2:2 (Moses); Judg. 13:3, 5, 7 (Samson); I Sam. 1:20 (Samuel); Isa. 8:3, 18 (Maher-shalal-hash-baz); but Isa. 7:14 has received most attention because of its messianic associations. One interpretation, calling attention to the promise of immediate fulfillment in Isa. 7:14-24, has denied any messianic reference altogether. Another view appeals to certain words in the formula to defend an exclusive reference to the Messiah. Delitzsch says hinneh ("behold") "is always used by Isaiah to introduce a future occurrence," but this is difficult to maintain in the light of Isa. 5:7; 8:18; 12:2; 20:6; 21:9; 37:36; 40:9 f.; 47:14; 48:10; 51:22; 59:9; 62:11; 65:6. Machen, insisting on the miraculous meaning of 'oth ("sign"), has followed early Christian apologists (Justin, Irenaeus, Origen) by failing to note the usage in the immediate context (Isa. 8:18) and other Old Testament passages.

The most vigorous discussion has been centered around the meaning of 'almah, which means a "marriageable girl, young woman (until the birth of her first child)." [19a] Those who are of the opinion that it always carries the connotation of an untouched virgin have great difficulty with Gen. 24:43; Ex. 2:8; Ps. 68:25; Prov. 30:19; S. of Sol. 1:3; 6:8, as well as with the usage of the Greek word parthenos in the LXX (cf. Gen. 34:3). The case is even more difficult when the adjective harah ("conceive") is examined (cf. Gen. 38:24; II Sam. 11:5). Since the time of Jerome a number of Christians, recognizing fully the immediate reference to a fulfillment in the time of Ahaz, have found it tenable to defend both the messianic reference of Isa. 7:14 and the virgin birth of Jesus, by noting the use of typological interpretation in the Gospel of Matthew (e.g., ch. 2:6, 15, 18, 23).

There is no decisive evidence that the narrative in Matthew based the virgin birth on Isa. 7:14. The quotation of the promise in Matt. 1:23 is only one of a number of Old Testament proof texts in this Gospel, and the teaching about the miraculous conception does not require the verse. Two facts establish the miracle: (*a*) after the betrothal and (*b*) before they came together, Mary was found to be with child "of the Holy Spirit" (Matt. 1:18, 20). Strack and Billerbeck have pointed out that this idea of the life-giving and creative power of the Holy Spirit is absolutely new and has no parallels in Jewish thought.

The Eshnunna Law Code (3800 B.C.) required "bride money" of the prospective groom and provided for a refund with 20 percent interest if the betrothed virgin died before the consummation of marriage. In early Old Testament times betrothal was effected by payment of *moher* ("fifty shekels") to the bride's father as a compensation for loss (Gen. 34:12; I Sam. 18:25) and presentation of gifts to the prospective bride (Ex. 22:16 f.; Ruth 4:5, 10). The bride made use of the time of betrothal to collect her trousseau and property, and the groom was exempt from military service for the year (Deut. 20:7). The marriage was complete after a marriage feast of joyous celebration (Matt. 25:1-13; John 2:1-11). Only after this ceremony could they live together as husband and wife (Matt. 1:18, 25), although they were considered husband and wife from the time of betrothal (Matt. 1:19 f.), and the woman was considered a widow if her husband died.

It is the statement that Jesus was conceived (Matt. 1:18) and born (v. 25) to Mary "before" she and Joseph had sexual contact that constitutes the second evidence for belief in the virgin birth. Even if Joseph knew he was not responsible for the conception, there was the law that demanded death by stoning for both man and woman in cases of seduction (Deut. 22:23-24) and death for the man in cases of rape (vs. 25-27). Joseph was not only "unwilling to put her to shame" (Matt. 1:19), but he also feared for his life. The strong verb in the phrase "as he considered this" (*enthumēthentos*), in Matt. 1:20, suggests this and explains why Joseph wanted to divorce her quietly (v. 19). This was difficult to do quietly, since an engagement could be terminated after betrothal only by divorce and the payment of a dowry. The narrative teaches clearly that the Holy Spirit, not Joseph, was the agency of

48

the conception of the child born to Mary.

Emmanuel ("God with us") is a major motif in Matthew. The miraculous conception, at the beginning of the Gospel, is the means by which the Shekinah, the tabernacling presence of God, came to be with us (Matt. 1:23); and the Great Commission, at the end, has the promise, "Lo, I am with you always, to the close of the age" (ch. 28:20). Several other passages indicate the belief that as the Shekinah was present in the study of the Torah, so there is "the presence of the Risen One in the Church." [20] This is particularly true in the promise, "For where two or three are gathered in my name, there am I in the midst of them" (ch. 18:20). This concern with the Shekinah continues in the birth narrative of Luke (ch. 1:35).

THE POWER OF THE MOST HIGH (LUKE)

Luke's Gospel has an interest in the Holy Spirit that is deep and distinct. Literary structure and theological interest are intertwined in an impressive way. B. H. Streeter's theory of Luke's composition, in *The Four Gospels*, first published by Macmillan in London in 1924, has received renewed attention in *The Structure of Luke and Acts*, by A. Q. Morton and G. H. C. MacGregor, published in 1964 by Hodder & Stoughton, Ltd., in London. The place of pneumatology in this structure requires attention for the understanding of the Gospel as well as for the distinctive view of the Spirit.

It is believed that Luke passed through two editions. While Paul was a prisoner in Caesarea for two years, the author of Luke-Acts was his companion. Luke at first collected some special materials (L) about the origins of Christianity. Then there came into his hands a collection known by both Caesarea and Antioch and found very much the same in Matthew, the Antioch Gospel, and Luke, the Caesarean Gospel. This material, known as Q, from the German word *Quelle*, meaning "source," does not appear at all in Mark, the Roman Gospel traced to the testimony of Simon Peter. Luke composed the first edition, called by Streeter "Proto-Luke," from these L and Q sources. A special section (Luke 9:51 to 18:14) is known as the Lucan travel narrative.

A final edition of Luke was composed in Rome. It has been said that Mark's Gospel came to hand and four large blocks of material were added with additional touches in the passion narrative. However, Luke's use of Mark is doubtful. A new introduction was added, chs. 1; 2, and the present Gospel of Luke was the result. When this framework is followed, the passages on the Holy Spirit appear near the beginning of each special part. The final edition has chs. 1; 2, the first edition chs. 3:1 to 4:30, and the travel narrative, chs. 10; 11.

The so-called Gospel of the Infancy (chs. 1; 2) that introduces the final edition in Rome has a fascinating theological structure. Three summaries (Luke 1:80; 2:40, 52) indicate a time of preparation. John the Baptist "grew and became strong in spirit, and he was in the wilderness till the day of his manifestation to Israel" (ch. 1:80). This is a possible reference to what is now known as his Essene background.[21] It is the time of preparation for "the prophet of the Most High" (v. 76).

The Lucan infancy narrative (chs. 1; 2) begins with a brief Prologue to the Gospel (ch. 1:1-4) in its final form. This is followed by the annunciation of the angel Gabriel that Zechariah would become the father of a great prophet (vs. 14-17).[22] His birth will be a wonder birth, and his ministry will be like that of Samson, the greatest of the *shophetim,* and Elijah, the greatest of the *n^ebhi'im.*

Parallels with Samson are unmistakable: barren parents, angelic visitor, the life of a Nazirite, the power of the Spirit. The power of the Spirit in him will be even greater than in Samson. It was not until Samson was in Mahaneh-dan that the Spirit began to stir him, but John will be "filled with the Holy Spirit, even from his mother's womb." This apparently came to pass when John leaped for joy in his mother's womb three months before he was born. This was when Elizabeth met Mary the mother of Jesus (Luke 1:41-44).

The first stanza about John the Baptist says (vs. 14 f.):

And you will have joy and gladness,
and many will rejoice at his birth;
for he will be great before the Lord,
and he shall drink no wine nor strong drink,
and he will be filled with the Holy Spirit,
even from his mother's womb.

His prophetic inspiration will not be derived from "wine and strong drink," as noted in the cultic prophets, but from the Holy Spirit.

The second stanza about this "prophet of the Most High" turns to parallels with Elijah. There was a widespread expectation that Elijah would return. When John later appeared, his dress and diet were those of Elijah. He denied, according to the Gospel of John (John 1:21), that he was Elijah, but Jesus spoke in a mysterious way about his message and mission in the world. "But I tell you," said Jesus, "that Elijah has come, and they did to him whatever they pleased, as it is written of him." (Mark 9:13.)

This second stanza of the hymn about John the Baptist says (Luke 1:16 f.):

And he will turn many of the sons of Israel to the Lord
    their God,
and he will go before him in the spirit and power of
    Elijah,
to turn the hearts of the fathers to the children,
and the disobedient to the wisdom of the just,
to make ready for the Lord a people prepared.

John stands between the Elijah of the Old Testament and the Elijah of the End (Mal. 4:5 f.; Rev. 11:6).

The miraculous conception in the Lucan nativity narrative, where Mary not Joseph is the central figure, contrasts the birth of John and Jesus. Special attention should be given to three units of contrast. The first contrast is between Elizabeth the old woman and Mary the young virgin (1:5-7,26 f.).

The second contrast is the manner in which John and Jesus

51

were conceived (1:18*b*,34*b*). The great age of Zechariah and Elizabeth raised Zechariah's question: "How shall I know this?" Mary's question was raised by the fact she had never had sexual relations with any man (1:34*b*). This is the crucial question: "How can this be?" The miraculous conception of Jesus is attributed to the Holy Spirit in contrast to the human agency in the conception of John.

The third contrast is between the filling of John with the Holy Spirit three months before he was born and the conception of Jesus by the Holy Spirit nine months before he was born (1:15,41,35). By the miraculous conception of Jesus in the womb of the virgin Mary the glory of God as the power and presence of the Most High came to dwell in the humanity of Jesus. That is the idea behind *episkiasei* ("will overshadow"). (Cf. Ex. 40:34-38; Luke 9:27-36.)

The time of preparation for "the Son of the Most High" (Luke 1:32) is even more pronounced than the time for "the prophet of the Most High." The laws of Moses on circumcision, purification, and presentation in the Temple are all strictly followed. After the presentation the parents returned to Nazareth with Jesus, and the next twelve years are packed into one summary: "And the child grew and became strong, filled with wisdom; and the favor of God was upon him" (ch. 2:40). At twelve, Jesus was again in the Temple with his parents, this time for Bar Mitzvah, to assume responsibility for keeping the law himself. The shift from Joseph as his legal father to God as his heavenly Father is crucial. Then again many years are packed into another summary: "And Jesus increased in wisdom and in stature, and in favor with God and man" (v. 52).

This time of preparation was marked by much prophetic inspiration. After the annunciations of the births of John the Baptist and Jesus, there are three occasions in which this inspiration is noted.

The first is the visitation of Elizabeth by Mary. The mother of John the Baptist was six months pregnant when the mother of Jesus, now pregnant, hurried to the hill country of Judah to be with those who would understand in some degree her miraculous conception and the coming birth of the Messiah.

On this occasion the prophecy about John's being filled with the Holy Spirit in his mother's womb was fulfilled, for "when Elizabeth heard the greeting of Mary, the babe leaped in her womb; and Elizabeth was filled with the Holy Spirit" (Luke 1:41). Under prophetic inspiration Elizabeth blessed Mary, and Mary responded in the magnificent hymn that has been called by the opening words in Latin, the Magnificat ("it magnifies") (vs. 42-55).

A second outburst of prophetic inspiration was the so-called Benedictus ("blessed") of Zechariah, the father of John the Baptist. Between the annunciation of the great prophet's birth by the angel Gabriel and the naming of John, the father Zechariah was dumb. After writing that his son was to be called John ("the Lord is gracious"), "Zechariah was filled with the Holy Spirit, and prophesied" (Luke 1:67). That hymn is a classic example of prophetic inspiration.

The third example of such inspiration was the so-called Nunc Dimittis ("now thou lettest depart") of Simeon and the thanksgiving of the prophetess Anna (ch. 2:22-38). This took place at the presentation of Jesus in the Temple for circumcision. The Holy Spirit "was upon" Simeon, much as was noted in both the *shophetim* (Judg. 3:10) and the n*e*bhi'im (II Kings 10:10). This concept later became a part of the messianic hope in both the Davidic (Isa. 11:2) and the Servant of the Lord (Isa. 40:1; 49:13; 58:6; 61:1) traditions.

Simeon received both revelation and inspiration by the Holy Spirit. It was revealed to him "that he should not see death before he had seen the Lord's Christ" (Luke 2:26), so the presentation of Jesus in the Temple made him ecstatic "in the Spirit" and filled him with prophetic inspiration (v. 27). The blessing of the Nunc Dimittis poured forth from Simeon (vs. 29-35), and the prophetess Anna had a like experience (vs. 36-38).

The second unit in Luke that has a special interest in the Holy Spirit is at the beginning of Proto-Luke, the first edition of Luke believed to have been composed by Luke while he stayed with Paul in Caesarea (Acts 23:31 to 26:32). This, according to Streeter's famous theory accepted in this analysis, was a conflation of some special materials, collected by Luke and known as L, with the materials found in Matthew and Luke and not in Mark, known as Q.

If it is remembered that Caesarea was the home of Philip the evangelist, with whom Luke and Paul once stayed and whose house was known for the prophetic inspiration of his four virgin daughters (Acts 21:8 f.), a clue may be found for the special concern with the Spirit in both the first and final editions of the Gospel. Prophetic inspiration in a remarkable way is found at the very source of Proto-Luke, and it found its way into the theological structure of the Gospel.

Prayer and prophetic inspiration are linked in Luke's account of the descent of the Spirit on Jesus at his baptism. He alone makes mention of the fact that Jesus "was praying" (Luke 3:21) when the Spirit descended. Prayer in the ministry of Jesus is of special interest to Luke (see also chs. 5:16; 6:12; 9:18, 28; 22:44), and this interest in prayer continues in the accounts of the early church (Acts 1:14; 2:42; 4:31; 6:4, 6; 8:15, 17; 9:11, 40; 10:4; 12:5; 13:3; 14:23).

Jesus was "full of the Holy Spirit" when he returned from the Jordan, as Luke 4:1 alone says. Mark's statement that the "Spirit immediately drove" Jesus into the wilderness (Mark 1:12) has been softened by Matthew to "led" (Matt. 4:1), but Luke has a special interest in the fact that Jesus went beyond the prophetic inspiration of prophets. The prophets were "filled" while they delivered their ecstatic utterances in the Spirit, but Jesus remained "full."

According to Hans Conzelmann, Luke's account of the temptation introduces the thesis that Satan did not tempt Jesus between his wilderness temptation and the betrayal of Judas Iscariot. After "the devil had ended every temptation, he departed from him until an opportune time" (Luke 4:13). This "opportune time" came when "Satan entered into Judas called Iscariot" (ch. 22:3). Jesus then instructs his disciples: "Pray that you may not enter into temptation" (vs. 40, 46).

A third unit in the Gospel of Luke that has a pneumatology near the beginning is the Lucan travel narrative, the special section in Luke 9:51 to 18:14. Teachings on the Holy Spirit are related to three topics: the return of the Seventy (ch. 10:17-22), answer to prayer (ch. 11:9-13), and the Beelzebul controversy (vs. 14-23).

The return of the Seventy was attended by the joyful discovery that the very name of Jesus was sufficient to command the demons, and Jesus is boldly portrayed as one who saw visions, much as he saw the descent of the dove and heard the voice of God at his baptism. His vision explains the power of Jesus' name in exorcisms: "I saw Satan fall like lightning from heaven" (Luke 10:18). Seeing visions and hearing voices were some of the chief characteristics of prophetic inspiration in the Old Testament, and the claim of this quality comes as no surprise.

The disclosure of the vision is followed by an oracle for the Seventy (vs. 19 f.):

Behold, I have given you authority to tread upon
     serpents and scorpions,
   and over all the power of the enemy;
     and nothing shall hurt you.
Nevertheless do not rejoice in this,
   that the spirits are subject to you;
     but rejoice that your names are written in heaven.

The authority by which Jesus cast out demons has again been transferred to his disciples who use his name, but authority over demons is not to be compared with citizenship in heaven.

This citizenship in heaven brings joy on earth. In ecstasy, an ecstasy wrought by the Holy Spirit, much like the ecstasy among the cultic prophets of the Old Testament, Jesus utters a two-stanza oracle that is a powerful example of *Patēr* ("father") pneumatology. Joachim Jeremias has shown convincingly how the address of God as *Abba* ("father") is a

55

distinctive teaching of Jesus.[23] None had dared previously to *address* God on such intimate terms, but Jesus did this and taught his disciples to do the same.

The Q source, the material in Luke and Matthew not in Mark, says (Luke 10:21 f.):

> I thank thee, Father, Lord of heaven and earth,
> that thou hast hidden these things from the wise and
>   understanding
> and revealed them to babes;
> yea, Father, for such was thy gracious will.
>
> All things have been delivered to me by my Father;
> and no one knows who the Son is except the Father,
> or who the Father is except the Son
> and any one to whom the Son chooses to reveal him.

The first stanza is addressed to God, the second a declaration to others, but both reveal the intimate relation between God the heavenly Father and Jesus Christ the Son full of the Holy Spirit.

The portrait of Jesus as one full of the Spirit, speaking and acting in the power of the Spirit, is a pneumatic Jesus, a charismatic Christ, who has authority and power, *exousia* and *dynamis*. His words are God's words, and his deeds are God's deeds. Ecstatic power and prophecy have come to perfection in the person of this Son of the Most High God who addresses him as "Abba." All three of the Synoptic Gospels report the Voice from heaven that declared this intimate relationship; all three reveal this in the prayer of Jesus in the Garden of Gethsemane; but this Q oracle relates it in a unique way to the ecstatic experience inspired by the Holy Spirit.

Authority over demons is not equal to this relationship. In Jesus and in the disciples the intimate relationship to the Father is the highest of all. The second section on the Spirit in the travel narrative interprets prayer as the practice of this relationship. Luke's special concern with prayer in the personal life of Jesus has already been noted. He was praying when the Spirit like a dove descended upon him, and it is in prayer that God, the heavenly Father, gives the Holy Spirit to those who take the name of Jesus.

A textual reading in the Lucan form of the Lord's Prayer has reference to the gift of the Holy Spirit through prayer. Luke 11:2 reads: "May the Holy Spirit come upon us and cleanse us" rather than "Thy kingdom come." No less a scholar than B. H. Streeter argued that this is original, and he has many followers.[24] This is possible, but Luke never equates the coming of the Kingdom with the gift of the Spirit. This reading, made famous by Gregory of Nyssa's treatise on the Lord's Prayer, seems more likely to be derived from the liturgical use of the Lord's Prayer in the laying on of hands after baptism.

The Beelzebul controversy has "the finger of God" in Luke 11:20 where Matt. 12:28 has "the Spirit of God." This at first is a surprise, but Luke is here comparing the exorcisms of Jesus with Moses, who wrought his wonders by "the finger of God" (Ex. 8:19). The Second Moses has come to lead the second exodus. The powers of the coming Kingdom have already "come upon" (*ephthasen*) them in the spoiling of the Strong One's goods.

At the end of the Gospel, Luke has joined the promise of the Spirit to prayer again (Luke 24:49): "And behold, I send the promise of my Father upon you; but stay in the city, until you are clothed with power from on high."

In the very act of blessing the disciples, Jesus ascends into heaven, and the disciples continued to bless God in the Temple until they were "clothed with power from on high" on the Day of Pentecost.

In summary, the Holy Spirit in Mark is a *power* by which Jesus defeated Satan in his temptations and spoiled his goods by exorcisms. Matthew's perspective is that of the Holy Spirit as the agent by which God was present in Jesus and continues his *presence* in the worshiping congregation. Luke extends the teachings on the Spirit into the *promise* of a definite future by which the disciples will be baptized "with power from on high."

3

THE GIFT OF THE HOLY SPIRIT IN ACTS

THE ACTS OF THE APOSTLES has long been recognized as "the Acts of the Holy Spirit"[1] or "the Gospel of the Holy Spirit."[2] Critical scholarship has served to sustain this devotional and lay approach to the only early history of the expanding church "in Jerusalem and in all Judea and Samaria and to the end of the earth" (Acts 1:8).

A significant study in the theology of Luke draws the conclusion that the initial stage of salvation took place in the Old Testament. The central event in this history of salvation was the appearance of Jesus, the fulfillment of the prophetic promise. The ascension of Jesus introduced the third stage in salvation history, after the Holy Spirit was given, to continue the work in the church which began in Jesus.[3]

It has already been seen that the Synoptic Gospels represent John the Baptist as preaching two baptisms, baptism with water and baptism with Spirit, but the time of this baptism of the Spirit remained indefinite until the end of the Gospel of Luke (ch. 24:49). There it is linked with a mission "to all nations" (v. 47), and this becomes the theme of Acts.

The witness begins in Jewish Christianity (Acts, chs. 1 to 12), in which there are three stages (chs. 6:7; 9:31; 12:24), then continues in Gentile Christianity (chs. 13 to 28) in three more stages (chs. 16:5; 19:20; 28:30 f.). In all of these stages the Holy Spirit is the motive power and inner life of the witnesses.

The relationship between literary structure and theological

58

tendencies is a difficult and unresolved problem in the study of Acts. Ernst Käsemann, of Tübingen, may be said to have fired the shot that precipitated the hottest battle. In 1960 he published the first volume of his essays in which he challenged the "early Catholicism" (*Frühkatholizismus*) of Luke-Acts.[4] The next year Ernst Haenchen published the thirteenth edition of a great commentary that helps the new start in the study of Acts. Already, strong voices have resisted Käsemann's attack on salvation history so obvious in the expanding church.[5]

In the survey of the Spirit in Acts, which follows, the writer is aware of the theological issues at stake, but the chief concern is to set forth the teachings on the Holy Spirit as they are found in the final structure of Acts. At times, however, the question of sources must be raised to understand the text. The twofold pattern of the Holy Spirit in the acts of Peter (Acts, chs. 1 to 12) and the Holy Spirit in the acts of Paul (chs. 13 to 28), associated with the commentary of R. B. Rackham, is helpful and no doubt represents an important stage in the composition of Acts. The Acts of Peter includes both the gathered church in Jerusalem (chs. 1:1 to 6:7) and the scattered church in all Judea and Samaria (chs. 6:8 to 12:24), so it seems best to use a threefold division, the clue to which is found in Acts 1:8: "witnesses in Jerusalem and in all Judea and Samaria and to the end of the earth."

"Witnesses in Jerusalem" (Acts 1:1 to 6:7)

The baptism with the Spirit had a time of preparation after the ascension. This was a time of obedience. Jesus had commanded the disciples to "stay in the city" until they were "clothed with power from on high" (Luke 24:49). Before he ascended "he had given commandments." This is repeated in Acts. Jesus was not "taken up" until "he had given commandment through the Holy Spirit to the apostles whom he had chosen" (Acts 1:2). This was the commandment not to depart from Jerusalem until the baptism with the Spirit, prom-

59

ised by John and renewed by Jesus, had taken place (v. 4).

This was also a time of promise. Obedience to the commandment prepared the way for the outpouring of power promised. "And you shall be my witnesses in Jerusalem and in all Judea and Samaria and to the end of the earth." (V. 8.) Power to witness as the church expands to the end of the earth is the purpose of Pentecost.

This was further a time of prayer. After the ascension the eleven disciples returned to the upper room where the Last Supper had taken place. "All these with one accord devoted themselves to prayer, together with the women and Mary the mother of Jesus, and with his brothers." (Acts 1:14.) This is believed to be the original beginning of the so-called Proto-Acts (vs. 12-14) before the final edition added the new preface (vs. 1-5) and the new beginning (vs. 6-11).[6]

Then this was a time of study. The final edition records the decision to replace Judas. The study of Ps. 69:25 and 109:8 convinced them that a successor to Judas should be chosen. Judas had a *kleros* (Acts 1:17, "charge"; cf. I Peter 5:3) in the *diakonia* ("ministry"), so his *episkope* (Acts 1:20, "office of overseer," episcopate) should be taken by another. This has led to endless argument about apostolic succession, but this should not be ignored or rejected with the charge of *Frühkatholizismus*. Judas alone had a successor, but bishops did emerge from the elders after the death of the apostles.

Finally, the period of preparation was a time of unity. The first edition noted that the meeting in the upper room was *homothumadon* (Acts 1:14, "with one mind"). The final edition says, "They were all together [*homou*] in one place" (Acts 2:1) on the day of Pentecost. Luke seems eager to emphasize this apostolic unity in the light of rising heresy and schism in his time.[7]

The power of Pentecost had many associations. The oldest was agricultural. Pentecost was the Feast of Weeks, i.e., a week of weeks with a celebration of the fiftieth day after Passover. Firstfruits from the harvest (a sheaf) were offered to the Lord at the beginning, 16th Nisan in April, and at the

60

end of the fifty days, at the beginning of June, firstfruits (two loaves made from new wheat) were again offered (Lev. 23:9-21). Very early the resurrection of Jesus was called "firstfruits" at the beginning of the fifty days (I Cor. 15:20, 23), so the harvest of three thousand souls at Pentecost was the firstfruits at the end. According to Paul, the full harvest would occur at the *parousia*.

The historical importance of Pentecost was the giving of the law to Moses (2 Chron. 15:10-12). Passover remembered the coming out from Egypt, but Pentecost was the feast of the law given on Sinai (*Pesachim* 68b). It was believed that the law was given in seventy languages.

> Although the ten commandments were promulgated with a single sound, it says, "all people heard the voices": it follows then that when the voice went forth it was divided into seven voices, and then went into seventy tongues, and every people received the law in their own language. (Midrash *Tahuma* 26c.)

At Shinar the seventy nations were "confounded" (Gen. 11:7), but this was reversed when the multitude was "confounded" at Pentecost (Acts 2:6).

The symbolic meaning of Pentecost is further signified by the wind and fire, two of the oldest symbols of God's presence. Fire attended the theophany at Sinai (Ex. 19:1-25; 20:18-21), and Spirit was related to such phenomena in the choice of the seventy elders (Num. 11:25). Wind and Spirit are almost synonyms in Ezek. 37:9-14. Both wind and fire are associated with the Spirit in Rabbinic Judaism.[8] A quake attended the filling with the Spirit in Acts 4:31. This physical phenomenon had led Harnack to regard the passage as a primitive doublet of the expanded and later story in Acts, ch. 2.[9]

Pentecostal power fulfilled the promise of the Father to clothe the disciples "with power from on high" (Luke 24:49). This clothing, reminiscent of primitive ecstasy (Judg. 6:34), was an endowment of power to witness in the world mission of the church (Acts 1:8). As the Holy Spirit came upon the Virgin Mary and "the power of the Most High" overshadowed her (Luke 1:35), so now the Holy Spirit has "come upon" (Acts 1:8) the disciples.

The phenomenon of glossolalia, speaking in tongues, has been interpreted in many ways. The first group of interpreters think tongues are intelligible languages. The church fathers are almost unanimous on foreign languages. Irenaeus spoke of many brethren in the church "who possess prophetic gifts and who through the Spirit speak all kinds of languages, and bring to light for the general benefit the hidden things of men, and declare the mysteries of God" (*Against Heresies* V.vi). If he meant tongues, many other fathers misunderstood him, for Origen, Gregory of Nazianzus, Gregory of Nyssa, Cyril of Alexandria, and Chrysostom among the Greek fathers, and Jerome, Rufinus, and Augustine among the Latin fathers, thought the apostles spoke in foreign languages.[10] The legend that the apostles composed the old Roman baptismal creed (the Apostles' Creed) grew out of this tradition.[11]

The notion that the language was no more than fiery eloquence has been advanced by W. Beyschlag,[12] and William Barclay suggests this theory still.[13] A mixture of foreign language and fiery eloquence is suggested by Burton Scott Easton and many others.[14]

Modern scholarship tends more and more to identify the phenomenon with the tongues and prophecy in I Cor., ch. 14. Some conservative scholars, taking the text as it is, have argued for an auditory miracle, a miracle in the hearing of the people.[15]

More critical scholarship finds a solution to the problem in the sources. The one word *heterais* ("other") in Acts 2:4 and the whole of vs. 6b-11 are assigned to a later "language" source. The rest leaves a picture identical with Acts 10:46; 19:6; and I Cor., ch. 14, where intelligible prophecy and tongues are mixed. By reducing the number of nations to twelve (dropping Judaea, Crete, and Arabia on critical grounds), one nation and one apostle are allocated to each sign of the Zodiac. This is based on a catalogue by Paul of Alexandria in A.D. 387 that is thought to go back to earlier times. The idea that the apostles spoke foreign languages would go back to the Rabbinic teachings on Gen. 11:1-9 and Ex., ch. 19.[16]

This line of thinking can go so far that the whole Pentecost story is reduced to a "tale" or a "myth," as M. D. Goulder suggests,[17] but the Rabbinic parallels are impressive. When Acts 2:6b-11 is separated from the context, there is no problem in seeing one consistent view in I Corinthians and Acts. Luke later adds a theological interpretation that foreshadows the future mission of the church to all nations. This does not mean that he is "theologizing" a legend constructed from Jewish lore. He has seen in the mixture of tongues and prophetic preaching the reversal of Babel and the unification of mankind in the salvation history of the church.[18]

In Acts 10:46, "They heard them speaking in tongues and extolling God." In ch. 19:6, "They spoke with tongues and prophesied." The two phenomena are identical with I Cor., ch. 14, in which Paul discussed in great detail the greater value of prophecy over tongues in the public worship of God. Aside from the pericope in Acts 2:6b-11, there is no suggestion of language. First Corinthians, ch. 14, is primitive and primary, not Acts 2:6b-11, so the earliest passage, not the secondary, should control interpretation.

The secondary theological universalism does not contradict the primary account of tongues and prophetic preaching (e.g., Peter's sermon) if the gift of interpretation was given to the people who *heard* in their own language, but language is a word that would not have been used apart from the Rabbinic backgrounds on Babel and Sinai. This is essentially the view expressed long ago by Kirsopp Lake.[19]

Peter's preaching at Pentecost is one of the seven sermons in Acts that illustrates the content of the primitive kerygma. Since C. H. Dodd published his influential book on *The Apostolic Preaching and Its Developments* (1936), there has been a growing agreement that early preachers fed their flock with a three-pronged fork. Their sermons had three points: the fulfillment of the Old Testament, the story of

Jesus, and a call to repentance.

Peter declares (Acts 2:14-21) the outpouring of the Holy Spirit to be the fulfillment of Joel's famous prophecy that God would pour out his Spirit on the righteous and the fire of judgment on the wicked (Joel 2:28-32). Then follows (Acts 2:22-36) the story of the life, death, resurrection, and exaltation of Jesus Christ with the crucial interpretation: "Being therefore exalted at the right hand of God, and having received from the Father the promise of the Holy Spirit, he has poured out this which you see and hear" (v. 33). The call to repentance concludes the speech (vs. 37-42).

The call to repentance contains a promise that has led to endless debate: "Repent, and be baptized every one of you in the name of Jesus Christ for the forgiveness of your sins; and you shall receive the gift of the Holy Spirit" (v. 38). At least four possibilities have been proposed for the understanding of how water baptism and Spirit baptism are related.

American dispensationalism attempts to relegate water baptism to the role of mere ritual and assign to Spirit baptism the place of "real baptism" as water baptism is abandoned in a dispensational scheme.[20] Radical criticism has followed the reverse order and claimed that the primitive church practiced Spirit baptism only and that water baptism came in as the glow of spiritual fervor died away.[21] Some sacramental views say that the Spirit is imparted by water baptism rather than by the laying on of hands or some other means.[22]

It seems more consistent with Acts in the present form to say that water baptism symbolizes Spirit baptism which is the spiritual substance that is normally expected with the symbol, but there are occasions when Spirit baptism is received before water baptism (ch. 10:44-48), and water baptism may be received before Spirit baptism (chs. 8:15 f.; 19:1-6). Every effort to establish a rigid order or an inseparable relation between the ritual acts does violence to the text of Acts as it now exists.

The principle of control is always repentance. When there is no repentance, there is no reception of the Spirit, but water baptism and/or laying on of hands may or may not be present. Arguments for their presence when not mentioned is special pleading, and the order is definitely different when they are mentioned.

The following verse has not been less controversial: "For the promise is to you and to your children and to all that are far off, every one whom the Lord our God calls to him" (Acts 2:39). On the basis of this passage and ch. 18:8 (perhaps also I Cor. 1:16) Joachim Jeremias has argued for infant baptism even in Jewish households.[23] To this, Baptists have been quick to reply that any evidence for infants receiving baptism and the Holy Spirit is evidence for them hearing the call of God and prophesying, for all of this is ascribed to children in the context (Acts 2:17, 39).[24]

After the initial blessing of baptism with the Holy Spirit, with the summary on their common life (vs. 43-47), the blessings of Pentecost are manifest in many ways. This first book continues in four literary sections (chs. 3:1 to 4:31; 4:36 to 5:11; 5:17-41) with four summaries (chs. 4:32-35; 5:12-15; 5:42; 6:7). In each section there is some special reference to the work of the Holy Spirit in Jerusalem. These four blessings are added to the power that came by baptism with the Holy Spirit.

The second, the blessing of boldness (*parrēsia*), was a special quality in the preaching of Peter and John (Acts 4:13), and Peter's preaching is specifically attributed to his being "filled with the Holy Spirit" (v. 8). This filling, unlike the event of Spirit baptism, may be frequent or continuous. It could be individual or corporate. The whole church met to pray for *parrēsia* to speak God's word (v. 29). In the passage Harnack took to be a more primitive account of the Pentecost experience, it is said: "And when they had prayed, the place in which they were gathered together was shaken; and they were all filled with the Holy Spirit and spoke the word of God with boldness" (v. 31). Even if one does not accept Harnack's source criticism, it is obvious that this is a close parallel to the power of Pentecost. The boldness (*parrēsia*) with which they spoke God's word was a freedom of speech flowing from the fullness of the Spirit.[25]

A third blessing of the Holy Spirit was that of fellowship (*koinōnia*). *Koinōnia* was both a way of worship and a way of life among these Jewish Christians. All faithful souls " devoted themselves to the apostles' teaching and fellowship, to the breaking of bread and the prayers " (Acts 2:42). The fellowship (*koinōnia*) was perhaps the collection of goods for those in need, so that the fellowship of the Spirit was also a fellowship of substance. The summary that follows (vs. 43-47) is a vivid picture of this charismatic community that "had all things in common " (*koina*, v. 44). Private ownership of homes and goods was practiced, but they gladly shared them with those in need.

A second summary on the common life (Acts 4:32-35) is followed by two case histories in vivid contrast. True *koinōnia* is illustrated by Barnabas, a man filled with the Holy Spirit (ch. 11:24), who "sold a field which belonged to him, and brought the money and laid it at the apostles' feet " (ch. 4:37). Then follows immediately the contrast of Ananias and Sapphira (ch. 5:1-11) who sold a piece of property but kept back some of the proceeds. In the common life of the Holy Spirit this was looked upon as being filled with Satan rather than the Spirit. Peter charges Ananias with lying to the Holy Spirit (v. 3), and the liar died. Three hours later Sapphira meets the same judgment after she is charged with tempting the Holy Spirit (v. 9). True *koinōnia*, the work of the Spirit, stands over against false *koinōnia*, the work of Satan. The concluding summary (vs. 12-15) calls attention to the fact that the power present to smite dead was also present to heal. Excommunication and isolation destroy, but fellowship heals and makes whole.

The fourth blessing of the Holy Spirit's baptism was that of witness (*martyria*). The primary purpose for the outpouring of the Holy Spirit at Pentecost was to make the disciples witnesses (Acts 1:8). The first section of the first book of Acts has a declaration of the apostles as witnesses of the resurrec-

66

tion of Jesus (ch. 2:32). This is repeated in the second section (ch. 3:15), but the fourth section unites the witness of the apostles with the witness of the Holy Spirit in a direct way (ch. 5:32): "And we are witnesses to these things, and so is the Holy Spirit whom God has given to those who obey him."

This second imprisonment of the apostles was legal action (Acts 5:17-32) after the legal warning at their first hearing (ch. 4:18). The failure of the apostles to heed the legal warning filled the Sadducees, those in charge of the Temple, with indignation (ch. 5:17), but they were met by men filled with the Holy Spirit who chose to obey God rather than men. It was this obedience to God that brought to them God's gift of the Holy Spirit. Repentance, the initial obedience of the believer, is followed by obedience to God's command to bear witness to the mighty work of God in Jesus Christ. This is not work righteousness but the obedience of faith.

The fifth blessing of the Holy Spirit is that of service or ministry (*diakonia*). A specialization in service soon developed in the Jerusalem church (Acts 6:1-6). It was impossible for all to do all in a developing community. Some division of labor was necessary. The selection of the Seven arose out of the decision of the apostles to make *diakonia* of the word the main thing and that which they were best qualified to do. It did not seem right for those equipped to be servants of the word to use their time "to serve [*diakonein*] tables" (v. 2). Serving tables was a service (*diakonia*, v. 1), but devotion to prayer and the *diakonia* of the word of God was the central thing in the apostolic ministry. Much modern thought and talk that discounts the value of the preaching ministry has not reached this stage of the primitive church. Man still does not live by bread alone but by the word of God.

The Seven were chosen to serve (*diakonein*) the tables in the administration of alms for widows, but they too needed the help of the Holy Spirit. As Bezalel and Oholiab needed to be filled with the Spirit in the building of the Tabernacle (Ex. 31:1-11; 35:30 ff.), so the Seven needed the Holy Spirit as table servants. The Spirit of God and the wisdom of God

67

are closely related, and the Seven needed both (Acts 6:3). Stephen, who is to play a special role in the spreading of the apostolic faith, is singled out as "a man full of faith and of the Holy Spirit" (v. 5).

The relationship between the laying on of hands (v. 6) and the imparting of the Holy Spirit has been as controversial as the relationship between water baptism and Spirit baptism. When the multitude murmured against Moses in the wilderness, seventy "elders" were chosen as assistants, and "the LORD came down in the cloud and spoke to him, and took some of the spirit that was upon him and put it upon the seventy elders" (Num. 11:25). Another instance tells how Moses "laid his hands upon" (ch. 27:23) Joshua, "a man in whom is the spirit" (v. 18). This was to invest Joshua with "authority" (v. 20). Ideas from both accounts appear in Acts 6:1-6, but the Seven already possessed the Spirit. In this they were like Joshua.

Other debated matters raise the question as to whether the Seven were "elders," "deacons," or Hellenistic parallels to the Twelve. The noun *diakonia* and the infinitive *diakonein* are used in reference to the Seven, but Stephen and Philip soon became servants of the word too. Later deacons (I Tim. 3:8-13) became in a very definite way table servants, both in the collection of funds and in assistance at the communion service, but the precise connection between their origin and the Seven is an unsolved problem.

Congregational Christianity has at times argued for congregational ordination on the basis of Acts 6:6 and 13:3. It is claimed that "the whole multitude" chose the Seven and set them aside by laying their hands on them. The whole multitude, according to most manuscripts, did "pick out" the Seven, but it makes little sense to say the multitude set the Seven "before the apostles" so that the multitude could lay hands on them. The grammar could be so construed from the plural participle and verb, but "apostles" that came immediately before is plural and did not need to be repeated. It is doubtful that this desperate expedient for congregational

68

ordination would be advanced were it not for historical circumstances since the Reformation. Until the Reformation the ordination of the Seven was understood as apostolic, not congregational. Those who are for congregational ordination usually resort to a presbyterial laying on of hands. More will be said on this point when Acts 13:3; I Tim. 4:14; 5:22; II Tim. 2:1-6 come up for discussion.

"AND IN ALL JUDEA AND SAMARIA"
(ACTS 6:8 TO 12:24)

The major manifestation of the Holy Spirit in book two of Acts (chs. 6:8 to 9:31) is the so-called Samaritan Pentecost (ch. 8:4-25). This is most closely associated with Philip, but the charismatic personalities of Stephen and Saul appear also.

The story of Stephen (chs. 6:8 to 8:3) is one of the turning points in Acts, but he is considered here only in relationship to the Holy Spirit. The dynamic of Stephen was indicated in the list of the Seven when he was singled out as "a man full of faith and of the Holy Spirit" (ch. 6:5). He is again called a man "full of grace and power," who "did great wonders and signs among the people" (v. 8). In the clash with the Dispersion Jews, perhaps descendants from the captives set free by Pompey, Stephen was so dynamic with the Holy Spirit that his opponents "could not withstand the wisdom and the Spirit with which he spoke" (v. 10). Luke perhaps intends to point out the fulfillment of the promise made by Jesus (Luke 21:15). The charge against Stephen is parallel to the charge against Jesus (Mark 14:56-58; John 2:19 ff.). The very face of Stephen, "like the face of an angel" (Acts 6:15), was like the countenance of Jesus praying at the transfiguration (Luke 9:29; cf. Ex. 34:29 ff.).

The defense of Stephen cut like Peter's preaching at Pentecost. His survey of Israel's salvation history finds a foreshadowing of the Jews' rejection of Jesus in the rejection of Joseph and Moses. Having rehearsed Israel's rebellion against God, Stephen charges them with the stinging words: "You stiff-necked people, uncircumcised in heart and ears, you always resist the Holy Spirit. As your fathers did, so do you" (Acts 7:51). Isaiah 63:10 recalled: "But they rebelled and grieved his holy Spirit; therefore he turned to be their enemy, and himself fought against them." Resistance to the Spirit is both possible and a danger, despite claims to the contrary (cf. Heb. 10:29).

The death of Stephen draws the most powerful parallel with the death of Jesus. His vision of "the glory of God, and Jesus standing at the right hand of God" came as he was "full of the Holy Spirit" (Acts 7:55). As heaven "opened" at Jesus' baptism, while he prayed (Luke 3:21), so at the death of Stephen "the heavens opened" so that the first Christian martyr saw "the Son of man standing at the right hand of God" (Acts 7:56). Stephen's prayer of forgiveness, again like Jesus' (Luke 23:34), is followed by his yielding up of his spirit (Acts 7:59), like Jesus to the end (Luke 23:46). There is no doubt that the charismatic martyr was a true servant of the charismatic Christ. Vision and ecstasy belonged to both.

The story of Philip (Acts 8:4-40) is in two parts. A very primitive source tells about his preaching mission among the Samaritans (vs. 4-25). This is the so-called Samaritan Pentecost. Many of the Samaritans believed and were baptized, but they did not receive the gift of the Holy Spirit as Peter's Pentecost sermon had promised (ch. 2:38 f.). The normal sequence of repentance or belief, baptism and the reception of the Spirit, was not complete. Among the Samaritans "there was much joy" (ch. 8:8) and many "signs and great miracles" were performed, but as yet the Spirit "had not yet fallen" as it did on the Jews at Pentecost in Jerusalem. The Holy Spirit was obviously at work, but there was no falling and filling.

It took the falling of the Spirit in power to confirm Philip's mission to this mongrel race so despised by the Jews in Jerusalem. Most of the debate for centuries on the relationship between the laying on of hands and the gift of the Spirit has begun with the passage:

Now when the apostles at Jerusalem heard that Samaria had received the word of God, they sent to them Peter and John, who came down and prayed for them that they might receive the Holy Spirit; for it had not yet fallen on any of them, but they had only been baptized in the name of the Lord Jesus. Then they laid their hands on them and they received the Holy Spirit. (Acts 8:14-17.)

By the beginning of the third century of Christianity various benefits in baptism had been assigned to the separate acts of the rite. Immersion in the name of the Trinity, administered threefold with the confession of the Apostles' Creed, signified the forgiveness of sin, but the reception of the Spirit was signified by the imposition of the bishop's hands or "consignation" (Tertullian, De baptismo 8). With the separation of immersion and the imposition of hands by several years, as infant immersion became more and more the custom, the odd notion that people could be forgiven Christians all this time without the Spirit developed. Anglican theologians have been particularly perplexed as to whether the imposition of hands is the initial gift of the Spirit or a strengthening of the gift, but some have linked the gift with baptism.[26]

After hundreds of years in this tradition, it is difficult not to see Peter and John as bishops going about their diocese administering confirmation for those who have been already baptized and have come to believe for themselves, but this picture has been vigorously challenged and that from within the Anglican communion.

The apostles were not visiting Samaria to "confirm" the baptised, like a modern bishop. They were confirming the extension of the mission to Samaria and ratifying Philip's preaching and baptisms.[27]

This was the Samaritan Pentecost.

The laying on of hands, first noted in the choice of the Seven (Acts 6:6) and not related to the reception of the Spirit, has still other associations in Acts (chs. 5:12; 9:17; 14:3; 19:11; 28:8). It will appear again after baptism and with the gift of tongues (ch. 19:6). The gift of tongues perhaps attended the Samaritan Pentecost, for Simon the Great "saw that the Spirit was given through the laying on of the apostles' hands" (ch. 8:18). The most likely thing for him to see was speaking in tongues and prophesying when the Spirit fell upon the Samaritans. This was most certainly the evidence in the Gentile Pentecost at Caesarea (chs. 10:44-48; 11:15). The Greek *epipeptōkōs* ("having fallen") indicates the Spirit had not taken possession of the Samaritans until the apostles laid their hands on them. The laying on of hands is the only factor not found at the Jerusalem Pentecost. Water baptism and Spirit baptism have now become linked with the laying on of hands.

Philip's encounter with the Ethiopian eunuch came under the guidance of the Holy Spirit (Acts 8:29 f.), and here the speaking of the Spirit and of the angel of the Lord seem synonymous (v. 26). After the eunuch believed and was baptized some texts say that he went on his way "rejoicing" (v. 39), an idea associated with the Spirit (ch. 13:52; cf. chs. 16:34; 2:46). The Western text says that the "Holy Spirit fell upon the eunuch, and an angel of the Lord caught away Philip." This falling of the Spirit would indicate the same experience as in Acts 8:16; 10:44; and 11:15, but there is no agreement on the value of the Western text. The text usually accepted speaks of a rapture of Philip by the Spirit much like that of Elijah (I Kings 18:12; II Kings 2:16). Whether in rapture or ecstasy the Holy Spirit was active.

The story of Saul's conversion relates the receiving of the Holy Spirit with both the laying on of hands and baptism, but nothing definite is said about tongues. The laying on of hands by Ananias brought both healing and the Holy Spirit to Saul, and this was some sign of Saul's inclusion in the community of believers (Acts 9:17). Baptism in this instance followed the laying on of hands and the gift of the Spirit (v. 18), and the reference to taking "food" (v. 19) may be more than a breaking of his baptismal fast. It could have reference to the breaking of bread in the Lord's Supper, as it is possible in ch. 16:34. Very early in the Christian movement baptism was followed immediately with the Lord's Supper or at least communion. (I Cor. 10:1-5; 10:16 f.; 11:17-33.) Charismatic power in Saul is most evident afterward (Acts 9:20-22).

The Gentile Pentecost is the major event in book three (Acts 9:32 to 12:24). The conversion of Cornelius in Caesarea is told with great emphasis on supernatural manifestations: both Cornelius and Peter see visions (chs. 10:3, 17, 19; 11:5), an angel of God appears to Cornelius (chs. 10:3, 11:13), and the Spirit speaks to Peter (ch. 10:19). Many features recall the events associated with the birth of John the Baptist and Jesus (Luke, chs. 1; 2), and Peter's preaching tells "how God anointed Jesus of Nazareth with the Holy Spirit and with power; how he went about doing good and healing all that were oppressed by the devil, for God was with him" (Acts 10:38). Now signs are to follow to indicate that God is with Peter in the expanding mission of the church.

The falling of the Spirit on Cornelius and all who heard the word is the crucial moment:

> While Peter was still saying this, the Holy Spirit fell on all who heard the word. And the believers from among the circumcised who came with Peter were amazed, because the gift of the Holy Spirit had been poured out even on the Gentiles. For they heard them speaking in tongues and extolling God. Then Peter declared, "Can any one forbid water for baptizing these people who have received the Holy Spirit just as we have?" And he commanded them to be baptized in the name of Jesus Christ. (Acts 10:44-48.)

If God baptized them with the Spirit, there was no reason why Peter should not baptize them with water.

As in the conversion of Saul, water baptism follows Spirit baptism, but no word is said about the laying on of hands. The Spirit had been given by the hand of God! Tongues and prophesying ("extolling God," v. 46) appear again, as on the Day of Pentecost in Jerusalem ("just as we have," v. 47; cf. ch. 11:15), and perhaps at the Samaritan Pentecost (ch. 8:16). Ecstatic utterances, unintelligible to most, are usually mingled

73

with prophetic utterances, intelligible to all (cf. ch. 19:6; I Cor., ch. 14).

At Antioch the Spirit was at work too. Barnabas, "a good man, full of the Holy Spirit and of faith" (Acts 11:24) was sent from Jerusalem to Antioch to investigate the work of God there among the Gentiles. A charismatic figure, the prophet Agabus (ch. 21:10), came also from Jerusalem, and it was in Antioch that he "foretold by the Spirit that there would be a great famine over all the world" (ch. 11:28). Roving prophets of this type were many in the expanding church. (Chs. 11:27; 13:1; 21:9.) Acts 11:19-30 should follow 12:24; apparently a page is out of place.

"AND TO THE END OF THE EARTH"
(ACTS 12:25 TO 28:31)

Paul has already been introduced as a charismatic person, but the second half of Acts (chs. 13 to 28) is especially concerned with him as the instrument of the Spirit in the increase of the word of God from Antioch to Rome. Spiritual power blended with spiritual guidance has been a dominant theme in the first part of Acts, but spiritual guidance is a special topic for part two.

Book four (chs. 12:25 to 16:5) traces the spread of the gospel from Antioch through Asia Minor with the Jerusalem conference as the climax. Five prophets and teachers in Antioch were worshiping God and fasting in prayer when a most unusual sense of guidance came to them. In simple directness the story says that the Holy Spirit told them to set aside Barnabas and Saul for a very special mission (ch. 13:2). This was what has been called Paul's first missionary journey.

The significance of the laying on of hands in this venture is different from the previous examples. Barnabas (Acts 11:24) and Saul (ch. 9:17), like the Seven (ch. 6:3, 5), had the gift of the Spirit and were charismatic prophets before the laying on of hands by their colleagues (ch. 13:1 f.). Why, then, did the three (Symeon, Lucius, Manaen) lay their hands on the two (Barnabas at the head of the list and Saul at the end)?

74

The laying on of hands always represents solidarity and self-identification, so here Barnabas and Saul are sent forth as "apostles" (ch. 14:14) to represent the apostolic church. The leaders of the church, the prophets and teachers, commission them with a solemn blessing. This sounds very much like the *Nasiim* sending forth apostles (*shelihim*) in the Great Sanhedrin.[28]

The congregational tradition, which at times finds expression among Baptists, makes the claim that Barnabas and Saul, as in the case of the Seven (ch. 6:6), were set aside by the whole congregation's laying hands on them.[29] This would be interesting and most unusual if it really happened, but one must bring this view to the text. It is not there in a way obvious enough for the church to discover until after the Protestant Reformation. The congregational claim would have " the whole multitude," more than five thousand people, lay hands on the Seven. Before Saul arrived in Antioch " a great number" (ch. 11:21) had turned to the Lord, so this would be another multitude laying hands on Barnabas and Saul if the whole church did so.

It must be remembered that " the church at Antioch " means all the Christians in Antioch. The New Testament never speaks of more than one church in a city. When they can meet in one house, the local church and the congregation are identical, but this is the only time the congregational view of the church is true. There are only four specific references to house churches in the New Testament (I Cor. 16:19; Rom. 16:5; Philemon 2; Col. 4:15). The great majority of references in the New Testament use church to mean all the Christians in a city, even though they meet in many places. This is obvious in Acts (chs. 5:11; 8:1, 3; 9:31; 11:22, 26; 12:1, 5; 13:1; 14:23, 27; 15:3, 4, 22, 41; 16:5; 18:22; 20:17; 20:28). When the plural is used, it has reference not to a city but to a province or larger area (I Cor. 7:17; 11:16; 14:33 f.; 16:1, 19; II Cor. 8:1, 18 f., 23 f.; 11:8, 28; 12:13; Gal. 1:2, 22; II Thess. 1:4; Rev. 1:4, 11, 20; 2:7, 11, 17, 23, 29; 22:16).

On two occasions during the missionary journey, Saul, now

75

called Paul, was able to defeat the false prophet Elymas, because Paul was "filled with the Holy Spirit" (Acts 13:9). This term has at this stage become normal to describe the inspiration of apostolic witnesses, but it is also basic in Luke's theology of mission. The disciples they made in Antioch of Pisidia were also "filled with joy and with the Holy Spirit" (v. 52), two ideas closely associated.

At the Jerusalem Council, Peter reviews his experience with Cornelius as justification for receiving Gentiles without circumcision. He testified:

> And God who knows the heart bore witness to them, giving them the Holy Spirit just as he did to us; and he made no distinction between us and them, but cleansed their hearts by faith. (Acts 15:8 f.)

The agreement of the Council "seemed good to the Holy Spirit" (v. 28). This last statement is the third instance in Acts when the Holy Spirit, usually spoken of as a power, is described in terms of a person. (Cf. 8:29; 13:2.)

Book five (chs. 16:6 to 19:20) ascribes personality to the Holy Spirit even more. As Paul and his company planned to evangelize Asia they were "forbidden by the Holy Spirit" (ch. 16:6), and "the Spirit of Jesus did not allow them" to go into Bithynia (v. 7). The term "Spirit of Jesus" is found nowhere else in the New Testament, but it indicates perhaps some identification between the historical Jesus and the Holy Spirit of God (cf. II Cor. 3:17). It could imply an actual vision of Jesus as in Acts 23:11. God's guidance was through the vision of the man of Macedonia (ch. 16:9). Vision and rapture are closely associated. The Trinitarian formulations remain for Paul and John to state more precisely.

Parallels in Acts 18:24 to 19:7 present what may be called the "Baptist Pentecost." Those who knew only the baptism of John the Baptist become integrated into the apostolic faith that had expanded from Jerusalem. Apollos, a learned and eloquent Alexandrian, represents one parallel and a group of twelve disciples represents the other.

Apollos is described in a way that has baffled expositors. "He was an eloquent man, well versed in the scriptures. He had been instructed in the way of the Lord; and being fervent in spirit, he spoke and taught accurately the things concerning Jesus, though he knew only the baptism of John." (Cf. 18:24 f.) All this is impressive, but two things are difficult to interpret.

The first is the phrase translated in the Revised Standard Version as "fervent in spirit." This would indicate that he was a boisterous Baptist with much learning. It seems to mean more than that, despite the number of commentaries that regard this as a reference to his human spirit. The Greek phrase *zeōn tōi pneumati* is very close to the *tōi pneumati zeontes* in Rom. 12:11, translated in the Revised Standard Version as "aglow with the Spirit." Many have suggested the thought that Apollos was "boiling over with the Holy Spirit" of God.[30] This is consistent and agrees with the context in all but one point.

If Apollos already had the gift of the Spirit, why is it said that "he knew only the baptism of John" (Acts 18:25)? Ernst Käsemann charges Luke with a strong tendency to write an "ideological theology of history" to integrate all independent movements into the Jerusalem movement.[31] He says flatly that this statement about his knowing only the baptism of John is a "fabrication" in the interest of the "doctrine of a legitimate Church."[32] G. H. C. MacGregor says Priscilla and Aquila "almost certainly" rebaptized Apollos.[33] These contradict, and neither is supported by the text.

There was one deficiency in the preaching of Apollos, but this was not enough to require the rebaptism of one already possessed of the Spirit. When Priscilla and Aquila heard his charismatic preaching they only "expounded to him the way of God more accurately" (v. 26). The word *akribesteron* ("more accurately") has been ruled out also as an effort to harmonize it with the claim that he knew only the baptism of John.[34] Yet there is an advance in the preaching of Apollos. Previously he "taught accurately the things concerning Jesus," the historical Jesus, but he sounded the new note afterward, "for he powerfully confuted the Jews in public, showing by the scriptures that the Christ was Jesus" (v. 28). His charismatic message had become messianic.

The evidence for a Baptist community that Luke seeks to integrate into "the legitimate church" may be accepted. Such "independents" as Philip the evangelist in Samaria, the conversion of Cornelius by Peter, and most of all the Pauline movement had to be assimilated into the one apostolic fellowship if Christianity maintained its unity. Luke is concerned with this, but he does not invent history to work out his theory of unity. References to John the Baptist in John's Gospel, the Ephesian Gospel, is enough to indicate a strong Baptist movement in Ephesus (John 1:6-8, 15-17, 19-42; 3:22-36; 4:1-3; 5:35 f.). Luke's Gospel said plainly that "all men questioned in their hearts concerning John, whether perhaps he were the Christ" (Luke 3:15). The belief did not die with John's martyrdom.

The parallel story about the twelve disciples illustrates the other side of the problem. Their faith was so defective that they were rebaptized. Why? Thy did not possess the Spirit and missed the messianic note in the preaching of John the Baptist. They are called "disciples" (Acts 19:1) and they had "believed" (v. 2), but they did not know "there is a Holy Spirit" (v. 3). After Paul instructed them about the Coming One, "they were baptized in the name of the Lord Jesus" (v. 5), even though they had been baptized "into John's baptism" (v. 3). This is the only instance of rebaptism in the New Testament, but later the Donatists and Anabaptists revived this for Catholics. Some Baptists insist on this for all who have not been baptized on the authority of a Baptist church. The full circle has been made. Once Baptists were rebaptized, but now Baptists do the rebaptizing!

The twelve disciples were not only rebaptized, but they also received the gift of the Spirit. "And when Paul had laid his hands upon them, the Holy Spirit came on them; and they spoke with tongues and prophesied." (Acts 19:6.) Baptism and laying on of hands again come before the gift of the

78

Spirit. Tongues and prophecy come together again (chs. 2:4, 11; 10:46). It is impossible to establish a fixed order with the following:

Repentance — baptism — no hands — Spirit (ch. 2:38).
Repentance — baptism — hands — Spirit (ch. 8:14 ff.).
Repentence — hands — Spirit — baptism (ch. 9:17-19).
Repentance — no hands — Spirit — baptism (ch. 10:44-48).
Repentance — baptism — hands — Spirit (ch. 19:1-6).

No fixed sequence and no sacramental slavery are to be found.

In the sixth book of Acts (chs. 19:21 to 28:31) the Holy Spirit leads the church to Rome. It was "in the Spirit" (ch. 19:21) that Paul resolved to pass through Macedonia and Achaia, then on to Jerusalem before he saw Rome. The journey to Jerusalem is described in language that recalls Jesus, when "he set his face to go to Jerusalem" (Luke 9:51).

Paul said:

> And now, behold, I am going to Jerusalem, bound in the Spirit, not knowing what shall befall me there; except that the Holy Spirit testifies to me in every city that imprisonment and afflictions await me. But I do not account my life of any value nor as precious to myself, if only I may accomplish my course and the ministry which I received from the Lord Jesus, to testify to the gospel of the grace of God. (Acts 20:22-24.)

The disciples of Tyre repeated Paul's prediction, but they urged him not to go to Jerusalem (21:4). The prophecy of Agabus, attributed also to the Holy Spirit, was a further confirmation of Paul's course (ch. 21:11). It was Paul, not his friends who begged him to avoid Jerusalem, who discerned the will of God (v. 12). In his readiness to die in Jerusalem he was never more like Jesus (vs. 13f.).

Paul's sermon to the Ephesian elders (ch. 20:17-35) represents also one of the important stages in the development of "the legitimate church" in opposition to the "independent" groups that were appearing. Salvation history and the structured fellowship are more of a necessity in defense against heresy and schism.

The necessity for a presbytery, elders to rule and teach the various group meetings of God's church, is clearly expressed in this admonition to the elders: "Take heed to yourselves and to all the flock, in which the Holy Spirit has made you guardians, to feed the church of the Lord which he obtained with his own blood" (v. 28). Those who are described as "guardians" (*episkopoi*, "overseers" or "bishops") were called elders (*presbyteroi*, "presbyters") in v. 17, so it may be concluded that the terms for elders and bishops meant the same at this stage of the developing ministry. It was not until a later time that "bishop" became the term for the single presiding elder of a church with a plurality of elders. There was one church in Ephesus with many meeting places and many elders. This was the work of the Holy Spirit to protect the church from the "fierce wolves," the independent heretics, who would seek "to draw away the disciples after them" (v. 30).

Controversy over the relationship between the charismatic and official ministers of the church was a lively issue in the early church as it is today.[35] Charismatic prophets have a place in the theology of Acts (chs. 11:27 f.; 13:1; 15:32; 20:22 f.; 21:9). The last reference is to Philip's "four unmarried daughters, who prophesied." These prophets were no threat to the unity of the church until they became false prophets, as the speech of Paul anticipates, but threats to the fellowship and faith of the church are to be met by the *presbyteroi-episkopoi* ("elder-bishops") appointed to this task by the Holy Spirit. *Charismata* ("spiritual gifts") without *taxis* ("order") leads to schism (cf. I Thess. 5:12-22; I Cor. 14:40; I Peter 5:1-11; Heb. 13:7, 17, 24).

As long as the church exists in history, there is need of structure and an ordered ministry. Much current opposition to this that appeals to primitive Paulinism for justification is strangely similar to early Gnosticism, not only in attacks upon the historical structure of the church, but in its denial of the bodily resurrection. In order to be abreast with the latest fad,

80

many seem unable to see that the battle of the early church against a false "spirituality" is being waged anew. The salvation history and structured life of Acts, noted first in ch. 6:1-6, has much to teach twentieth-century Christians.

The gift of the Spirit in Acts is set within the framework of salvation history, the central events of which were the anointment of Jesus with the Spirit in his ministry and the outpouring of the Spirit upon the disciples at Pentecost. The literary structure of six books, built on the twofold structure of the acts of Peter and the acts of Paul, and the unity of the threefold witness from Jerusalem to the end of the earth constitute a perspective in which the acts of the church in the power of the Spirit are seen as the history of salvation.

4

THE SPIRIT OF LIFE
IN EARLY PAULINE WRITINGS (I)

TEACHINGS on the Holy Spirit in the Pauline writings are in abundance. These writings form five groups: the letters to the Thessalonians, to the Corinthians, to the Galatians and the Romans, the Prison Letters, and the Pastoral Letters. This chapter is confined to the first two groups, a second to Galatians and Romans, and a third to the last two. Brief background studies appear, but the bulk of the material attempts to interpret the statements about the Spirit in their literary setting.

In the Biblical passages considered thus far the Holy Spirit has for the most part been interpreted as a power in the present pointing to the future. This is still true in the Pauline writings, but the period of mission, developed in the Lucan writings, has become the age of the church, the time for the formation of the body of Christ and the living of the life of salvation. The present is more than a prelude and the power of the Spirit is more than the presage of Final Judgment.[1] It is the age of the Spirit.

THE HOLY SPIRIT AND PROCLAMATION
(I, II THESSALONIANS)

In the earliest of Paul's extant letters the teachings on the Holy Spirit are vitally related to proclamation. These teachings are not highly developed, but their early date, about A.D. 50, and the missionary situation give them great impor-

82

tance. This preaching in a pioneer situation may be grouped under two headings: apostolic preaching and prophetic preaching.

The apostolic preaching by Paul and his associates planted the gospel in a pagan situation, and out of this situation the gospel took on relevant form. It was first of all evangelistic, in the original meaning of *euangelion*, " good news."

Their proclamation was dynamic and persuasive. The dynamic came not from human eloquence and artful rhetoric. It came to the people " not only in word, but also in power and in the Holy Spirit and with full conviction" (I Thess. 1:5). Preaching in word only is as dead as a naked symbol; it is perhaps deader, for meaningful symbols are by their very concreteness more powerful than abstract sounds. When sounds are both abstract and dead few things are so flat.

Sounds can become dynamic, as symbols can take on power when understood, believed, and, most especially, blessed by the action of God. This is as important to remember in preaching as in Baptism and the Lord's Supper. It is the " also," the " also in power and in the Holy Spirit and with full conviction " that makes the difference between throwing shibboleths and proclaiming the word of God. When the word is preached " in power and in the Holy Spirit " it brings " full conviction." The power (*dynamis*) is derived from the Holy Spirit. There is as much difference between preaching " in the Holy Spirit " and preaching by human strength alone as there is between living " in the Spirit " and living " in the flesh."

The full conviction (*plērophoria*) opened the hearts of the people to the preaching of the gospel. Paul could say:

> And you became imitators of us and of the Lord, for you received the word in much affliction, with joy inspired by the Holy Spirit; so that you became an example to all the believers in Macedonia and Achaia. (I Thess. 1:6 f.)

Paul and his associates imitated the Lord, and the people imitated them and the Lord.

The outward circumstances by which they received the

word were full of affliction. With three weeks of synagogue preaching that Jesus is the Christ, the place was in an uproar. The Jews brought the accusation before the city authorities that Paul and his companions were men who "turned the world upside down" (Acts 17:6). In the midst of all this, however, the people received the word "with joy inspired by the Holy Spirit" (I Thess. 1:6).

Much of this inward joy came from the content of the apostolic preaching. The people "turned to God from idols, to serve a living and true God, and to wait for his Son from heaven, whom he raised from the dead, Jesus who delivers us from the wrath to come" (vs. 9 f.). This is the same as the "work of faith and labor of love and steadfastness of hope in our Lord Jesus Christ" (v. 3). In the history of the church the hope of glory and the Holy Spirit often stimulated great joy.

The apostolic preaching was also strongly ethical. Evangelistic preaching that does not come to grips with great ethical issues is not apostolic. The most radical issue confronted in Thessalonica was sanctification. Greek paganism thought of the body as evil, so the sanctity of the body was strange to them. Fornication was as free as in the *Playboy* Philosophy of the present.

Sanctification of the body was the will of God for Paul, and this ruled out fornication (I Thess. 4:3-8). Sanctification means three things: abstaining from fornication (v. 3), controlling the passions of the body (vs. 4 f.), and respect for the marriage relation (v. 6a). This was a radical ethic for people given to immorality.

The reasons for sanctification were: God's judgment on human sin (v. 6b), the call to consecration (v. 7), and the gift of the Holy Spirit (v. 8). "Therefore whoever disregards this, disregards not man but God, who gives his Holy Spirit to you." (V. 8.) This last reason comes as a climax to the whole appeal, and it is crucial for the Christian concept of sexual sanctity. The human body in which the Holy Spirit dwells is holy, and fornication is forbidden.

Sanctification is also the act of God. It is his act understood

84

both as gradual process and as a final state. Sanctification is both *hagiōsunē* (I Thess. 3:13), the final state, and *hagiasmos* (ch. 4:3), the present process that leads to the final state. The Holy Spirit works in the whole process to make the total life holy. Salvation and sanctification are a process (present, past, and future) "because God chose you from the beginning to be saved, through sanctification by the Spirit and belief in the truth" (II Thess. 2:13).

Apostolic preaching, in the third place, was eschatological. Listen to the apostolic benediction on the Thessalonians: "May the God of peace himself sanctify you wholly; and may your spirit and soul and body be kept sound and blameless at the coming of our Lord Jesus Christ" (I Thess. 5:23). Sanctification by the Spirit is no isolated spasm that does the work of God in a moment. It is a spiritual process, beginning when the Holy Spirit takes up his abode in the human body and completed only at the *parousia*, the second coming of our Lord Jesus Christ. Salvation history is sanctification history, and he who is being saved is being sanctified.

Prophetic preaching which builds the church follows the apostolic preaching that planted the church. The building of the church required both structure and spiritual dynamic, but some tension developed between these two. The first believers came out of the synagogue (Acts 17:1), in which the leaders or rulers were elders (*presbyteroi*). The first leaders of the church in Thessalonica had a similar function, but they were called rulers (*proistamenoi*), a functional term for those in a ruling capacity (Rom. 12:8; I Tim. 3:4 f., 15; 5:17).

It is possible that the tension between the synagogue and the church caused Paul to use the functional term *proistamenoi* rather than the official term "elder."[2] The same type of leaders are called *hēgoumenoi* ("leaders") in Hebrews (ch. 13:7, 17, 24) and *presbyteroi* ("elders") in I Peter (ch. 5:1). Paul speaks of *episkopoi* ("bishops") in Philippians (ch. 1:1), and *presbyteroi* are found in I Timothy (ch. 5:17; cf. Titus 1:5; Acts 11:30; 14:23). Least order is found in Corinth, but even there "such men" (I Cor. 16:16, 18) as "devoted themselves to the service of the saints" (v. 15) are to be found. By the time of First Timothy there were three types of leaders: deacons, elders, and the position of Timothy which was called "bishop" no later than Ignatius of Antioch.

Tension in Thessalonica first developed between the *proistamenoi* and the *adelphoi* ("brethren") (I Thess. 5:12, 14). The brethren were admonished "to respect those who labor among you and are over you in the Lord and admonish you" (v. 12). They were exhorted to join in the oversight of the church and to "admonish the idle, encourage the fainthearted, help the weak, be patient with them all" (v. 14). This makes at least three groups in the church: rulers, brethren, and the immature.

The real tension in Thessalonica was between the official ministers described above and the charismatic ministries so common in the primitive churches. The exhortations suddenly take on the structure of a hymn:

Always rejoice!
   1. Without ceasing, pray!
      2. In all circumstances, give thanks! (for this is the will of God in Christ Jesus for you.)
   1. The Spirit, do not quench!
      2. Prophesyings, do not despise!
   1. All things, prove them!
      2. The good, hold fast! (Abstain from every form of evil.)

The numbered lines are parallels, the rest are introduction or title and two comments, the last taken from Job 1:8; 2:3.

The six lines of the hymn yield very much the picture of Christian worship to be seen in greater detail in First Corinthians. Quenching the Spirit, which Paul forbids, sounds very much like the gift of tongues in First Corinthians, which Paul practiced (ch. 14:18) in private and permitted in public worship under regulations (vs. 26-32). First Corinthians 14:39 is almost a rephrasing of I Thess. 5:19 f. in reverse order: "So, my brethren, earnestly desire to prophesy, and do not forbid speaking in tongues."

In the setting of prayer and thanksgiving, two very important elements in Christian worship: the Spirit is not to be quenched, and prophecy is not to be despised. Both of these are attributed to the moving of the Spirit. God is not the author of confusion that may attend the disorderly worship, but room is to be given for the charismatic gifts that build the church. Rigid leaders should not pour cold water on the charismatic fires.

This does not mean that the church is to accept all claims of inspiration. They are to "test everything" and "hold fast what is good." Among the charismatic Quakers the meeting always practiced discernment when any claimed to be moved by the Spirit. There are true prophets and false prophets.

False prophets were among the Thessalonians. Paul's preaching of the *parousia* had been so misunderstood that some prophets were preaching a "realized eschatology" that said "the day of the Lord has come" (II Thess. 2:1 f.). The people are warned "not to be quickly shaken in mind or excited, either by spirit or by word, or by letter purporting" to be by Paul (v. 2). No date had been attached to the *parousia* in I Thess. 4:13 to 5:11, but the false prophets said it had already come. Paul corrects this with a seven-stage apocalypse (II Thess. 2:1-12).[3]

THE HOLY SPIRIT AND EDIFICATION
(I, II CORINTHIANS)

If there is a distinctive term to describe spiritual growth in the Corinthian church it is "edification" (*oikodomē*, "building up").[4] The church is God's *oikodomē* (I Cor. 3:9), and the value of any spiritual gifts is measured by their use in building the church (chs. 14:3, 4, 5, 12, 17). Ethical behavior is likewise measured in this manner (chs. 8:1; 10:23). Paul's guiding principle is: "Let all things be done for edification" (ch. 14:26; cf. I Thess. 5:11; II Cor. 10:8; 12:19; 13:10; Rom. 14:19; 15:2; Eph. 4:12, 16, 29). This is applied to a complex of problems related to the Holy Spirit.

The first major problem was immorality. The theological thrust of sanctification, noted in the Thessalonian letters, is developed even more in the Corinthian letters. The key concept is that of temple or sanctuary. The church is the temple of the Holy Spirit first, then the human body is. Sanctification by the Holy Spirit is basic in both. The concept of the people of God as the sanctuary of God comes into full focus in what is believed to be a fragment of Paul's first letter to the Corinthians (II Cor. 6:14 to 7:1). God's people are God's temple because God indwells them.

God's indwelling of his people by the Holy Spirit appears in the next letter. After describing the church as God's field (I Cor. 3:5-9) and God's building (vs. 10-15), the concept of the temple comes as a climax (vs. 16 f.):

Do you not know that you are God's temple and that God's Spirit dwells in you? If any one destroys God's temple, God will destroy him. For God's temple is holy, and that temple you are.

The plural is used each time in this passage, so the "you" always means the people as a whole, the church, rather than the human body of one individual. The holiness of the temple is derived from the indwelling Spirit. The Spirit is holy, so those in whom he dwells are holy too. Desecration of this temple, by schism and sin, is such a sacrilege that God will destroy those responsible for it. Physical death is looked upon as God's judgment upon the desecrators (I Cor. 5:5; 11:29 f.).

Each human body in which the Holy Spirit dwells is also holy. Sanctification is first of all separation from sin. After a catalogue of ten sins, half of them perversions of the human body, comes the comment (ch. 6:11): "And such were some of you. But you were washed, you were sanctified, you were justified in the name of the Lord Jesus Christ and in the Spirit of our God." The sanctity of the body excludes fornication, adultery, homosexuality (two Greek words), and drunkenness.

Sanctification is more than separation from human vice. Separation alone would be negative puritanism. Sanctification is also positive consecration to Christ. Gnostic libertines argued that food and sex did not raise moral issues. They thought one could be joined to God with his human spirit and joined to a prostitute with his body without raising a question of morals. Paul believed the human body as well as the human spirit became united to Christ when the Holy Spirit was received.

These issues indicate a fundamental difference between the Christian and the pagan view of the human body. In pagan thought the body was a tomb from which a soul, by nature immortal, would escape for redemption. For Paul, man as a whole was mortal, but the human spirit and the human body could *receive* immortality. His conclusion, on the basis of his presuppositions, was most logical:

> Do you not know that your body is a temple of the Holy Spirit within you, which you have from God? You are not your own; you were bought with a price. So glorify God in your body. (I Cor. 6:19 f.)

The second major problem was immaturity. This was expressed in the need for spiritual growth and in the exercise of spiritual gifts. Spiritual maturity is reached primarily by growth in knowledge and love. Knowledge without love produces pride (ch. 8:1), but true love includes knowledge (ch. 13:8-13). Knowledge through spiritual growth begins with wisdom.

There are two types of wisdom — the wisdom of man and the wisdom of God, earthly and heavenly (cf. James 3:13-18). Paul resisted all temptations to employ worldly wisdom in the proclamation of the gospel. This resistance was based upon the very nature of God's revelation in the crucified Christ. Manner and message are intertwined, so he reminded the Corinthians that he preached "not in plausible words of wisdom, but in demonstration of the Spirit and power" that their "faith might not rest in the wisdom of men but in the power of God" (I Cor. 2:4 f.).

His preaching was a paradox of grace. Human weakness was more manifest than human wisdom. His fears were so many that it took a heavenly voice to give him assurance (Acts 18:9). Paul's demonstration (*apodeixis*), a technical term in rhetoric, was that power which the Spirit gave. His preaching was abundant proof that "the kingdom of God does not consist in talk but in power" (I Cor. 4:20).

God's wisdom was revealed through the Spirit in three stages. It was first hidden from this present evil age and those who conform to its ways and are dominated by its demonic powers (ch. 2:6-9). The crucifixion of Jesus, the Shekinah glory of God in human flesh, is evidence for this hiddenness.

God's wisdom is revealed in the dialogue between God and man created by the Holy Spirit (vs. 10-13). God's Spirit knows the profoundest things of God. The "deep things" (*ta bathē*) come out of God's *bathos*, a word which means "depth," the deepest water. Before this mystery Paul exclaimed: "O the depth [*bathos*] of the riches and wisdom and knowledge of God! How unsearchable are his judgments and how inscrutable his ways!" (Rom. 11:33).

Using a psychological analogy, later explored in Augustine's psychological Trinity (*De Trinitate*), Paul indicates the manner of God's self-disclosure: "For what person knows a man's thoughts except the spirit of the man which is in him? So also no one comprehends the thoughts of God except the Spirit of God" (I Cor. 2:11).

We receive the Spirit of God that we may *know* the things that God has given to us from his mysterious depths (v. 14). The spirit of the world, the demonic power that dominates this age and its rulers, knows only "the deep things of Satan" (cf. Rev. 2:24). The things of God are known and *made known* by the Spirit. Reception and impartation are impossible without that personal power that goes forth from God. "And we impart this in words not taught by human wisdom but taught by the Spirit, interpreting spiritual truths to those who possess the Spirit." (I Cor. 2:13.)

God's wisdom is hidden from those who do not possess the Spirit, but it is revealed to those who do. The reception of the revelation, therefore, divides men into two main groups: the

90

natural and the spiritual. " The natural man does not receive the gifts of the Spirit of God, for they are folly to him, and he is not able to understand them because they are spiritually discerned." (V. 14.) It is as impossible for this *psychikos anthrōpos* ("natural man") to discern spiritual things as it is for a man without a radio to receive a broadcast. The receiver is not there.

The *pneumatikos anthrōpos* ("spiritual man") is the mature Christian, but he may appear odd to those who listen to only one side of his dialogue. It is like trying to make sense out of a telephone conversation when only one end of the conversation is heard. The judgment of the natural man, knowing nothing about spiritual things, cannot be accepted. "The spiritual man judges all things, but is himself to be judged by no one." (V. 15.)

There is a third man, however, in the reception. Many commentaries identify the carnal men of I Cor. 3:1 with the natural man of ch. 2:14, but this is impossible. The carnal men are plainly called "babes in Christ." This could never be said of a natural man who had never received the Spirit. Babes in Christ are immature Christians, people who have received Christ and the Spirit, but they have not developed to maturity. They are able to drink milk, the elementary things of the Christian life, but the deeper things of the Christian faith, the solid food, they are not able to eat.

This distinction between the carnal and spiritual Christian, the immature and the mature, points up the basic cause of schism in the church of Corinth. There was so much jealousy and strife among them that Paul rebuked them for "behaving like ordinary men," men who did not possess the Spirit at all. Two main parties, those for Paul and those for Apollos, had developed. It is possible that a group for Cephas and a party for Christ made a four-way split. It was much like the hard-pressed preacher who declared he would have the largest cradle roll in the land when church members become classified according to their spiritual growth.

The Holy Spirit enables the spiritual men to make practical

application of God's wisdom. Paul attributes this assistance to the Spirit in his advice about second marriages. Second marriage, after the decease of the first husband, is allowed, provided the second husband is a Christian, but he thinks the unmarried state best. In this judgment he said: "And I think that I have the Spirit of God" (I Cor. 7:40).

The problem of spiritual gifts may also have some connection with the Apollos party. If Apollos were "boiling over with the Spirit," even before he met Priscilla and Aquila, then he may have been a leader in the charismatic revival in Corinth. To say the least, the Corinthians were "not lacking in any spiritual gift" (ch. 1:7), and the exercise of spiritual gifts was as much a problem as the lack of spiritual growth. The two have a close relation as Paul seeks the edification of the church.

One of the questions sent to Paul from Corinth was "concerning spiritual gifts" (ch. 12:1), and his reply to this question is the *locus classicus* on the *charismata* ("spiritual gifts"). Until the second century the term itself is found outside of Paul only in Philo (*De leg. alleg.* iii. 30) and I Peter 4:10. Paul uses the singular in reference to redemption (Rom. 5:15 f.; 6:23), gifts that may be an endowment (I Cor. 1:7), a capacity (ch. 7:7), a favor (II Cor. 1:11), or truth (Rom. 1:11), and to the ministry (I Tim. 4:14; II Tim. 1:6), but the special use in the plural usually has reference to the Holy Spirit (I Cor. 12:4, 9, 28, 30 f.; Rom. 12:6; cf. Rom. 11:29).

The general presentation of the *charismata* in I Cor., ch. 12, is in two parts, both of which are central in Paul's theology. The manifestation of the Spirit (vs. 1-11) begins with a confession that connects two words: *KYRIOS IĒSOUS* ("Lord Jesus"). This acclamation arose in the Hellenistic Gentile Christian church, but its confessional form (cf. Rom. 10:9a) and appearance in the pre-Pauline hymn in Phil. 2:11 makes it very early. It first belonged to liturgical worship, but it was later the confession of the persecuted who made this confession rather than *KYRIOS KAISAR* ("Lord Caesar").[5]

The Corinthians were once "led astray to dumb idols," but

the Holy Spirit enabled them to abandon their heathen ways and make the KYRIOS confession. "Therefore I want you to understand that no one speaking by the Spirit of God ever says 'Jesus be cursed!' and no one can say 'Jesus is Lord' except by the Holy Spirit." (I Cor. 12:3.) The Aramaic *anathema* ("cursed") may reflect the Jewish opposition to Paul's preaching. Luke's account of Paul's preaching "that the Christ was Jesus" (Acts 18:5) indicates a similar situation.

The manifestation of the Spirit was unity in the midst of variety. The unity is found in the Triune God (cf. II Cor. 13:14), as indicated in the liturgical hymn:

> Now there are varieties of gifts [*charismatōn*],
>   but the same Spirit;
> and there are varieties of services [*diakoniōn*],
>   but the same Lord;
> and there are varieties of workings [*energomatōn*],
>   but the same God
> (who inspires them all in every one).

The gifts, services, and works are not three different groups, as Spirit, Lord, and God are not three different gods. There is a oneness in threeness in the gifts as there is a oneness in threeness in God.

There are varieties in the unity of the spiritual gifts. "To each is given the manifestation of the Spirit for the common good." (I Cor. 12:7.) The nine gifts are threefold in their manifestation. The gifts manifested in thought are wisdom and knowledge. The *logos sophias* ("utterance of wisdom") is insight into mystery. It enables one to discern in the dramas of history the *sod* (Hebrew for "counsel") of God. Even in the Old Testament it was only the wise man who could discern wisdom and put it to practice (Prov., chs. 1 to 9), so now the Crucified One may be discerned as the *sophia* of God by the Spirit alone (I Cor. 1:18 to 2:16). He who has the Spirit of God has the mind of Christ (ch. 2:12, 16). Wisdom, often united with knowledge, becomes more comprehensive in

93

later Pauline writings (Rom. 11:33; Col. 1:9, 28; 2:3, 23; 4:5; Eph. 1:9, 17; 3:10).

The *logos gnōseōs* ("utterance of knowledge") is mystical vision. It soars above the clouds of history in mystical contemplation. The Corinthians "were enriched in him with all speech and all knowledge" (I Cor. 1:5), but this, apart from love, led to spiritual pride. "'Knowledge' puffs up, but love builds up." (Ch. 8:1.) Knowledge (*gnōsis*) was not possessed by all believers (v. 7), so a weak brother could meet spiritual disaster by the example of the stronger brother who had *gnōsis* (vs. 7-13). He who has knowledge without love is nothing (ch. 13:2), yet knowledge has value in Christian worship (ch. 14:6) and life (II Cor. 2:14; 4:6; 6:6; 8:7; 10:5; 11:6). This continues too in the Pauline writings (Phil. 3:8; Col. 2:3), but *gnōsis* may turn out to be false (I Tim. 6:20).

The gifts manifested in action are miraculous faith, healing, and the working of miracles. The very close relation between *gnōsis* and this miraculous faith is seen in the following chapter:

And if I have prophetic powers, and understand all mysteries and all knowledge, and if I have all faith, so as to remove mountains, but have not love, I am nothing. (I Cor. 13:2.)

It is not saving faith, the acceptance of God's initial grace, in which one continues to walk. It is miraculous faith measured out by God, and it has much of the danger that attends knowledge.

For by the grace given to me I bid every one among you not to think of himself more highly than he ought to think, but to think with sober judgment, each according to the measure of faith which God has assigned him. (Rom. 12:3.)

Healings have reference to human life. The healings of body and mind so central in the ministry of Jesus (Mark 5:34; 10:52), continue in his body, the church. These healing pow-

94

ers are present in the mystical body of Christ according to God's grace and man's response to that grace, but not all members of the body possess this gift (I Cor. 12:28, 30). Quackery that excludes modern medicine, on the part of misguided advocates, and panic, on the part of those who are skeptical, have all but eliminated this ministry so normal in the apostolic age (James 5:14 f.). The healing team of faith and science is too seldom seen, but this is being corrected in some places.

The workings of powers in the wider order of creation were abundant in the ministry of Jesus (Mark 9:23; 11:22; Matt. 11:20; Luke 5:17; 17:6). Hellenistic Jewish Christianity saw Jesus as one to whom God " bore witness by signs and wonders and various miracles and by gifts of the Holy Spirit distributed according to his own will " (Heb. 2:4). Paul's own ministry among the Gentiles was confirmed by God's supply of the Spirit and miracles (Gal. 3:3; Rom. 15:18 f.). Does the church of the present manifest the body of Christ fully when the powers are seldom present?

The third group of spiritual gifts are manifest in speech. The gifts of prophecy and discerning of spirits belong together as do kinds of tongues and interpretation of tongues. Inspired prophets were many in the early church. They are mentioned in Acts (chs. 11:27; 13:1; 15:32; 21:9), and Paul discloses their function in the worship of the church. Women as well as men exercised the gift (I Cor. 11:4; cf. Acts 21:10), and this was a normal part of public worship in Corinth at least (I Cor. 14:3; cf. Rom. 12:8). The Didache, an early church manual, has detailed regulations about the conduct of prophets (11:7-12). They are often connected with teachers (Acts 13:1) and apostles (Eph. 2:20; 3:5; Didache, 11:3-12).

This does not mean that the early church accepted all claims to inspired prophecy as valid. They were acutely aware of the dangers of false prophets (Mark 13:22; Matt. 7:15; 24:11, 24; Acts 13:6; Rev. 16:13; 19:20; 20:10). The false prophets under the guise of Gnosticism were recognized as antichrists preparing the way for *the* Antichrist, and I John 4:1-6 indicates the discernment of spirits which enabled the church to detect them.

The gift of tongues has been noted in Acts (Jerusalem, Samaria, Caesarea, Ephesus), and it became a special problem in Corinth that called for careful regulation and evaluation. This and the gift of interpretation complete the nine gifts of I Cor. 12:8-10, but they call for more consideration shortly.

The manifestation of the Spirit in the members of the body of Christ is applied to the threat of schism and the need of order in the church (I Cor. 12:12-31). This is introduced by a second confession. The basic confession that said " Jesus is Lord " is supplemented by the confession which briefly stated is, " One body and one Spirit " (Eph. 4:4). The longer form is:

> For just as the body is one and has many members, and all the members of the body, though many, are one body, so it is with Christ. For by one Spirit we were all baptized into one body — Jews or Greeks, slaves or free — and all were made to drink of one Spirit. (I Cor. 12:12 f.)

As there is one human body for one human spirit, so there is only one body for the Holy Spirit.

This baptism with the Spirit and drinking of the Spirit is an antitype of which the exodus from Egypt was a type. The fathers "were baptized into Moses in the cloud and in the sea, and all ate the same spiritual food and all drank the same spiritual drink. For they drank from the spiritual Rock which followed them, and the Rock was Christ " (I Cor. 10:2-4). By the one Spirit believers are baptized into Christ or the body of Christ. This is the antitype of the Red Sea crossing. This baptism of the Spirit is not repeated, but filling with the Spirit is. Drinking from the Rock came later in the wilderness, and filling with the Spirit often comes later in the body of Christ. Paul would not have used the term " drink one Spirit " had he not been following this type of the wilderness experience.

Twice the " one body " is mentioned (ch. 12:12 f.), and twice the phrase " one Spirit " is used. The very idea of even two

96

bodies of Christ (Jews and Greeks, slaves and free), to say nothing about thousands, was an impossible thought for Paul. It was as impossible as the idea of two Spirits or ten thousand Spirits. Therefore, schism in the body of Christ must be avoided at all cost. "God has so adjusted the body, giving greater honor to the inferior part, that there may be no schism in the body, but that members may have the same care for one another." (Vs. 24 f.)

To argue that each congregation is a separate body of Christ on the basis of the one example (sole example of the New Testament) of the missing article (*sōma Christou*) in v. 27 is separatism staging a desperate defense. *Sōma Christou* means "Christ's body." Christ's body is Christ (cf. v. 12). Becoming a member of the body and putting on Christ mean the same. If one is *in* Christ, he is *in* the body. Schism in the body is sin against Christ. That is the burden of vs. 14-26.

The work of God in the body of Christ is a work of order, not schism. That is the burden of vs. 27-31. God has not only "set" (*etheto*) the organs in the body (v. 18); he has also "set" (*etheto*) order (v. 28): "First apostles, second prophets, third teachers, then workers of miracles, then healers, helpers, administrators, speakers in various kinds of tongues" (vs. 28-30). Apostles and teachers, helpers and administrators were not among the nine gifts. The seven gifts of Rom. 12:6-8 have five more (ministry, exhorting, giving, ruling, showing mercy). Evangelists and pastors-teachers appear for the first time in Eph. 4:11. This list of twenty gifts in four different groups, none of them the same, should warn against all rigidity.

In the growing concept of the ministry, ordination was later performed by the laying of hands on both elders and deacons, but many charismatic ministries were never "ordered" by ordination. Deacons and elders gave order to the helpers (deacons) and administrators (elders) of I Cor. 12:28 and to the giving (deacons) and ruling (elders) of Rom. 12:8, but this does not appear until the Pastoral Letters.[6]

The special presentation of the *charismata* was called forth

97

by the problem of tongues. Order in the church was observed in I Thess. 5:12-20, but the regulations for the gift of tongues introduced the term *taxis* ("order," I Cor. 14:40), later to designate the structure of the church. As a step in church order and as the only analysis and evaluation of tongues in the New Testament, I Cor., ch. 14, demands attention.

Speaking in tongues (vs. 1-19) has a place in relation to both prophecy (vs. 1-12) and worship (vs. 13-19), but there is an order of value. That which edifies most is worth most. Two comparisons between prophecy and tongues indicate prophecy as the higher and greater gift: (1) He who speaks in uninterpreted tongues speaks only to God, but he who prophesies speaks also to man (vs. 2 f.); (2) he who speaks in uninterpreted tongues edifies only himself, "but he who prophesies edifies the church" (vs. 4 f.). Evaluation is guided by edification, so prophecy is of greater value.

Two illustrations support this conclusion. Musical instruments are of value only when their sound has meaning. "So with yourselves; if you in a tongue utter speech that is not intelligible, how will any one know what is said?" (V. 9.) Foreign languages likewise are of no value to those who do not understand them (vs. 10-12). The Greeks called all who spoke other languages "people who go *barbar*" ("barbarians," Thayer), and this is the way one responds to uninterpreted tongues. Paul is not here calling tongues foreign languages; he is comparing them to a foreign language not understood by the hearer.

Tongues still are tolerated by Paul in worship (vs. 13-19), but they must always be interpreted to edify the church. Three forms of worship are mentioned: prayer (vs. 13-15), thanksgiving (vs. 16 f.), and instruction (vs. 18 f.). One may pray with his *pneuma* ("human spirit") only, but Paul wants him to use his *nous* ("human mind") also.

The distinction between human *pneuma* and human *nous* is very close to the modern distinction between unconscious (or subconscious) and the conscious, and the observation of tongues suggests that sounds are pouring out of the unconscious without any "censor" from the conscious. Inarticulate sounds, articulate sounds resembling words, coined words and phrases, and foreign words and phrases have been heard. In all of these the person is left with a sense of purification and integration. Interpretations of the source of these phenomena differ sharply, but the phenomena have been observed.

The same distinction between *pneuma* and *nous* is applied to giving of thanks, either in general or at the Eucharist. At the end of thanksgiving the congregation responded with the "Amen," as in Old Testament worship (Neh. 8:6; I Chron. 16:36; Ps. 106:48), but one is not able to "Amen" uninterpreted tongues. Only the one who prays in the tongues is edified when there is no interpreter.

Tongues do not edify unless there is "some revelation or knowledge or prophecy or teaching" (I Cor. 14:6). Instruction that edified the church was the main thing. Paul then said:

> I thank God that I speak in tongues more than you all; nevertheless, in church I would rather speak five words with my mind, in order to instruct others, than ten thousand words in a tongue. (Vs. 18 f.)

The significance of tongues (vs. 20-25) is stated in reference to Scripture (vs. 20-22) and the church (vs. 23-25). Isaiah 28:11 f. was a warning to Israel. If they rejected Isaiah's message, the Assyrians would invade the land and speak to them in a foreign language. This quotation has been used as demonstration that tongues are foreign languages, but it is only an illustration. "Thus, tongues are a sign not for believers but for unbelievers, while prophecy is not for unbelievers but for believers." (I Cor. 14:22.)

The above is difficult to harmonize with that which follows in reference to the church (vs. 23-25). It sounds now as if tongues are not for unbelievers and that prophecy is for both believers, to edify, and for unbelievers, to convict. Two approaches have been made to this problem. Some have dismissed vs. 21 f. as an interpolation, a comment that did not originally belong to the letter. The alternative explanation says tongues are for unbelievers *when interpreted*. They will think one "mad" (v. 23, "you rave") if there is no interpreter.

The regulation of tongues (vs. 26-40) calls for edification. A variety of hymns, lessons from the Old Testament, special revelations, and even tongues and interpretations are permitted, but one rule prevails: "Let all things be done for edification" (v. 26). Two or three may speak in tongues provided they speak in turn and one interprets, but one is to keep silent in the church "and speak to himself and to God" if there is no interpreter (vs. 27 f.). Prophets do not need interpreters, but the principle of order applies to them too: "For God is not a God of confusion but of peace" (v. 33).

Women present a special problem in Corinth. The Pastoral Letters, following the law of the synagogue, forbid a woman to exercise the functions of an elder (teaching and ruling, I Tim. 2:12), but Paul allowed women to pray and prophesy provided they covered their heads (I Cor. 11:5). What does he mean by the silence of women in I Cor. 14:34? The synagogue order had not yet developed in Corinth, so the rule in I Tim. 2:12 does not apply. He does not mean they are forbidden to pray and prophesy, unless he contradicts himself. Eduard Schweizer thinks vs. 34 f. a later addition based on I Tim. 2:11-15.[6a]

The only suggestion left is that he forbids them to speak in tongues in the church. He has already told those men who talked in tongues to be silent (*sigatō*, I Cor. 14:28) when there is no interpreter, and the prophets are to remain silent (*sigatō*, v. 30) while another is speaking. Now he says "the women should keep silence [*sigatōsan*] in the churches" (v. 34). If he does not have reference to tongues, then it could be the discussion of the prophecy uttered by orderly prophets. One thing is sure: Paul is not the suppressor of women he is often pointed up to be (cf. Rom. 16:1 f., 3, 6, 12 f., 15; Phil. 4:2 f.). Acts sustains this better picture even more (chs. 16:1, 14 f.; 17:4, 12, 34).

In summary, Paul seeks to regulate tongues, not to eliminate

100

them. Modern crusaders who seek to drive from the church all who receive the gift of tongues and loudly proclaim the New Testament as their "only rule of faith and order" confront difficulties with Paul who said: "Now I want you all to speak in tongues, but even more to prophesy" (I Cor. 14:5). Then: "I thank God that I speak in tongues more than you all" (v. 18). Finally: "So, my brethren, earnestly desire to prophesy, and do not forbid speaking in tongues; but all things should be done decently and in order" (vs. 39 f.).

Pentecostals who major on the examples in Acts and minimize the evaluations and regulations of I Cor., ch. 14, bring upon themselves many of their calamities. Aggressive advocates seem to overlook the fact of "higher gifts" (ch. 12:31) and Paul's principle of edification (ch. 14:26). They ignore his regulations that speaking in tongues in public worship should always be interpreted and even then no more than two or three should speak in turn. Women should remain silent, yet most "disorder" observed in modern tongues comes from women. One wonders if ever a balance between suppressors and aggressors will be reached.[7]

The problem of immaturity occupies more space in the Corinthian letters than even immorality, yet there is a third major problem that is confronted. Sexual drives and spiritual babes and babbling may be difficult to direct, but man's greatest problem is death. This indeed is "the last enemy to be destroyed" (I Cor. 15:26). After sexual and spiritual aberrations have subsided, the grim reaper stands there alone.

That third problem is immortality. At some time while Paul was in Ephesus he looked death in the face. He knew himself to be in "peril every hour"; he died "every day" and "fought with beasts at Ephesus" (I Cor. 15:30-32). Many scholars believe this had reference to an Ephesian imprisonment and trial not mentioned specifically in Acts.[8] After Paul got to Macedonia he wrote about afflictions "experienced in Asia" in which he was "utterly, unbearably crushed" and "despaired of life itself." He and his companions felt they "had received the sentence of death" (II Cor. 1:8 f.).

101

Against this background of the immediate possibility of death, Paul's thought had evidently brooded much on present mortality and the prospects for immortality beyond earthly existence. The full story of things said and done at Troas, first finding an open door for preaching Christ and then pressing on to Macedonia looking for Titus, is not known. The arrival of Titus in Macedonia, perhaps at Philippi, was the occasion for the glad letter (II Cor., chs. 1 to 9), full of joy and hope, that is such a contrast to chs. 10 to 13, perhaps the grievous letter hotly dispatched before leaving Ephesus (ch. 2:1-11).

Meditations on the hope of immortal glory are based on three Semitic words that reflect the Old Testament sources for Paul's view of the Holy Spirit. The first Semitic word is the "Amen" already noted in Paul's evaluation of tongues in public worship (I Cor. 14:16). This solemn affirmation, meaning "so be it," was the usual response to the doxology in the synagogue, and this was followed in the New Testament in many places.[9]

The Corinthians charged Paul with vacillation when he wavered in his plans to visit them. This was the setting for the inspired aside so full of meaning (II Cor. 1:18-22):

> As surely as God is faithful, our word to you has not been Yes and No. For the Son of God, Jesus Christ, whom we preached among you, Silvanus and Timothy and I, was not Yes and No; but in him it is always Yes. For all the promises of God find their Yes in him. That is why we utter the Amen through him, to the glory of God. But it is God who establishes us with you in Christ, and has anointed us; he has put his seal upon us and given us his Spirit as a guarantee.

Christ is the answer, the affirmative answer, to all God's promises to Israel. When the church responds with the "Amen," it endorses this belief. Those who bless in the name of God know that Christ is the answer, for God establishes and confirms such preaching and worship by the Holy Spirit.

102

The threefold cluster of Semitic ideas explains why the church responds with the warm and fervent "Amen." The cluster includes anointing, sealing, and the down payment or guarantee.

The "Amen," that the leader of worship so often today must say himself, comes like a rumble of thunder from the apostolic congregation. They say, "Amen" because they have been anointed with the Holy Spirit. As prophets, priests, and kings were anointed with oil in Old Testament times, to signify that they were commissioned to be God's representatives, so now all of God's people are prophets, priests, and kings commissioned to be his representatives. As "God anointed Jesus of Nazareth with the Holy Spirit and with power" (Acts 10:38), so now he anoints those who find God's answer in Jesus.

Then the people in the congregation respond, "Amen" because they have been sealed with the Holy Spirit. Tombs, documents, books, etc., were sealed as a means of attestation and security, so God gives the seal of the Spirit as assurance of ownership and future inheritance (Eph. 1:13; 4:30). As long as the seal goes unbroken, there is security and assurance that all God's promises in this life and the life to come will be fulfilled.

Finally, the people in the congregation say, "Amen" because they have the guarantee, the *arrabōn*. The *arrabōn* was the old Phoenician word used for a down payment that guaranteed the full payment later. God has given the foretaste of the heavenly inheritance by the gift of the Spirit, and this is the guarantee that the future payment will be made in full (II Cor. 5:5; Eph. 1:14; cf. Titus 3:4–7).

The second major Semitic word is translated *doxa* ("glory"), but the Semitic *kabod,* meaning "weight" or "honor," furnishes the content. Second Corinthians, ch. 3, is actually a Christian midrash (commentary) on the *kabod* of God that appeared on the face of Moses (Ex. 34: 29-35). Paul stayed in Ephesus until Pentecost (I Cor. 16:8), the time when the giving of the law to Moses was celebrated, and II Cor., ch. 3, indicates how the *kabod,* along with the "Amen," was interpreted in Christian initiation. Jewels of Christian catechism stud II Cor., chs. 1 to 5.

The work of the Spirit in the transforming process of glory is compared with the writing of a letter (II Cor. 3:1-3), the giving of life (vs. 4-11), and the setting at liberty (vs. 12-18). No letters of recommendation were needed by Paul, for the Corinthians were his letter. Christ sent the letter; Paul delivered it; and it was written "with the Spirit of the living God" upon human hearts. This is more than letters written on paper with ink or carved on stone tablets. They are "servants of a new covenant, not of the written code, but of the Spirit" (v. 6).

The stone tablets have reference to the law of Moses, and this suggests the contrast between the written code which kills and the Spirit which gives life, the former being the old covenant and the latter the new. To Paul, Christ as the Last Adam, risen from the dead, "became a life-giving spirit" (I Cor. 15:45). Now he takes a step beyond that to describe the Holy Spirit as the agent by which Christ gives this life. The Nicene Creed has incorporated the idea in the statement: "We believe . . . in the Holy Spirit, the Lord and the Life-giver."

The reference to the Holy Spirit as "Lord" comes also from this chapter of Second Corinthians (ch. 3:18). This does not identify the risen Lord and the Holy Spirit, as is often argued. Such identification would contradict the strong Trinitarianism of the confession in I Cor. 12:4-6 and the apostolic benediction of II Cor. 13:14. The risen Lord is identical with the historical Jesus. The risen Lord and the Holy Spirit are of the same nature, but they are distinguished as persons in the Godhead. Paul could have confessed the Nicene Creed without mental reservations.

The unity between the risen Lord and the Holy Spirit is manifested in setting the captives at liberty and putting them in the process of the transforming glory.

Now the Lord is the Spirit, and where the Spirit of the Lord is, there is freedom. And we all, with unveiled face, beholding the glory of the Lord, are being changed into

104

his image from one degree of glory to another; for this comes from the Lord who is the Spirit. (II Cor. 3:17 f.)

The text does say, "The Lord is the Spirit," but this has reference to the Lord in Ex. 34:34, quoted in the previous verse (II Cor. 3:16). The idea of the Last Adam as "a life-giving spirit" allows this interpretation of an Old Testament text, and the reference to "the Spirit of the Lord" as a synonym immediately afterward makes this view most likely. The transformation of the beholder who has turned to the Lord (i.e., the Spirit) is the work of the Spirit in setting man free (cf. Rom. 8:2).

The transformation, spiritual metamorphosis, that begins with repentance, turning to the Lord, comes to completion at the resurrection of the dead. The fifth parallel in the ten-line hymn on the two Adams in I Cor. 15:45-49 states this clearly (v. 49):

Just as we have borne the image of the man of dust, we shall also bear the image of the man of heaven.[10]

All this "comes from the Lord who is the Spirit" (II Cor. 3:18), still identifying the Lord of Ex. 34:34 with the Holy Spirit that sets man free (cf. Rom. 8:2) and starts him on the way to immortal glory.[11]

The third Semitic word employed in the service of immortality is the old Semitic word *arrabōn*, already noted in II Cor. 1:22. It is the climax of ch. 5:1-5 where the hope of immortality comes into full bloom. The threat of death was met by the belief that the destruction of "the earthly house [*oikia*] of this tent," the human body, would be followed by a "house [*oikia*] not made with hands, eternal in the heavens" (v. 1). This is clearly a state of being "absent from the body" (v. 8), so "the house not made with hands" is not the resurrection body.

The transition from the tent of the human body to the heavenly house does not strip us naked. It is the moment of transition from the groanings and anxieties in the earthly house to immortality. It is the clothing of the human spirit with immortality, as the human body will be clothed with immortality at the resurrection (I Cor. 15:51-57). The mortal is "swallowed up by life" (II Cor. 5:4). The Spirit is the *arrabōn*, the down payment, that guarantees the clothing of the human spirit with immortality at death and the putting on of immortality by the body at the resurrection.[12]

The perils and paradoxes of the present life do not cause the earthen vessel to crumble. Therefore, between ten perils and ten paradoxes, Paul possesses eight powers: "purity, knowledge, forbearance, kindness, the Holy Spirit, genuine love, truthful speech, and the power of God" (II Cor. 6:6 f.). The Holy Spirit makes all the other powers possible.

The apostolic benediction in II Cor. 13:14 has already been mentioned with I Cor. 12:4-6 as an important step in the formulation of the doctrine of the Holy Trinity, both functional and ontological, but "the *koinōnia* of the Holy Spirit" summarizes Paul's view of the church as he wrestles with the problems presented by Corinth.

The famous yoke passage in II Cor., chs. 6:14 to 7:1, perhaps a part of the letter mentioned in I Cor. 5:9, rebuked the Corinthians for failing to make a clear distinction between the *koinōnia* of light and the darkness (II Cor. 6:14). The second letter reminded them that God had called them "into the *koinōnia* of his Son, Jesus Christ" (I Cor. 1:9) and that the loaf they broke at communion was "*koinōnia* in the body of Christ" (ch. 10:16). Now the grievous letter pronounces the benediction:

> The grace of the Lord Jesus Christ
> and the love of God
> and the fellowship of the Holy Spirit
> be with you all.

5

THE SPIRIT OF LIFE
IN EARLY PAULINE WRITINGS (II)

THE TEACHINGS on the Holy Spirit in Galatians and Romans have much in common, but the style of the two letters is very different. Galatians was written to Paul's own converts in Galatia, but the location of Galatia is debated. Once it was thought that the letter was to Christians in the interior of Asia Minor where Gauls had settled in the third century B.C. Exponents of this theory date the letter as late as A.D. 57–58.

There is no independent evidence that Paul ever preached in North Galatia, so many modern scholars argue for South Galatia, the scene of Paul's activities on his first missionary journey (Acts, chs. 13; 14). Since the writings of W. M. Ramsay on this issue, the date has been set as early as A.D. 49, before the Jerusalem conference of A.D. 50. The conference is not mentioned in Galatians, so it is argued, and the issue was settled later at Jerusalem.

The more general view vacillates in date between A.D. 51, from Corinth on the second missionary journey (*The Westminster Study Edition of The Holy Bible*), and A.D. 55, on the third missionary journey (*Oxford Annotated Bible*). The date A.D. 54 seems best. If from Ephesus, which seems most likely, the similarities with II Cor., chs. 10 to 13, are made clearer. If later from Corinth, it was written within three months of Romans (Acts 20:3).

There is little doubt that the letter to the Romans went forth from Corinth (Rom. 15:25-27), about A.D. 55. The first readers of it were people Paul had never seen rather than his converts. The polemics of Galatians had been replaced by peaceful persuasion.

In Galatia a crisis developed on the question of man's right relationship to God. Paul had evangelized the territory, teaching that the right relationship to God is one of faith, obedient trust, and that this relationship can be established without the works of the law. After his departure certain Judaizers put forth the propaganda that circumcision was required before man could be just before God.

Wavering between the two ways of justification threatened Paul's gospel among his Galatian converts, but Paul was in no mood to waver with them. In blunt language he told them:

> I am astonished that you are so quickly deserting him who called you in the grace of Christ and turning to a different gospel — not that there is another gospel, but there are some who trouble you and want to pervert the gospel of Christ. (Gal. 1:6 f.)

Deserting the gospel would make them a "turncoat" to the true gospel.

The function of the Holy Spirit in justification is introduced in the context of faith, freedom, and fulfillment. The place of faith in the experience of the Holy Spirit appears in a constellation of five probing questions (ch. 3:1-5).

The first question was: "O foolish Galatians! Who has bewitched you, before whose eyes Jesus Christ was publicly portrayed as crucified?" To bewitch one was to cast the spell of the evil eye upon him, and this was the disastrous result of a perverted gospel. In the language of the marketplace, Paul had put Christ before them on a placard, yet the evil eye was casting a spell that would bring spiritual ruin.

The second question sharpens the issue more: "Let me ask you only this: Did you receive the Spirit by works of the law, or by hearing with faith?" The question is enough to shake their enchantment, for the Galatians knew very well

108

that the manifestation of the Spirit followed the preaching of the cross, not circumcision. Faith came by hearing the gospel, and the Spirit was received in the obedient submission of faith in Christ. "The joy belonged to the reception of the gospel and the Spirit had disappeared. This fact alone should convince the Galatians that they had been robbed of their great possession."[1]

The third question makes them fools: "Are you so foolish? Having begun with the Spirit, are you now ending with the flesh?" "Beginning" (*enarchesthai*) and "ending" (*epiteleisthai*) are words of sacrifice, the first being "the word for scattering the grains of barley on and around the victim which was the first act of sacrifice," and the other the "word used for fully completing the ritual of any sacrifice."[2] It is sheer folly, warns Paul, to begin the crucified life in the Spirit and attempt to finish it in the flesh. Spirit and flesh for Paul are the very opposites, as the cryptic Greek so well expresses it: *pneumati nun sarki* ("in the Spirit now in the flesh").

The fourth question is filled with pathos: "Did you experience so many things in vain? — if it really is in vain." The Galatians had experienced the great variety of spiritual gifts, the many manifestations of the Holy Spirit, now they are about to substitute circumcision for the charismatic life. The question could also have reference to their many sufferings for Christ, for the verb *epathete* means "to experience good or ill." In any case any effort to put circumcision in the place of Christ would make all this experience vain.

The fifth question most certainly has reference to charismatic and miraculous manifestations of the Spirit: "Does he who supplies the Spirit to you and works miracles among you do so by works of the law, or by hearing with faith?" The verb *epichorēgōn* ("supplying") has reference to the Greek chorus (*chorēgia*), a display of generosity on the part of the sponsor. God's generosity had poured out the Spirit in the preaching of Paul. The mention of miracles is rare in Paul (but see Rom. 15:19), and the appeal to them here is proof positive that God's approval rested on the preaching of justification by grace through faith and not on works of the law such as circumcision.

Abraham, to whom the gospel was preached before circumcision was given, is the true example of the justified man (Gal. 3:6-29). He had neither the ceremonial of law nor the moral law when he was accepted by faith alone. God's purpose was "that in Christ Jesus the blessing of Abraham might come upon the Gentiles, that we might receive the promise of the Spirit through faith" (v. 14).

Freedom and the Holy Spirit have a common source in God's grace. To the Corinthians, Paul declared: "Now the Lord is the Spirit, and where the Spirit of the Lord is, there is freedom" (II Cor. 3:17). This theme is expanded in Paul's exhortations to the Galatians.

Two possibilities are visualized in man's relation to God (Gal. 4:1-11). The first is a movement from slavery to sonship (vs. 1-7). Men are in bondage until God acts in history and in the human heart. His act in history was the sending of his Son to redeem men from bondage. "But when the time had fully come, God sent forth his Son, born of woman, born under the law, to redeem those who were under the law, so that we might receive adoption as sons." (Vs. 4 f.)

A second sending is assurance that one has passed from a state of slavery into a state of sonship. "And because you are sons, God has sent the Spirit of his Son into our hearts, crying, 'Abba! Father!'" (V. 6.) *Abba* is the Aramaic word for "father," and the cry is on the lips of Jesus in the Garden of Gethsemane (Mark 14:36), but here the cry is heard pouring forth from the hearts of those who receive the Spirit. "When we cry, 'Abba! Father!' it is the Spirit himself bearing witness with our spirit that we are children of God." (Rom. 8:15 f.)

Their present status is now established. "So through God you are no longer a slave but a son, and if a son then an heir." (Gal. 4:7.) Yet another possibility is feared. This is the danger that the enchantment of the Judaizers may tempt them to go from sonship back into slavery.

110

The question is dreadful and should not be ignored in the interest of preconceived notions. Let them sink into the wavering heart:

> Formerly, when you did not know God, you were in bondage to beings that by nature are no gods; but now that you have come to know God, or rather to be known by God, how can you turn back again to the weak and beggarly elemental spirits, whose slaves you want to be once more? (Vs. 8 f.)

The allegory of Hagar and Sarah (vs. 21-31) illustrates the difference between slavery and freedom. The two women are two covenants, one from Mt. Sinai and the other from the Jerusalem above. The two sons, Ishmael of a slave and Isaac of a free woman, are the slavery of the law and the freedom of faith. Isaac, "born according to the Spirit" (v. 29), was the child of promise and received the inheritance. So it is with those who are justified by faith and who have been set free by Christ. However, as Ishmael persecuted Isaac, it is suggested that those who live *kata sarka* ("according to the flesh") will persecute those who live *kata pneuma* ("according to the Spirit").

The issue of spiritual freedom or legalistic bondage is the central concern of Galatians. Paul exhorts them: "For freedom Christ has set us free; stand fast therefore, and do not submit again to a yoke of slavery" (Gal. 5:1). He warns them: "You are severed from Christ, you who would be justified by the law; you have fallen out of grace" (v. 4, A. T. Robertson). He rebukes them: "You were running well; who hindered you from obeying the truth?" (v. 7).

Freedom from the bondage of the law is freedom to fulfill the requirements of the law. "For through the Spirit, by faith, we wait for the hope of righteousness. For in Christ Jesus neither circumcision nor uncircumcision is of any avail, but faith working through love." (Vs. 5 f.) Freedom must not be used as an opportunity to indulge the desires of the fallen and self-centered nature, the flesh. The true expression of freedom is love, freedom for our neighbor as well as freedom

111

from the law. Love for our neighbor is the one word that fulfills the law (vs. 13 f.).

This fulfillment of the law by neighborly love is the Christian *halakah* ("rule for daily living"). Many rules constituted the Jewish *halakah*, but there is only one rule for Christians: "You shall love your neighbor as yourself" (Lev. 19:18; Gal. 5:14; cf. Rom. 13:8-10). When Paul says "walk by the Spirit" (Gal. 5:16, 25), he translates the Hebrew *halak* ("walk"). Two other ways to express this are "led by the Spirit" (v. 18) and "live by the Spirit" (v. 25). Love is the expression of this leading and living. This is the rule by which those in the new creation walk (ch. 6:15 f.).

The one rule does not exclude norms, the normal course of action under similar circumstances. The rule of love has normal applications in situations that are the same. This has been thrown out of focus by some forms of "situation ethics" that have a hankering for abnormal predicaments.[3] Life is a choice between two sets of desires, those that have their source in the flesh, man's nature in estrangement from neighbor and God, and those that flow from the Spirit and the dominant sentiment of love.

Rabbinic thought spoke of the *yetzer ha-ra*, the evil desires located on man's left side, and the *yetzer ha-tob*, the good desires on the right.[4] A Christian adaptation and refinement of this explains the frustrations in the fulfillment of law through love.

> For the desires of the flesh are against the Spirit, and the desires of the Spirit are against the flesh; for these are opposed to each other, to prevent you from doing what you would. (Gal. 5:17.)

The works of the flesh that gratify the flesh are very different from the fruit of the Spirit. Paul put them plainly: "immorality, impurity, licentiousness, idolatry, sorcery, enmity, strife, jealousy, anger, selfishness, dissension, party spirit, envy, drunkenness, carousing, and the like" (vs. 19-21). He is so sure that these are not the desires of the Spirit and

112

the expression of love that he continues: "I warn you, as I warned you before, that those who do such things shall not inherit the kingdom of God" (v. 21). This is true in most situations!

The Christian life bears "the fruit of the Spirit" (vs. 22 f.). These are those who "walk by the Spirit," who are "led by the Spirit" and "live by the Spirit." This fruit is expressed in relation to self, our neighbor, and God.

True fulfillment of faith and freedom is the fruit of the Spirit, and this fruit is expressed in nine "graces." These nine graces are no less important than the nine gifts. The gifts are manifestations of the Spirit for the edification of the body, the whole church; the graces are ethical norms that give evidence that the Spirit has become the new principle of life. The graces are our gifts to God, the sacrificial fruit offered in love. This fruit may be grouped into the inward (love, joy, peace), the outward (patience, kindness, goodness), and the upward (faithfulness, meekness, self-control). The inward has reference to self, the outward to others, the upward to God.

Love is the first grace of a life being fulfilled. This is authentic life. The primacy of love in the primitive church is well illustrated by the hymns that they sang. First Corinthians, ch. 13, is a three-stanza hymn on love, and the portrait of love in the second stanza (vs. 4-7) portrays the ethical qualities of Jesus. Love is like Jesus. The power of love for one who abides in Christ is praised in another hymn in Rom. 8:31-39. The first two stanzas (vs. 31-34) of this song of sovereign love speak of "no condemnation." The last two (vs. 35-39), viewing the dangers of this world and the next, give assurance of no separation from God's love for those who remain in Christ as their refuge.

Joy is a second quality of the self living in the Spirit. Joy comes with the Holy Spirit (I Thess. 1:6) and is retained in the Holy Spirit (Rom. 14:17). This joy is found in devotion to Christ and in detachment from external circumstances. Philippians does not have much about the Spirit, but joy, the fruit of the Spirit, is its major theme. In devotion to

113

Christ there is "a bountiful supply of the Spirit of Jesus Christ" (Phil. 1:19, Williams) that fills life with joy. The "fellowship of the Spirit" (ch. 2:1), in imitation of the humility of Christ, enables one to adapt to the circumstances of life. Joy of this type is experienced in jail (ch. 4:4-20). Inward communion compensates for outward circumstances.

Peace is harmony within, for harmony with God and man is associated with the heart (Col. 3:15). It is the peace which is beyond ordinary understanding (Phil. 4:7). Peace with God is the source of this peace, for it comes when " God's love has been poured into our hearts through the Holy Spirit which has been given to us " (Rom. 5:5). Peace with people is found in the temple of God by which one enters in the Spirit, through Christ, to God the Father (Eph. 2:18). Harmony in the heart leads to the harmony of the new humanity in Christ. Joy and peace come with the power of the Spirit (Rom. 15:13).

Patience is long-suffering. He who offers a life of patience to God returns that which he has received. God's patience brings us to repentance (Rom. 2:4), and God's patience endures even those who refuse God's grace and glory (ch. 9:22). Godly living under the guidance of the Spirit gives back to God this quality that is missing in the self-centered person. Abundance of spiritual power and abundance of patience belong together.

Kindness helps those in need. It, too, is celebrated in song by the New Testament disciples. A hymn of God's grace in Eph. 2:4-10 views the coming ages as an arena for "the immeasurable riches of his grace in kindness toward us in Christ Jesus" (v. 7). A baptismal hymn pictures God as a plutocrat and a philanthropist who comes to the help of sinful man in his kindness (Titus 3:4-7). In Greek the noun for "Christ" (*Christos*) and the adjective for "kind" (*chrēstos*) were often mixed. The fruit of the Spirit mixes them even more.

"Goodness" is one of those words so close to God that it is difficult to define otherwise. A good person is transparent with God. God's Spirit fills his life like light flooding through a window. *Agathōsunē* lives in the light of God. The self-righteous are goody-good; they must turn on their artificial light. The righteous are just good and notice not the natural glow of their lives.

Faithfulness is what the Hebrews called *emunah*. Psalm 89 alone mentions God's faithfulness seven times. God can be trusted in preservation, temptation, and salvation. The faithfulness of God is almost a proverb for Paul (I Thess. 5:23 f.; I Cor. 1:9, 18; 10:13). This dependable quality grows in those who walk by the Spirit, and the unfaithful have no claim to spiritual maturity. It is striking to notice how Paul magnifies faithfulness in his friends, not only in their devotion to him but in their service to God.

"Gentleness" is a better translation than "meekness" in these days when people think of a mouse when they hear the word "meek." Moses and Christ stand out as the models of meekness, but people know more about mice than about Moses. It is that quality one finds in a gentle animal. That is why Jesus could say: "Take my yoke upon you, and learn from me; for I am gentle and lowly in heart, and you will find rest for your souls" (Matt. 11:29). This life of the yoke he requires of those who follow him.

Self-control belongs to this gentle life. Paul's use of the term has reference to the whole of life, but he applies it to the control of sex and self in particular. Sex is to be controlled, and this principle undergirds his advice for both married and unmarried people (I Cor., ch. 7). He is perhaps hardest on himself as he disciplines himself, lest he be disqualified in God's great game of life (I Cor. 9:24-27).

Most of the moral life as Paul conceived it could be embraced by this concept of the fruit of the Spirit, for the fulfillment of the ethical demands of God are not possible without the love of God imparted by the Spirit. The spiritual (*pneumatikoi*) are called to a life of concern for him who "is overtaken in any trespass" (Gal. 6:1). Life is a sowing and a reaping, and "he who sows to the Spirit will from the Spirit reap eternal life" (v. 8). This is the right relation to God in faith and freedom. This is the fulfillment of life in love.[5]

The Holy Spirit and Salvation (Romans)

Much that was introduced in Galatians, written perhaps from Ephesus around A.D. 55, is expanded in Romans, a letter written from Corinth a few months later. From the beginning to the end of Romans the Holy Spirit is a central teaching.

At the very beginning the comments of Paul on what may be a formula going back to even Palestinian Jewish Christianity interprets the resurrection of Christ and his designation as the eschatological judge (cf. Acts 3:20; 10:42; 17:31) in terms of the power of the Holy Spirit.[6] The formula, with the Hellenistic additions in parentheses, follows (Rom. 1:3 f.):

> Born of the seed of David
> (according to the flesh),
> Designated Son of God from the resurrection of the dead
> (*in power* according to the Spirit of holiness).

The phrase "in power" may be the only Pauline addition to this Jewish-Christian formula. The power of the Spirit in the present points to the position of Jesus as judge in the future.

The polemic of Paul against circumcision in Galatians has developed into a declaration that "the true Jew is he who is such inwardly, and the true circumcision is of the heart, directed not by written precepts but by the Spirit" (Rom. 2:29, NEB). It is possible to translate the *en pneumati* ("by" or "in the Spirit") as "spiritual," as in RSV, but this seems to weaken the phrase too much. The contrast here is again between the written code which kills and the Spirit which gives life (II Cor. 3:6).

This is repeated yet again in Rom. 7:6, which declares: "But now we are discharged from the law, dead to that which held us captive, so that we serve not in the oldness of the written code but in the newness of the Spirit." After the analogy of marriage, in which a woman is not bound to her deceased husband, those who have been set free from sin by the Spirit are no longer bound by the law.

116

The similarity of the three passages may indicate a common creedal tradition.

ou grammatos alla pneumatos (II Cor. 3:6)
not in a written code but in the Spirit

en pneumati ou grammati (Rom. 2:29)
in the Spirit not in the written code

en kainotēti pneumatos kai ou palaiotēti grammatos (Rom. 7:6) in newness of the Spirit and not in the oldness of the written code.

The passages in Rom. 2:29; 7:6 restate the passage in II Cor. 3:6 previously written to Corinth. Romans 7:6 combines the structure of II Cor. 3:6 and Rom. 2:29. Romans is written from Corinth. This creed is echoed again in Phil. 3:3 (*hoi pneumati . . . ouk en sarki*, who in the Spirit . . . not in the flesh), but so is Gal. 5:16-26.

The passage that takes Paul's thought beyond the idea of justification to salvation has been passed by until now.

> Therefore, since we are justified by faith, we have peace with God through our Lord Jesus Christ. Through him we have obtained access to this grace in which we stand, and we rejoice in our hope of sharing the glory of God. More than that, we rejoice in our sufferings, knowing that suffering produces endurance, and endurance produces character, and character produces hope, and hope does not disappoint us, because God's love has been poured into our hearts through the Holy Spirit which has been given to us. (Rom. 5:1-5.)

This pouring (*ekkechutai*) is a continuous action of God.

Justification by faith and the hope of eschatological salvation are linked by God's love which has been poured, not only into history as a prelude to the *parousia*, but "into our hearts through the Holy Spirit" as the power of salvation. The three tenses of salvation, past faith (v. 1), future hope (v. 2), and present love (v. 5), embrace the whole of the Christian life. It is true that eschatological "salvation is nearer to us now than when we first believed" (ch. 13:11), but the power of

117

the Spirit is proof that "in this hope we were saved" (ch. 8:24) when we "first believed."

If Galatians is the Magna Carta of Christian liberty, then Romans is the charter of the Christian life as salvation. This salvation delivers from the written code that kills (II Cor. 3:6; Rom. 2:28 f.; 7:6) and sets men free to live. Romans 8:1-27, in almost systematic development, explores this imparting of life with eight great themes.

The first is the law of the Spirit (vs. 1-4). Love is the law of Christ (Gal. 6:2), and there is a dependable law of the Spirit. It is best stated in relation to two other laws. The law of sin and death operates in Adam, so that all who are in Adam die (I Cor. 15:22; Rom. 5:12-21). This is the corporate experience of mankind, but the law of sin and death is at work in the flesh, the fallen nature, of each individual (Rom. 7:7-25). Metaphors of this law are found in sowing and reaping (Gal. 6:7 f.) and in working and wages (Rom. 6:23).

The law of Sinai, given to Moses, is unable to break the bondage of sin and death. This law of Moses is holy, but it serves only to awaken the consciousness of sin (Rom. 7:7-13). As a sleeping soldier awakes from his slumber in time of danger, so sin moves from the unconscious to the conscious. It is aroused by God's holy law. The law of Moses is spiritual, but it is helpless to set the prisoner free when, in the marketplace of the mind, he is sold under sin (vs. 14-25).

The law of the Spirit of life, operating in the realm of Christ Jesus, is able to set those free who yield to him. The steps of faith, freedom, and fulfillment, so central in Galatians, are in the background in Romans (chs. 3:31; 7:24; 6:14). Spiritual law sets free "in order that the just requirement of the law might be fulfilled in us, who walk not according to the flesh but according to the Spirit" (ch. 8:4). This is no automatic operation that happens once for all time. It belongs to man's personal response to the Spirit in the daily conduct of life ("who walk").

The second theme about the Holy Spirit in Rom. 8:1-27 is the mind of the Spirit (vs. 5-8). Mind in the normal sense of *nous* has a very important function in the spiritual life. Spirituality is no emotional orgy, and the experience of tongues that does not employ the mind is of less value than prophecy, prayer, and singing which do (I Cor. 14:2, 14, 18).

The mind-set (*phronēma*) may be that of the flesh or that of the Spirit. The mind-set of the flesh is death and hostility, but the mind-set of the Spirit is "life and peace" (Rom. 8:6). The mind of the flesh is set on the things that belong to the inauthentic life, lived in estrangement from God. Romans 1:18-32 is a detailed description of the ungodliness and unrighteousness that characterize this fallen human existence. "And since they did not see fit to acknowledge God, God gave them up to a base mind and to improper conduct." (V. 28.) In deadly estrangement from God and living in hostility toward God and man the mind becomes futile. In this futility "they are darkened in their understanding, alienated from the life of God because of the ignorance that is in them, due to their hardness of heart" (Eph. 4:18).

The mind-set of the Spirit is a remolding of the mind. The reprobate mind that had no place for God is renewed by the Holy Spirit, and this becomes the normal Christian life. A new mind is prepared for the new age of the Spirit. "Do not be conformed to this world but be transformed by the renewal of your mind, that you may prove what is the will of God, what is good and acceptable and perfect." (Rom. 12:2.)

The cleavage between mind and spiritual life has often led to fanatical emotionalism, and this has been disastrous. More and more it becomes evident that a healthy mind and healthy religion are inseparable. One is impossible without the other.

The third theme is the dwelling of the Spirit (Rom. 8:9-11). This has already been noted in the corporate life of the church (I Cor. 3:16) and in the body of a believer (ch. 6:19). It will be noted as a central topic in Ephesians (ch. 2:22). The epitome of experience in Rom. 8:9-11 traces three stages of the Spirit's indwelling.

The first stage is past for the believer. He has already moved out of the fallen state of the flesh into the life of renewal in

119

the Spirit. "But you are not in the flesh, you are in the Spirit, if the Spirit of God really dwells in you. Any one who does not have the Spirit of Christ does not belong to him." (V. 9.) Paul's Trinitarian pattern of thought, as he views life in Christ, allows him to use the terms "the Spirit of God" and "the Spirit of Christ" as synonyms. This new position "in the Spirit" results from the new possession of the Spirit.

Most modern translations of Romans 8:10 are in error, but the King James Version is correct! "And if Christ be in you, the body is dead because of sin; but the Spirit is life because of righteousness." This means that the human body is destined to become a corpse, for "the wages of sin is death" (6:23), but the present possession of the Spirit means the future redemption of the human body (8:11,23).

The future stage of the Spirit's indwelling is the resurrection of the body. "If the Spirit of him who raised Jesus from the dead dwells in you, he who raised Christ Jesus from the dead will give life to your mortal bodies also through his Spirit which dwells in you." (V. 11.) If God raised Jesus, he can raise us; the fact that he raised Jesus is basic for believing he will raise all in Christ Jesus to a life of immortality. Mortal bodies will become immortal (I Cor. 15:53).

The fourth theme is life in the Spirit (Rom. 8:12 f.). This, too, has been noted in earlier writings of Paul. It is really a brief summary of Gal. 5:19-24. Those who live life according to the desires of fallen flesh are on the road to death. Life in estrangement from God is death already, but it leads to eternal death, eternal estrangement from God. This is more than cessation of physical life; it is the total dissolution of authentic life.

Life according to the Spirit leads to life (cf. 8:11). Total life involves "the redemption of our body" (8:23). This is necessary for the salvation of the total self. Belief in the redemption of the body has strong ethical implications. If the body too is subject to redemption, the evil "deeds of the body" should be put to death (v. 13). Life according to the Spirit is a process of putting

120

to death that which does not belong to the redeemed life.

This putting to death is portrayed in Christian baptism. "We were buried therefore with him by baptism into death, so that as Christ was raised from the dead by the glory of the Father, we too might walk in newness of life." (Rom. 6:4.) Later letters go into great details as to what is to be put to death and what is to be put on in the Christian life (Col. 3:5-17; Eph. 4:17-31). In the early church this was very soon dramatically demonstrated by the stripping off of the old garments before baptism and the putting on of the white robe, the symbol of Christ, after baptism (cf. Gal. 3:27).

The fifth theme is the leading of the Spirit. "For all who are led by the Spirit of God are sons of God. For you did not receive the spirit of slavery to fall back into fear, but you have received the spirit of sonship." (Rom. 8:14 f.) This again restates the thundering theme of Gal., chs. 4 and 5, but there are some new insights.

The spirit of slavery causes one to cringe back into the grips of fear. Fear is the father of hate, and hate is the father of murder. Fear is that self-preserving, other-destroying drive in the fallen nature of man, the flesh, that threatens all human life. In the grips of fear man is a hideous monster of destruction, because he is under the control of the father of hate and death.

The spirit of sonship is the Spirit of God as the spirit of slavery is Satan. Both of them are "received." There is a "prince of the power of the air, the spirit that is now at work in the sons of disobedience" (Eph. 2:2), but there is also the Spirit, God's Spirit, that works in man and creates a new life in man. Those who put on the new man, Christ, are urged to keep on being "renewed by the Spirit in your mind" (Eph. 4:23, *my translation*). This is the same as "the mind set of the Spirit" (Rom. 8:6,27, *my translation*). The Holy Spirit renews the mind in love. The sons of God are so led and renewed.

Present possession of this Spirit of sonship is the status of adoption. The Greek word for sonship *huiothesia* belongs to the oldest text in Rom. 8:15, where the present status of sonship is the subject (cf. Gal. 4:6), but the oldest collection of Paul's letters, P 46, does not have the Greek word in 8:23 where the reference is to the future. This conclusion was reached before reading the same in Pierre Benoit, *Jesus and the Gospel*, Vol. 2, pp. 40-50.

The sixth theme is the witness of the Spirit of God with the spirit of man. "When we cry, 'Abba! Father!' it is the Spirit himself bearing witness with our spirit that we are children of God, and if children, then heirs, heirs of God and fellow heirs with Christ, provided we suffer with him in order that we may also be glorified with him." (Rom. 8:15-17.)

Paul uses both "sons of God" and "children of God" to designate believers in Christ, but the first may have reference to the idea of adoption while the other may indicate more the divine begetting. In the Johannine writings Jesus alone is called Son of God, and he is never begotten (the AV translation is in error in John 1:12); those who are begotten are always believers, and they are called children of God.

Those who enjoy the blessings of God's children in the present have hope for a future inheritance, so they are also heirs of God. This is no "pie in the sky" idea, for those who share the glory must also share the suffering (Rom. 8:17; cf. ch. 5:2 f.). Where there is no cross, there is no crown.

The evidence that we are both children and heirs is the witness of the Spirit. This cry of God's children, as already noted, was first on the lips of Jesus Christ. It is the Holy Spirit that puts it on the lips of God's children. At this point, Calvin, who made much of the internal testimony of the Spirit, went beyond Augustine, who had little place for this in his doctrine of predestination. Both of them left us a nest of problems, but Calvin's theology was made more comfortable for the children of God by giving attention to the Spirit's witness.[7]

The seventh theme is the firstfruits of the Spirit (Rom. 8:18-25). The resurrection of Christ by the power of the Spirit was and is the firstfruits that point toward a future harvest in the redemption of the human body (cf. 1 Cor. 15:23; Rom. 8:11).

Creation's groan is joined by the groaning of God's children.

Sufferings in the present are endured in remembrance of the initial experience of salvation in the past and the anticipation of sharing the glory of God in the future (vs. 22-25).

The firstfruits indicate not only a future redemption of the body, now groaning in a fallen creation, but this belief is rooted in the more comprehensive concept of cosmic redemption. There is no problem in believing that the body can be redeemed if the created order in which it now exists is redeemed too.

The eighth and final theme is the intercession of the Spirit (vs. 26 f.). The Spirit's help comes into the midst of man's infirmity and ignorance. He helps the weakness that is common to man as a creature of God. Sufferings crown him in his finitude and freedom. Weakness is a way of life for us in the space-time world, but things are worse under the curse of creation and living in sinful and fallen flesh.

Ignorance compounds the circumstances. Limitations of knowledge look out upon the created work as a vast enigma. Modern science seems only to deepen the mystery and becloud the confusion. Man's needs as well as man's nature remain hidden, "for we do not know how to pray as we ought" (v. 26).

The Spirit's mind is made known to God in his intercessions for man to God. The "sighs too deep for words" may have some reference to the ecstatic experience in which the unconscious human spirit prays without the conscious human mind, but the words are unutterable in any case. God understands when man does not, so the deepest form of intercessory prayer is yielding completely to the Holy Spirit that our needs may be expressed to God.

The discussion on predestination in Romans 9—11 has only one reference to the Holy Spirit, but it is an interesting statement on how the moral law of conscience stated in Rom. 2:14-16 is strengthened and guided more clearly by the witness of the Holy Spirit (9:1).

The profoundest transformation of life includes the mind. As sin's dominion is made manifest in the reprobate mind

123

(Rom. 1:28), so the Spirit's dynamic renews the mind (ch. 12:2).

Ethical imperatives spring from the soil of this eschatological salvation. The pilgrim perspective is a powerful motivation in the Christian life of service to God and man. This spiritual motivation appears in five ways in the final and most practical section of Romans. They are the glow (ch. 12:11), joy (ch. 14:17), power (ch. 15:13, 18 f.), sanctification (v. 16), and love (v. 30) of the Spirit of God.

The glow of the Spirit appears in the midst of a stanza that is related to both enthusiasm and eschatology (ch. 12:11).

> Never flag in zeal,
> be aglow with the Spirit,
> seize your opportunities.

The last line is adopted from William Barclay, and this reading is strongly supported in the more detailed commentary by Franz J. Leenhardt.[8]

This is based on the Western text, which reads *kairōi* for *kyriōi*, but the greater support may be found in the context of the eschatological ethic which follows immediately (v. 12):

> Rejoice in your hope,
> be patient in tribulation,
> be constant in prayer.

The idea is later repeated in Eph. 5:16 ("making the most of the time"). The literary structure in Rom. 12:11 f. and the context of Eph. 5:16 would suggest part of a hymn used in Christian worship.

Romans was written in Corinth, and this was the scene of action for the ardent Apollos shortly before. It has already been argued that the correct translation should indicate in both Rom. 12:11 and Acts 18:25 that the glow is that of the Holy Spirit of God. Human spirits may glow too when set on fire by the Holy Spirit, but here the reference seems best when translated as in the RSV: "Be aglow with the Spirit." Human enthusiasm and the eschatological hope keep burning with this spiritual glow.

So much modern religion is just more go-go with no glow in it at all. As artificial logs, twirling with the twinkle of a low-watt bulb, are substituted for hickory logs giving forth real warmth and light, so now the "planned program" takes the place of the spiritual glow that creates zeal and hope.

The joy of the Spirit (Rom. 14:17) appears in a chapter concerned with Christian scruples about eating meat (v. 2), Sabbath observance (vs. 5 f.), and drinking wine (v. 21). To many "weak" Christians, there were serious problems in the Christian life, while "stronger" Christians treated them as *adiaphora*, matters of indifference in Christian liberty. It was these "strong" Christians who caused their weak brothers to stumble that Paul reminded: "For the kingdom of God does not mean food and drink but righteousness and peace and joy in the Holy Spirit; he who thus serves Christ is acceptable to God and approved by men" (vs. 17 f.).

Freedom should never be used to destroy the faith of another brother. Notice the words "stumbling block" (v. 13; cf. vs. 20 f.), "hindrance" (v. 13), "injured" (v. 15), "ruin" (v. 15), "destroy" (v. 20). This spiritual tragedy can be avoided by putting "righteousness and peace and joy" first. All three of these in this context have reference to the right relations among Christian brothers when matters of conscience are involved. They seem to be in order, for the right relationships between brethren bring about the harmony which is peace that the joy of the Spirit may be received.

The great principle of edification (*oikodomē*) is again exalted, and this time above the freedom (*eleutheria*) that the Galatian letter defended so vehemently! "Let us then pursue what makes for peace and mutual upbuilding." (Rom. 14:19.) That will make the joy of the Spirit possible.

The power of the Spirit follows from this peace and joy, as a benediction implies: "May the God of hope fill you with all joy and peace in believing, so that by the power of the Holy Spirit you may abound in hope" (ch. 15:13). Here again eschatological hope embraces the whole, and it is the power of the Holy Spirit that keeps this hope alive. The debate over diet fades into insignificance in the evening glow of the great consummation.

In the interim between the temporary hardness of Israel's heart toward Christ, Paul would give himself to the gathering of the Gentiles. The fullness of the Gentiles, according to Paul, comes before the fullness of Israel (ch. 11:12, 25).⁹ Therefore, Paul resolved:

> I will not venture to speak of anything except what Christ has wrought through me to win obedience from the Gentiles, by word and deed, by the power of signs and wonders, by the power of the Holy Spirit, so that from Jerusalem and as far round as Illyricum I have fully preached the gospel of Christ. (Ch. 15:18 f.)

In the power of the Spirit the *plērōma*, the final fullness of both Israel and the Gentiles, will be accomplished.

The sanctification of the Spirit (v. 16) in Romans has a very different application from that found in the earlier letters. Morality was central in both the Thessalonian and Corinthian letters, but it is mission that dominates in Romans. Previously, Paul was a prophet thundering against pagan morals; now he is a priest offering a sacrifice to God.

It is a sacrifice of Gentile souls that Paul would offer to God. He is a *leitourgos,* a liturgical minister approaching God "in the priestly service [*hierourgounta*] of the gospel of God" (v. 16). Earlier he was calling all Christians to offer up the spirtual sacrifices of their bodies to God (ch. 12:1 f.), but now he would offer others, his converts, to God. The sacrifice of our bodies is to be "holy and acceptable to God"; so also Paul hopes his offering of others will be "sanctified by the Holy Spirit" (ch. 15:16). As he puts them on the altar he hopes the fire will fall and that God will claim them for his own.

Here again Paul's Trinitarianism appears in the usual pattern of his thought:

> To be a minister *of Christ Jesus* to the Gentiles in the
126

priestly service of the gospel *of God,* so that the offering of the Gentiles may be acceptable, sanctified *by the Holy Spirit.*

The love of the Spirit (v. 30), in the final appeal, is also Trinitarian: "I appeal to you, brethren, *by our Lord Jesus Christ* and by the love *of the Spirit,* to strive together with me in your prayers *to God* on my behalf." Romans 5:5 elaborated the concept of God's love "poured into our hearts through the Holy Spirit," and now the last reference speaks of "the love of the Spirit." This is more unconscious than accidental. Love and the Spirit were never separated in Paul's thought. To be filled with the Spirit was to be filled with love, and to be filled with love was to be filled with the Spirit.

6

THE SPIRIT OF UNITY
IN THE LATER PAULINE WRITINGS

THREE GROUPS of Pauline writings have been examined for their teachings on the Holy Spirit. Galatians and Romans belong as much together as do the letters to Thessalonica and Corinth. All the letters, with the possible exception of Galatians, were written either to or from Corinth, that great center of charismatic Christianity, and the most comprehensive concept has been the Spirit as life-giver. Only Second Thessalonians has been seriously questioned as a letter of Paul's. Romans brings this pneumatic panorama to lofty heights and grand unity of thought.

The transition from these Pauline writings to the so-called Prison Letters and Pastoral Letters introduces new concepts of the Spirit that have been one of the reasons why these writings have been called Deutero-Pauline, i.e., writings not by Paul himself but by members of the Pauline school who were deeply in debt to Paul.[1] It is possible that the years of imprisonment in Caesarea and Rome and the changed circumstances account for these different teachings on the Spirit, but this is another question of authorship and date that can quote great names on both sides. It is not necessary to settle the question of authorship and date to recognize these writings as a second stage in the Pauline conception of the Spirit.

The differences between the Prison Letters and the Pastorals are as great as those between earlier Pauline writings, but the question of Christian unity dominates both groups. In the Prison Letters a spiritual unity is to the fore, while an organic

128

union, an institutional organization of clergy and creed into which one is initiated by baptism, emerges in the Pastorals.

Since the first edition of this book the belief that the Prison Letters of Philippians (with the exception of 3:16 to 4:9), Colossians, Philemon, and Ephesians were written from Caesarea, A.D. 55-57, has become more and more plausible. Arguments from style lose their great importance when the role of Paul's amanuenses, the composers of his letters, is given further consideration.

This also puts the Pastoral Letters of Titus and 1, 2 Timothy in a new setting. It is a bit old-fashioned to say so, but the composition of Titus in Macedonia (1 Timothy 1:3) and 1 Timothy from Nicopolis (Titus 3:12) before 2 Timothy was written in Rome (1:18), all A.D. 64-65, does not appear incredible. This revision in chronology, however, does not change the conclusions about the Holy Spirit.

INTRODUCTION (PHILIPPIANS, COLOSSIANS)

It is certain that the question of unity is to the fore in Philippians, for all four references to *pneuma* are concerned with this question (Phil. 1:19, 27; 2:1; 3:3).

The supply of the Spirit (ch. 1:19) to Paul in prison will enable him to rejoice in the preaching of the gospel by even his opponents. These were perhaps the Jewish Christians who were hostile to Paul's Gentile Christianity. Another group of believers, mostly Gentiles perhaps, demonstrated genuine love, and Paul was encouraged by them. His words reflect his joy even in the partisan preaching of the gospel: "Yes, and I shall rejoice. For I know that through your supplication and the supply of the Spirit of Jesus Christ this will turn out for my deliverance."

This concept of the supply (*epichorēgōn*) of the Spirit was met in Gal. 3:5. It will be recalled that the *chorēgia* was the chorus equipped and supplied by a generous donor. God is the donor of the Spirit to Paul, but the supplication of devoted friends was the secondary source of this supply. Through their intercessions Paul was strengthened by the Spirit.

He was confident that their supplication and the supply

129

of the Spirit would lead to his salvation, i.e., deliverance either from prison or this world or both. A theology of martyrdom, by which God supplies the Spirit in a special way to martyrs, may be found here. In any case, the supply of the Spirit made him triumphant in all circumstances. The relationship between the supplication of his brethren and the supply of the Spirit caused Paul to make frequent requests for prayers (I Thess. 5:25; II Thess. 3:1, 2; II Cor. 1:11; Rom. 15:30-32; Philemon 22). The connection between the two is so close in his mind that only one article is used in the Greek text.

The steadfast *pneuma* (Phil. 1:27) has reference perhaps to the human spirit, but the problem of unity is still central. The Philippians are exhorted:

> Only let your manner of life be worthy of the gospel of Christ, so that whether I come and see you or am absent, I may hear of you that you stand firm in one spirit, with one mind striving side by side for the faith of the gospel, and not frightened in anything by your opponents. (Vs. 27 f.)

As the citizens of Philippi united to defend their colony from attack, so Christians, the colony of heaven (ch. 3:20), are called to unite against all sectarianism.

The fellowship of the Spirit (ch. 2:1) has definite reference to the Spirit of God which creates *koinōnia* among human spirits participating in this new energy of life. This *koinōnia* of the Spirit was first met in the apostolic benediction (II Cor. 13:14), but here the appeal for unity on this basis is more explicit.

Charles B. Williams has brought this forth with this translation:

> So if there is any appeal in our union with Christ, if there is any persuasive power of love, if we have any common share in the Spirit, if you have any tenderheartedness and sympathy, fill up my cup of joy by living in harmony, by fostering the same disposition of love, your hearts beating in unison, your minds set on one purpose. (Phil. 2:1 f.)

Those "who worship God in Spirit" (ch. 3:3) are called "the circumcision" in contrast to those "dogs" and "evil-workers" reproached as "the mutilation" (v. 2). This is clearly a distinction between Christianity and Judaism, not Gentile and Jewish Christians as in the first two chapters. The difference here is so great that many have thought this another letter that begins at v. 2, with v. 1 the farewell of the more joyful letter. Polycarp of Smyrna, in his letter to the Philippians, did speak of "letters" that Paul wrote to Philippi (iii.ii).

The phrase *hoi pneumati theou latreuontes* (literally, "the in Spirit of God worshiping" ones), since *theou* is not in some manuscripts, could be interpreted as another reference to the human spirit, as in Rom. 1:9, but the idea seems to be closer to Rom. 8:26 f., where the human spirit is impossible. The presence of the same teaching in John 4:23 f. may indicate an Ephesian creed behind both the Pauline and Johannine traditions. Some think Philippians was written from Ephesus.[2]

The teaching on the true circumcision is clearly that of Rom. 2:28 f.:

> For he is not a real Jew who is one outwardly, nor is true circumcision something external and physical. He is a Jew who is one inwardly, and real circumcision is a matter of the heart, in the Spirit and not in the written code.

Colossians has only one passage on the Spirit (ch. 1:8). The description of the love of the Colossians "for all the saints" (v. 4) as "love in the Spirit" (v. 8) is very close to "the love of the Spirit" in Rom. 15:30, and the meaning is about the same too. God's Spirit creates love as the bond of unity in the church. The relationship between love and the Spirit is frequent in the previous Pauline letters (I Cor. 12:31; 13:1-13; Gal. 5:22; Rom. 5:5; 15:30).

The Holy Spirit and Recapitulation (Ephesians)

Ephesians stands among the Prison Letters as Romans stands among the previous Pauline letters. This again is especially true in regard to the teachings on the Holy Spirit. The unity created by the Holy Spirit in the church and in the whole creation has long been summarized with the Latin word *recapitulatio* which translates the Greek *anakephalaiōsis* (" summary," " gathering together into one ").

If the word "recapitulation" sounds strange, it is due to neglect of a great New Testament teaching. The infinitive form appears in Eph. 1:10, a comment of Paul's in the midst of a great hymn, and this comment states the main theme of the majestic Ephesian letter: "To unite all things in him, things in heaven and things on earth." "To unite" (*anakephalaiōsasthai*) — this is God's purpose in the church, the body of Christ.

No theological idea was more important in holding Christians together in the second century. Gnostic heresies and sinful schisms threatened the very life of Christianity. Then it was that a noble son of Ephesus, planting the gospel in the frontier city of Lyon, worked out for himself and for the profit of generations to come the meaning of Christ and the church. Recapitulation was his central concept.[3] Irenaeus interpreted Paul to mean that God would not only restore fallen humanity to communion with God, through the death of Christ, but he completed all previous revelations and would perfect the whole creation in Christ.

The present situation in Christianity requires a return to this great purpose of God. A return requires careful consideration of the work of the Holy Spirit in this process of unification, beginning in Christ, then continuing in the church, and moving on to the completion of the whole creation in the consummation. This whole plan must be kept in mind as special consideration is given to the specific passages on the Holy Spirit.[4]

The references to *pneuma* ("spirit") in Ephesians disclose several usages. One speaks of the evil spirit, "the spirit that is now at work in the sons of disobedience" (ch. 2:2). This demonic power becomes prominent in the struggle of the church described in ch. 6:11-13. Two references speak of the human spirit, man's point

132

of contact with the Holy Spirit of God. Man is a living soul, the whole man, but he has a spirit that relates him to God as his body relates him to the material world. When the God-man relation is in harmony, the Father of glory gives to each one "a spirit of wisdom and of revelation in the knowledge of him" (ch. 1:17). Even this *pneuma* is given by God, very much as "the spirit of wisdom" in the Old Testament was (Deut. 34:9; Isa. 11:2; cf. Acts 6:3,10). This is a process of growth, so Paul says to his readers: Go on being "renewed in the spirit of your minds" (Eph. 4:23). However, it is possible to interpret the two passages as references to the Holy Spirit by seeing the Holy Spirit as the giver of wisdom and the renewal of the mind as "the mind-set of the Spirit" (cf. 8:5,27). The translation "the Spirit of your minds" is possible in 4:23.

Nine other passages on *pneuma* remain, and they seem all to have reference to the Holy Spirit of God. Four of them appear in what has been called the doctrinal section (chs. 1:13; 2:22; 3:5, 16) and five in the practical (chs. 4:3 f., 30; 5:18; 6:17, 18). They are discussed in this order.

The seal of the Spirit (ch. 1:13) has become a part of the great doxology, the three-stanza hymn at the beginning of Ephesians (vs. 3-14). The third stanza is on the Holy Spirit, as the first is on God the Father and the second is on the Son. Perhaps the original was:

In whom, by the Holy Spirit,
    we heard the gospel of salvation;
    we believed the word of truth;
    we were sealed to the redemption of the possession,
      according to the good pleasure of thy will,
        to the praise of thy glory.

Sealing by the Spirit was first noted in II Cor. 1:22 ("he has put his seal upon us and given us his Spirit in our hearts as a guarantee").

Very soon the idea became associated with baptism, when believers were stamped as the possession of God; but it is related to the Spirit from the beginning.[5] This Oriental custom means more than attestation. The cabinet or document could not be opened until the seal was broken. Of course the seal could be broken, as the seal on the tomb of Jesus most certainly was (Matt. 27:66; cf. Rev. 5:2,5,9; 6:1,3,5,7,9,12; 8:1).

Paul's comment on the hymn makes the meaning clearer still. This sealing is called a guarantee (*arrabōn*). The *arrabōn* was a down payment by which the purchaser assured the seller that the rest would be paid later. This applied well to the Holy Spirit, "who is a deposit guaranteeing our inheritance until the redemption of those who are God's possession" (Eph. 1:14, *New International Version*, © 1973, New York Bible Society International, published by Zondervan: Grand Rapids, 1973.

The habitation of the Holy Spirit (ch. 2:22) is that holy temple, built by God and in which every redeemed person has a place. It is by the cross of Christ, by which human barriers are broken down, that any person makes peace with God and becomes part of the temple, "for through him we both have access in one Spirit to the Father" (v. 18).

The background to this figure of the temple of the Holy Trinity (Spirit, Son, Father) was the Temple in Jerusalem. A dividing wall separated the Court of the Women from the Court of the Gentiles, and on that wall was a warning that Gentiles going beyond that point would be killed. Christ by his cross destroyed that wall, and all men may now become the very sanctuary, the holy place itself, "a dwelling place of God in the Spirit" (v. 22).

The physiological metaphor of the church as the body of Christ is enriched with the political metaphor of a commonwealth and the architectural metaphor of a temple.[6] The church of God is the City of God, as Augustine's *City of God* celebrated it in a time of world crisis not unlike our own. This city where there are "no longer strangers and sojourners," in contrast with the city of this world, he described as follows:

> Accordingly, two cities have been formed by two loves; the earthly by the love of self, even to the contempt of God; the heavenly by the love of God, even to the contempt of self. (xiv. 28.)

134

This City of God is also the household of God, for there all men are "kinsmen." This household is that holy temple of God, "built upon the foundation of the apostles and prophets, Christ Jesus himself being the cornerstone, in whom the whole structure is joined together and grows into a holy temple in the Lord" (Eph. 2:20 f.). All local congregations, the several buildings, become one great temple, "the dwelling place of God in the Spirit" (v. 22).

The revelation of the Holy Spirit (ch. 3:5) is the source of the church's message. Paul said:

> When you read this you can perceive my insight into the mystery of Christ, which was not made known to the sons of men in other generations as it has now been revealed to his holy apostles and prophets by the Spirit. (Vs. 4 f.) (Literally: "in the Spirit," as in 2:18,22.)

These "holy apostles and prophets" have reference to those with unusual charismatic and prophetic powers in the church, not to the Twelve and the Old Testament prophets.

The revelation of this mystery is indeed the message of the church, and the manner of this revelation indicates how the Holy Spirit works in inspiration. A mystery is on the boundary between God and man. It is partly known, but it is so profound that it can not be fully known in history.[7] Revelation is God's self-disclosure and the disclosure of his purpose that is so "unsearchable" (v. 8) and "manifold" (v. 10). That which is made known is the message: "That is, how the Gentiles are fellow heirs, members of the same body, and partakers of the promise in Christ Jesus through the gospel" (v. 6). It is only "in the Spirit," the revealer, that a message will and can be realized in the church. He alone can unite all mankind in a fellowship of love and understanding.

The power of the Holy Spirit (v. 16) comes through prayer. The first prayer in Ephesians is a prayer for knowledge, that the eyes of the heart may be "enlightened" (ch. 1:18), but there is need for more than knowledge. Power is needed to do what we know.

> For this reason I bow my knees before the Father, from
> whom every family in heaven and on earth is named,
> that according to the riches of his glory he may grant
> you to be strengthened with might through his Spirit
> in the inner man. (Ch. 3:14-16.)

The " inner man " is the true self that does not pass away by
the process of human decay. " Wherefore we faint not; but
though our outward man is decaying, yet our inward man is
renewed day by day." (II Cor. 4:16, ASV.) Even in the contradiction of the flesh, man delights in " the law of God after
the inward man " (Rom. 7:22, ASV).

In this inmost self the Holy Spirit supplies power to meet
the outward pressures of life and to accomplish God's mission
in the world. The power of God's Spirit and the power of
God's love are so blended in the blessing of God that one never
finds one without the other. Where they are found, a benediction is added to the blessings:

> Now to him who by the power at work within us is able
> to do far more abundantly than all that we ask or think,
> to him be glory in the church and in Christ Jesus to all
> generations, for ever and ever. Amen. (Eph. 3:20 f.)

This "power at work" is the Spirit at work.

The unity of the Spirit (ch. 4:3 f.) penetrates some of the
most practical problems in the church. Unity is the worthy
walk of Christians. The Holy Spirit is the creator of unity, not
discord, but there are many hindrances to unity that must be
removed before this unity in Christ is made manifest. Human
pride that puts self before Christ and his church is one of the
most difficult barriers to get over. Therefore, Paul prescribes
a liberal portion of lowliness and meekness, patience and fore-
bearance (vs. 2 f.). Eagerness to maintain unity does not come
until pride goes.

Unbelief is another barrier that must be broken down before
there is manifest unity. That is one of the reasons why a confession of sevenfold unity is prescribed in vs. 4-6. The opening
words (" one body and one Spirit "), following the analogy of

one human body for one human spirit, reflect a very early belief about the Holy Spirit and the church. There could be only one body of Christ, because there is only one Holy Spirit in which we are baptized into that body. The New Testament never speaks of many bodies of Christ, any more than it could speak of many Holy Spirits (cf. 1 Cor. 12:13).

The addition of five more strands of unity in the body of Christ prepares the way for the unity of faith (v. 13). Where there is a unity of knowledge and love there is a road to the unity of belief. True unity includes both "the unity of the Spirit" and "the unity of the faith," and the unity of the Spirit cannot be maintained where immature Christians are "tossed to and fro and carried about with every wind of doctrine, by the cunning of men, by their craftiness in deceitful wiles" (v. 14).

The grief of the Spirit (v. 30) is a remembrance to those familiar with the Old Testament of a terrible tragedy. Grieving the Spirit is mentioned only once in the Old Testament and once in the New, and the latter is based on the former where it is said of Israel when they came out of Egypt (Isa. 63:10):

> But they rebelled
>   and grieved his holy Spirit;
> therefore he turned to be their enemy,
>   and himself fought against them.

They were almost in the Promised Land, then turned for most of them to perish in the wilderness.

The outrage of this willful sin of unbelief, after full knowledge of the truth, is very near in meaning to this grieving of the Spirit.

> A man who has violated the law of Moses dies without mercy at the testimony of two or three witnesses. How much worse punishment do you think will be deserved by the man who has spurned the Son of God, and profaned the blood of the covenant by which he was sanctified, and outraged the Spirit of grace? (Heb. 10:28 f.)

Those warned against grieving had the seal of the Spirit, the

137

seal that marked them for God's very own and pointed them to the day of redemption. Notice that Eph. 4:30 does not say "until the day of redemption" but "unto" (*eis*, "pointing toward"). The same is true in ch. 1:14 (*eis apolutrōsin*, "pointing toward redemption"). Remember that seals can be broken. The one on the tomb of Jesus and those in Revelation were! Grieving and sealing do not contradict.

The filling of the Spirit (Eph. 5:18), so prominent in Acts, appears in a setting of worship in Ephesians.

> And do not get drunk with wine, for that is debauchery; but be filled with the Spirit, addressing one another in psalms and hymns and spiritual songs, singing and making melody to the Lord with all your heart, always and for everything giving thanks in the name of our Lord Jesus Christ to God the Father. (Vs. 18-20.) [8]

Salvation (*sōteria*) was found in debauchery in the cult of Dionysus, for salvation meant for them release from tension. Sex and salvation were closely related in this orgy of relaxation!

This concept of salvation was repulsive to Paul. The experience of salvation was intoxicating for him, but it was the fullness of the Spirit expressed in worship. At Pentecost this fullness of the Spirit was confused with intoxication too (Acts 2:13). Much of our modern worship would panic in a first-century service. Even today the very suggestion that there is a need for the filling of the Holy Spirit is met with a fortress of opposition. One could believe this staid opposition to be drugged but it would hardly be called drunk.

Part of the opposition may grow out of a punctiliar fallacy committed by "Spirit-filled" advocates. The present tense in Greek does not mean "get filled with the Spirit" in one experience, but "keep on being filled in the Spirit" in all experience and daily living. Once Protestantism had a rigid taboo of sex, but now there is a deadness due to a taboo of the Spirit.

Baptism in the Spirit is only once (Eph. 4:5), as baptism with water should be only once, but the filling of the Spirit

138

may be continual and best of all, on the highest level, continuous. Filling in the Spirit may be repeated in the same person on many occasions. Perhaps only the very mature and steadfast should be described as "full of the Spirit" (cf. Acts 6:5; 11:24).

The sword of the Spirit (Eph. 6:17) means the sword that the Spirit uses. The Spirit, like a soldier, takes the word of God and wages war against the demonic powers of darkness. It was said of the Davidic king: "He shall smite the earth with the rod of his mouth, and with the breath of his lips he shall slay the wicked" (Isa. 11:4). Now the church, following the Messiah, is to take "the sword of the Spirit, which is the word of God," and engage in spiritual warfare.

Warfare was often used to describe the witness of the church. Very soon the church was viewed as God's *militia*. Christians took an oath of obedience to Christ at baptism, as Roman soldiers placed their hands inside that of their general and swore obedience to death. This was the original meaning of a *sacramentum.*

Prayer "in the Spirit" (Eph. 6:18) gave the soldiers of the cross their strength. Four alerts are sounded for prayer. The first is the piety of prayer: "with *all* prayer and supplication." The second is the practice of prayer: "Pray at *all* times in the Spirit." The third is the perseverance of prayer: "To that end keep alert with *all* perseverance." Finally, there is the purpose of prayer: "making supplication for *all* the saints." This is the third time in Ephesians that prayer has become prominent. This indicates how important prayer is in that growth of unity by which all things are to be brought under the headship of Christ.

THE HOLY SPIRIT AND ORGANIZATION
(PASTORAL LETTERS)

The passages on the Holy Spirit in the Pastoral Letters are few, but they touch on three of the liveliest issues in the history of theology: (1) regeneration in relation to baptism, (2) ordination in relation to the laying on of hands, and (3) inspiration in relation to prophecy and Scripture. All of these belong to the church as an organization, the first to initiation, the second to its leadership, and the third to its order. It is impossible to be definite in the dating of the letters, for they have been assigned to a period as early as the seventh decade and as late as A.D. 120. The earlier date can claim such names as Parry, Lock, Meinertz, Spicq, Jeremias, Simpson, Guthrie, and Kelly, but it is opposed by Harrison, Scott, Dibelius, Gealy, and Higgins. On this, as on many other New Testament problems, Jeremias is persuasive, but it is here left an open issue. I am inclined toward A.D. 64-65.

Initiation into the organization or church order of the Pastorals was by baptism. Another one of the hymns of epiphany belongs to the baptismal liturgy. The second of the ten parallels says that God saved (Titus 3:5):

> By the washing of regeneration
> and renewal in the Holy Spirit.

Loutron ("washing"), *louein* ("to wash") and *apolouein* ("to wash away") "are commonly used in direct or indirect connection with Christian baptism." [19] Regeneration (*palingenesia*) is used in the New Testament only here and in Matt. 19:28 where it has reference to a new order in history.

The Greek supports the claim that both regeneration and renewal (*anakainōsis*) are "in the Holy Spirit." There is no *dia* ("by," "through") before *anakainōseōs*. The dynamic symbolism of Acts is present in this hymn. The Holy Spirit is "poured out upon us richly through Jesus Christ our Savior, so that we might be justified by his grace and become heirs in hope of eternal life" (Titus 3:6 f.). The unity of charismatic power and eschatological hope are present as they were when the Holy Spirit was "poured out" to fulfill the prophecy of Joel on the day of Pentecost (Acts 2:17, 33).

The close relationship between the visible sign of washing and the inward grace of regeneration and renewal degenerates into a false view of baptismal regeneration when the Holy Spirit is neglected. This did happen in Rome by the time

140

of Justin Martyr (*I Apology*, 61). The remedy for this situation, however, is a renewed emphasis on the Holy Spirit, not a devaluation of baptism. The reaction of "mere symbolism" to "baptismal regeneration" has made the symbol even more naked and less meaningful. The visible sign and the spiritual substance have been so completely severed that baptism is reduced to no more than a declarative act.

Baptism in the New Testament is a symbol, but it is a symbol with power. In the Pauline writings one became the possession of him in whose "name" he was baptized (I Cor. 1:13-17). It was the sign of the putting off of the old man of fallen humanity. "For as many of you as were baptized into Christ have put on Christ." (Gal. 3:27.) "We were buried therefore with him by baptism into death, so that as Christ was raised from the dead by the glory of the Father, we too might walk in newness of life." (Rom. 6:4.) The whole of Christian life is symbolized in this dramatic act (cf. Col. 2:11-15; 3:1-17; Eph. 4:17 to 5:14).

Both magical sacramentalism and mere symbolism miss the meaning of Titus 3:5. The former has interpreted the passage in such a way that "the washing of regeneration" has been applied to infant baptism and the "renewal in the Holy Spirit" to confirmation by the episcopal laying on of hands many years later. On exegetical grounds regeneration and renewal are inseparable. On exegetical and historical grounds G. W. H. Lampe has well-nigh wrecked this view by searching criticisms, but he has gone almost too far in relating the Holy Spirit to baptism.[20] Mere symbolism has rejoiced prematurely at these attacks from within the Anglican communion, for Professor Lampe's light will blind Baptist eyes that see no more than a naked symbol in baptism. The punctiliar fallacy that says all happens at one moment of "decision" and nothing happens in or after baptism received in faith is not the dynamic symbolism, the union of visible sign and spiritual substance, in Titus 3:5.[21] Initiation is a dynamic process in which the action of God through his Spirit is present for the response of faith.

141

The teachings on the Holy Spirit and organization correct one of the major Christian perversions. Sectarianism is based on the false assumption that the Holy Spirit can work only through individuals and never through institutions.[22] Institutions are persons in permanent relation, in covenant relation, and the vitality of the Spirit may be expressed even more through the group than through the same individuals in isolation and conflict. Radical distinctions between fellowship and institution threaten Christian unity, but unity of thought establishes unity of life and work.

Earlier Pauline writings assume the inspiration of prophets and of the Old Testament writings. Inspired prophecy finds its profoundest description in I Cor., ch. 14, but there is little that would help formulate a theory of the inspiration of the New Testament writers. The nearest approach would perhaps be Paul's interesting comment on his advice about remarriage: "And I think that I have the Spirit of God" (I Cor. 7:40).

The one reference to inspired prophecy in the Pastorals is I Tim. 4:1-3:

> Now the Spirit expressly says that in later times some will depart from the faith by giving heed to deceitful spirits and doctrines of demons, through the pretensions of liars whose consciences are seared, who forbid marriage and enjoin abstinence from foods which God created to be received with thanksgiving by those who believe and know the truth.

Other prophetic utterances, no doubt inspired by the Spirit, are mentioned (I Tim. 1:18; 4:14).

Eduard Schweizer is correct in saying this is "a wholly traditional way of speaking of the prophetic Spirit."[9] There are other matters to note. Apostasy (*apostēnai*) in Heb. 3:12 is "to fall away from the living God," but here (I Tim. 4:1) it is apostasy (*apostēsontai*) from "the faith" and "the truth." Faith has moved beyond trust in God to "giving heed" to doctrines. True doctrine is inspired by the Holy Spirit, but false doctrine is inspired by "deceitful spirits" or "demons." Prophecy may be either divine or demonic, and the criterion for distinguishing is *didaskalia* ("doctrine").

The earliest letters of Paul did have the idea of a great apostasy that would be followed by the man of sin, the lawless one. This, too, would be "the activity of Satan . . . with all power and with pretended signs and wonders, and with all wicked deception for those who are to perish, because they refused to love the truth and so be saved" (II Thess. 2:9 f.). If Paul wrote this earlier, the belief that he wrote the later statement over fifteen years later is not unreasonable.

A reference to the inspiration of Scripture, formed after the pattern of Rom. 15:4, which does not use the word *pneuma* ("spirit") but *theopneustos* ("inspired"), implies the work of the Spirit.

> All scripture is inspired by God and profitable for teaching, for reproof, for correction, and for training in righteousness, that the man of God may be complete, equipped for every good work.

The "Scripture" means the Old Testament, as in about fifty instances in the New Testament. Only once in the New Testament, and that in speaking of the letters of Paul (II Peter 3:15 f.), are New Testament writings so described. It is not wrong, however, to apply the verse to all the Bible.

Calvinism has built on those passages the doctrine of verbal inspiration, the infallibility of Scripture in every detail. John Calvin himself said that "we owe to the Scripture the same reverence which we owe God; because it has proceeded from him alone, and has nothing belonging to man mixed with it." [10] This view of Scripture has often been blasted as bibliolatry, and it has confronted difficulties as modern science has upset Biblical cosmology and chronology, to say nothing of theological issues, but a major denomination subscribed to this view in 1962. [11]

Inspired Scripture (*graphē theopneustos*) is the same as the "sacred writings" (*hiera grammata*), the Old Testament, with which Timothy had been acquainted since childhood and which were able to instruct him "for salvation through faith in Christ Jesus" (II Tim. 3:15). This is a high view of the Old

Testament that has been sustained by the most critical and historical type of research, but it is doubtful that a doctrine of verbal inspiration can be demonstrated here, for it does not have reference to the Hebrew autographs but to Timothy's Greek Old Testament.

Protestantism has no doubt been right in giving the primacy to Scripture, both Old Testament and New, over the ecclesiastical traditions that have developed beyond the apostolic traditions found in the New Testament, but the doctrine of inspiration developed in the sixteenth century must be understood in its prescientific setting and in opposition to what was later declared a dogma, papal infallibility, in 1870. The same views of Scripture were adopted by the Roman Catholic Church in the sixteenth century, but this did not establish Biblical theology over tradition.

The appeal to the sacred writings or to inspired Scripture in II Tim. 3:16 f. distinguished the Old Testament from profane works used by false teachers. Historical revelation is exalted over fantastic mythologies, genealogies, and ascetic doctrine propounded by false teachers, both Jewish and pagan. It is precisely the unhistorical and uncritical mind that falls for fancy and fanatical interpretations.

The Scriptures do have the breath of God in them, not in part but in the whole, but they must be studied for what they teach about God in relation to man rather than as a substitute for science. Biblical theology belongs to the I-Thou dimension, not to the I-It dimension of natural science. "All scripture is inspired by God and profitable for teaching, for reproof, for correction, and for training in righteousness, that the man of God may be complete, equipped for every good work." It is not profitable to refute scientific studies. The Bible is more than a book by the Spirit; it is a book about the Spirit.

Ordination by the laying on of hands is a practice rooted in the Old Testament. Some have traced this practice of the laying on of hands to the *sim* or *shith* tradition. These two words are used as synonyms in Israel's blessing of Ephraim and Manasseh in Gen. 48:14-17. Blessing by the laying on of hands

144

is found in the New Testament, when Jesus heals the sick (Mark 6:5) and blesses children (ch. 10:16). It may also have some influence on the reception of the Spirit by the laying on of hands before (Acts 9:17) or after baptism (chs. 8:17; 19:6; Heb. 6:2). In the early church, baptism was understood as the ordination of the laity to the priesthood of all believers.[12]

Most scholars, however, have seen the *semikhah* tradition of the Old Testament in the background of New Testament ordination.[13] The noun *semikhah* is derived from the verb *sāmākh*, used three times to describe the ordination of Joshua as the successor of Moses (Num. 27:18, 23; Deut. 34:9). By the laying on of hands Moses "put his honor [*hod*] upon him" (Num. 27:23). Hands were laid on the seventy elders to impart Moses' *ruach* ("spirit") to them (Num. 11:16-30), but Joshua possessed the Spirit before Moses laid his hands on him (Num. 27:18; Deut. 34:9). It was the *hod*, not the *ruach*, that was added.

This was almost exactly the condition of the Seven, table servants (deacons), when the apostles laid hands on them (Acts 6:6). Barnabas and Saul also possessed the Spirit before the prophets and teachers of Antioch laid hands on them, but this is more like the sending forth of apostles (*shelihim*) by the *Nasiim* in late Judaism.[14] Barnabas and Saul were called apostles too (Acts 14:14). They even appointed successors (v. 23, *cheirotonēsantes*).

The laying on of hands in the Pastorals is more charismatic than the transfer of legal authority by the *Nasiim*, but there are striking similarities between the two. It seems safer to say that both developed from the Old Testament rather than to make the direct connection defended by David Daube.[15] The form by which Rabbinic authority was communicated is nearer to the Pastoral practice than the content.

Many see a problem in the Pastorals between the apostolic laying on of hands in II Tim. 1:6 and the presbyterial practice in I Tim. 4:14. Early Christianity solved the problem by having both the bishop and the presbytery lay on hands.[16] This is not impossible in the Pastorals.

145

The apostolic ordination in II Tim. 1:6 has been interpreted as confirmation after baptism, but the context indicates the teaching office (vs. 7, 14). Timothy received the *charisma* ("gift") when Paul laid his hands on him. This does not mean that Timothy did not possess the Spirit before his ordination, but there is more than authority in the gift. It is also much more than the ministry of the whole church objectified. It is indeed "*an act of the Church which brings to a focus the nature of the Church's own ministry,*" [17] but an object lesson does not say enough to explain the laying on of hands in the Pastorals.

A charismatic element is in the *charisma!* Paul says to Timothy: "Hence I remind you to rekindle the gift of God that is within you through the laying on of my hands; for God did not give us a spirit of timidity but a spirit of power and love and self-control" (II Tim. 1:6 f.). The *dia tēs epitheseōs* ("through the laying on") is genitive singular and indicates the intercessory gesture by which Paul prayed for a donation and reception of the *charisma*. The RSV quoted above interprets the "spirit" as human or less than the Holy Spirit. This may be the case, but there is more in the context.

After a hymn (vs. 9 f.), one of the ten great hymns of epiphany in the Pastorals, the testimony of Paul makes clear the setting of the teaching office that Timothy fills. The indwelling Spirit is unmistakable there. A cluster of Greek words indicates Timothy's role:

> But I am not ashamed, for I know whom I have believed, and I am sure that he is able to guard until that Day what has been entrusted to me [*parathēkēn mou*, "my deposit"]. Follow the pattern of the sound words [*hugiainontōn logōn*] which you have heard from me, in the faith and love which are in Christ Jesus; guard the truth that has been entrusted [*kalēn parathēkēn*, "good deposit"] to you by the Holy Spirit who dwells within us. (Vs. 12-14.)

The Authorized Version translation of v. 12 ("which I have

146

committed unto him") is refuted by v. 14 where both the deposit (*paratheke*) and the Holy Spirit are with Timothy. The Greek clearly means the guarding of the deposit, not the giving. It is guarded by the Holy Spirit (*dia pneumatos*, v. 14), but the giving of the *charisma* was through the laying on (*dia tes epitheseos*, v. 6) of Paul's hands. The very close connection between *charisma* and *pneuma* justified the thought that both the giving of the gift and the guarding of the deposit are not possible without the action of God through the Spirit.

The *paratheke* (cf. I Tim. 6:20) and the *pistis* ("faith," found more than thirty times) in the Pastorals mean doctrine (*didaskalia*, found fifteen times). The threat of heresy has made it necessary to set aside by the laying on of hands certain charismatic men to be guardians of the faith and to impart sound doctrine to those in a less robust state of spiritual health. Therefore, Paul says:

Avoid such godless chatter, for it will lead people into more and more ungodliness, and their talk will eat its way like gangrene. Among them are Hymenaeus and Philetus, who have swerved from the truth by holding that the resurrection is past already. They are upsetting the faith of some. (II Tim. 2:16-18; cf. I Tim. 1:19 f.)

"Truth" (*aletheia*, used thirteen times) means "doctrine" also in the Pastorals.

It becomes abundantly clear that the laying on of hands in the Pastorals, with the added charismatic content, had a parallel in the Rabbinic *semikhah*. Both attempt to guard the true teaching against heresy. All the lashing attacks against "the guardians of the faith" and the Protestant devaluation of the Pastorals do not destroy the evidence. There is a strange mentality that gives the impression that any movement away from the eschatological and charismatic community of Corinth is a step toward apostasy.

After all, the *parousia*, second coming, has not yet taken place and the church is forced to be a historical fellowship with institution and office if she does not want to lose her

holiness, separateness from the world, and vanish into a neb-
ulous cloud of secularization. It is odd indeed to hear those
seeking to do service to the church by declaring a dead God
who has vanished into humanity and a dead church that
should now vanish into the world.

The church order in First Timothy is a step forward, not
backward, in the organization of the charismatic fellowship
into a historical institution with ordered worship (ch. 2:1-15)
and a developed hymnology (I Tim. 1:17; 2:5 f.; 3:16; 6:15b f.;
II Tim. 1:9 f., 18; 2:11-13; 4:1-8; Titus 2:11-14; 3:4-7). There
was "the office of bishop" (*episkopē*, I Tim. 3:1) with the
"deacons" as his assistants (v. 8). There was an order of
widows who were enrolled after a pledge (ch. 5:12) and elders who ruled and taught, received a salary, double if they did
their work well, and who fell into sin (vs. 17-22). All this was
intended as a "bulwark of the truth" (ch. 3:15) against Gnostic asceticism and their speculative mythologies (chs. 4:3, 7;
6:20).

There were so many presbyters (elders) that they adopted
the Jewish idea of a presbytery (*presbyterion*, I Tim. 4:14;
cf. Luke 22:66; Acts 22:5). It has already been noted that
charismatic prophecy is not dead in the Pastorals. Some prophetic utterance had pointed to Timothy as the presiding elder
of Ephesus (I Tim. 1:18). This is most clearly indicated in
the presbytery passage when Paul says: "Do not neglect the
spiritual gift within you, which was bestowed upon you
through prophetic utterance with the laying on of hands by the
presbytery" (ch. 4:14, New American Standard Bible).

If this laying on of hands was both apostolic as in II Tim.
1:6 and presbyterial as in I Tim. 4:14 the *dia tēs epitheseōs*
("through the laying on") of the former and the *meta epitheseōs* ("with the laying on") took place at the same time.
The argument for accusative plural ("because of prophecies")
instead of genitive singular ("through prophecy") does not
change the meaning, and it is probably an incorrect translation.

Timothy's main task was that of *pastor pastorum* ("pastor of

148

the pastors "), the chief presbyter of the presbytery. He was to look after their honorarium, not honor as incorrectly translated, exercise severe disciplines when an elder was proved guilty of sin, and ordain other elders (I Tim. 5:17-22). The instruction "Do not be hasty in the laying on of hands" has reference also to ordination (v. 22). It has been interpreted in the light of a third-century practice that restored penitents by the laying on of hands, but the context is in favor of ordination. Timothy and the elders ordained as Paul and the elders had ordained Timothy.[18] It is interesting to note that Luke-Acts was known when 1 Timothy was written, for Luke 10:7 is quoted in I Tim. 5:18, and the view of elders and ordination in the Pastorals is the same as that noted in Acts (cf. Acts 11:30; 14:23; 15:2,4,6,22 f.; 16:4; 20:17; 21:18 with I Tim. 4:14; 5:17,19; Titus 1:5). It is also in I Peter 5:1-5, written from Rome, James 5:14, and in Asia (II John 1; III John 1; Rev. 4:4,10; 5:11,14; 7:13) that the New Testament has similar examples of elders.

In Antioch, where there were the Five (prophets and teachers, Acts 13:1-3), and in Asia the structure of church leadership into deacons, elders, and bishops was very soon established. Before A.D. 117, Ignatius was "bishop of Syria" (Ign., *To the Romans* ii.ii), Polycarp of Smyrna (Ign., *To Polycarp* i.i.; *To the Magnesians* xv.i), Onesimus of Ephesus (Ign., *To the Ephesians* i.iii), Damas of Magnesia (Ign., *To the Magnesians* ii.i), and Polybius of Tralles (Ign., *To the Trallians* ii.i). Those who still claim the New Testament as the only rule of faith and order need to ponder this situation. Those who follow the most pragmatic and expedient structure of the church will adopt the most recent secular patterns.

7

THE SPIRIT OF TRUTH
IN THE JOHANNINE GOSPEL AND FIRST LETTER

SINCE THE TIME of Clement of Alexandria, in the second century, the Gospel of John has been called the "spiritual Gospel."[1] It is not necessary to adopt Clement's "spiritualizing" exegesis to see why this impression is given. There is far more about the Holy Spirit in John than in all three of the Synoptic Gospels. A dozen passages on the Spirit almost dominate the other themes. The Logos doctrine, introduced in a hymn (John 1:1, 3-5, 10 f., 14,18), has often been given this prominence, but even this is subordinate to the Spirit. The First Epistle of John, so similar in theology in other ways to the Gospel, continues this concern with the Spirit. By grouping the two writings the Holy Spirit may be surveyed under three headings: the Spirit as a power upon Jesus, the Paraclete as a person among the disciples, and the *koinōnia* as the presence of the Father and the Son in the believers.

THE SPIRIT (JOHN, CHS. 1 TO 7)

The first six passages on the Spirit, those that have reference to the acts of the Spirit before Jesus is glorified by his death-resurrection-ascension, speak of the Spirit as a power with a peculiar relationship to the ministry of Jesus. It is not until after Jesus is glorified (lifted up by death, resurrection, and ascension) that the Spirit has a special ministry in the disciples.

The first passage relates the Spirit to the true baptizer (John 1:32 f.). The water baptism of John was a purification rite,

150

preparing the people for the manifestation of the Messiah (vs. 25, 31, 33). It was believed, according to Mal. 3:1, that the Messiah would be manifest suddenly. Until that time he was hidden (cf. John 1:26,31,33). John came baptizing in water, having been told by God that the Spirit would descend as a dove upon the Messiah. John's Gospel does not say specifically that John baptized Jesus, but it is implied.

The Messiah would baptize in the Holy Spirit, not in water. It may be argued from John 3:22 that Jesus himself did baptize in water ("there he remained with them and baptized"), but this is carefully corrected in ch. 4:2 ("although Jesus himself did not baptize, but only his disciples"). Spirit baptism is the true baptism of the Messiah. John the Baptist testified:

> I saw the Spirit descend as a dove from heaven, and it remained on him. I myself did not know him; but he who sent me to baptize with water said to me, " He on whom you see the Spirit descend and remain, this is he who baptizes with the Holy Spirit." And I have seen and have borne witness that this is the Son of God. (Ch. 1:32-34.)

It is better to translate "in water" and "in Spirit." Some manuscripts say, "the Chosen One of God."

This testimony of John's deepens the significance of the dove's descent, already noted in the Synoptic Gospels. The descending of the dove still recalls the brooding of the Spirit over the waters of chaos (Gen. 1:2), as order was established in creation, but the idea of a new order in the new creation is even more pronounced. The materials are even arranged in a week (John 1:29, 35, 43; 2:1), like unto the seven days of creation.[2] C. K. Barrett is too cautious when he discounts the dove as " traditional imagery taken over from the earlier gospels." [3] It is not even certain that John knew the Synoptic Gospels.[4] E. C. Hoskyns shows more insight when he says: " The attention of the Evangelist is concentrated upon the dove, upon its descent, and upon its resting upon Jesus." [5]

The abiding of the Spirit upon Jesus identifies him as the Messiah and distinguishes him from those in the Old Testament who were anointed with the Spirit for special tasks. The historical Jesus became the holy temple in which the Holy Spirit came to dwell in all his fullness and power. Plato saw the human body as the tomb of the soul, from which death alone was the release (*Gorgias,* 493a), but John's Gospel thinks of the human body of Jesus as a temple for the Spirit that would also come to dwell in all who believe (ch. 2:21). Here again Barrett is strangely squeamish and Hoskyns is right when he interprets the saying at the cleansing of the Temple as a sign that the flesh of Jesus is "the abiding place of the Spirit," as well as "the tabernacle of the Word" and "the shrine of the presence of God." [6]

Arguments for baptismal incarnation, the incarnation of the Son of God in the human Jesus at his baptism, are not supported by this narrative. E. C. Colwell and Eric L. Titus give this interpretation of the dove's descent:

> It means that in this event lies the real beginning of the Johannine story of the Son of God; that prior to this, Jesus was the man from Nazareth and nothing more; that the ministry of the Son of God can only begin subsequent to the Spirit's descent when this man from Nazareth has been infused and transformed by the Holy Spirit in such a way that he has become a divine being.[7]

Most commentaries focus attention on the Logos Christology and assume that the incarnation took place at birth. If this assumption is correct, for Paul previously placed the incarnation at birth rather than baptism (Gal. 4:4-6), then the descent of the Spirit is an anointment (cf. Isa. 42:1; Acts 10:38). The dove's descent is a witness that Jesus is already the Son of God, not an incarnation. The argument for baptismal incarnation is based on silence. Colwell and Titus say John follows Paul's view of the Spirit, and it seems that he does not depart from Paul on the time of incarnation.

The second passage explains the Spirit as the source of the true begetting. This dialogue between Jesus and Nicodemus teaches both the necessity for and the nature of a spiritual birth for those who would enter the Kingdom of God (John

3:1-8). In order to present a tentative solution to a difficult textual problem the following translation is offered of vs. 3-5:

3. Jesus answered and said to him,
    Amen, amen, I say to you
        unless one is begotten from above
        he cannot see the kingdom of God
4. Nicodemus said to him, "How can a man be begotten when he is old? Can he enter a second time into his mother's womb and be begotten?"
5. Jesus answered,
    Amen, amen, I say to you
        unless one is begotten of the Spirit,
        he cannot enter the kingdom of God.

This states the necessity for the new birth in two stanzas of three lines each.

The two stanzas in which Jesus answers Nicodemus (vs. 3, 5) are synonymous parallelism. It will be noted that the first lines in each stanza are identical, a solemn assurance that what follows is true. The second lines differ in only one way. *Anōthen* ("from above," the same word as in ch. 3:31; 19:11, 23) in ch. 3:3 has become *ex pneumatos* ("of the Spirit") in v. 5. The third line again differs in only one word. The infinitive *idein* ("to see") has become *eiselthein* ("to enter"). In each case the words are synonyms. To be born "from above" is to be born "of the Spirit," and "to see" the Kingdom of God is "to enter" the Kingdom of God. That which is "above" is "Spirit" in John. That is the view of the two realms. The reference to the Kingdom of God reflects the Synoptic view of two ages, the present age dominated by the demonic and the coming age of glory. When the glory of the Kingdom is revealed, then those born from above will enter it, but the Kingdom of God and Christ does not belong to this world order (*kosmos;* cf. ch. 18:36). When the present world order has passed away, then the Kingdom of God will be seen and entered. God's Kingdom in John is otherworldly ("not of this world"). God's Spirit represents his present action in the world.

153

The omission of the phrase "water and" (*hydatos kai*) must be justified. This is not easy, but the literary structure printed above is a beginning. When *hydatos kai* in ch. 3:5 is added, the balance of the line is disturbed. It is no longer in the form of v. 3, and the meaning does not agree with v. 6 ("that which is born of the Spirit is spirit"). If "water and" appeared originally in v. 5, then it would be logical to say "that which is born of water and the Spirit is spirit" in v. 6, but there is no textual support for that addition. The phrase *hydatos kai* is definitely an alien element from the literary point of view.

It is often said that "there is no textual evidence whatsoever against the genuineness of the phrase" *hydatos kai*,[8] but this is not exactly true. It is true that no manuscript thus far supports the omission, not even the Bodmer papyruses, but a growing number of New Testament scholars, both Protestant and Catholic, support the omission.[9] The Nestle text notes four sources that omit *hydatos kai*. Two Latin manuscripts, Harleianus and 1028, do not translate the words, so their Greek text must not have had them. Justin Martyr quotes a conflation of texts ("Except you are begotten again you will not enter the kingdom of heaven"). The context is baptism (*I Apology*, 61), and it is difficult to believe he would have omitted the reference to water if his text had had it. Origen quotes v. 5 at times with and at times without the water, so this fluctuation indicates different readings. In the light of the literary structure and these sources it is possible that *hydatos kai* was not a part of the original text and was added by a redactor.[10] Some manuscripts (Sinaiticus, Old Latin, the Sinai and Cureton Syriac) have *tou hydatos kai* ("of water and") in v. 8, but all editors reject it there. It perhaps should be rejected in v. 5.

When *hydatos kai* was added to v. 5 it perhaps had reference to baptism, for baptismal regeneration became pronounced by the time of Origen. The theory for water being the natural birth, argued from the parallelism of v. 6 ("That which is begotten of flesh is flesh and that which is begotten of Spirit is spirit"), as well as the more widely adopted view

154

that thinks water is a synonym for the word of God (cf. ch. 15:3), are not without merit, but the theory of baptismal redaction is gaining ground. If it is true, much debate on ch. 3:5 has been wasted effort, and the endless argument for water baptism as an absolute essential for salvation is badly shaken.

The nature of this spiritual begetting follows (vs. 6-8), but this has two lines to the stanza:

6. That which is begotten of flesh is flesh
and that which is begotten of Spirit is spirit.
7. Do not marvel that I said to you,
"You must be begotten from above."
8. The wind blows where it wills,
and you hear the sound of it,
but you do not know whence it comes or whither it goes;
so is every one who is begotten of the Spirit.

This begetting, then, is of the Spirit in vs. 6, 8, as in v. 5. It is, therefore, the begetting from above (v. 3), the realm of Spirit, as flesh is the realm below.

The Spirit's begetting (regeneration) is the same as God's begetting, also found in Johannine theology (John 1:13; I John 2:29; 3:9; 4:7; 5:1, 4, 18). In Johannine thought Jesus is the only Son of God, unbegotten but who becomes flesh, but believers are begotten. Those begotten are called children of God (*tekna theou*, John 1:12; I John 3:1, 2; 5:2), never "sons." [11]

"Wind" and "Spirit" are the same word in Greek (*pneuma*), so the illustration of wind is fitting for the mystery of the Spirit's begetting of the new life, the life eternal. That which is begotten of the flesh participates in the weakness and mortality, not necessarily sin, of the creature, but that which is begotten of the Spirit participates in the eternal life of God the Creator. Flesh passes away, but spirit abides.

The third passage interprets the Spirit as the seal of the true God (John 3:33 f.). The narrative background is John the Baptist's parable of the bridegroom (vs. 22-30). The marriage metaphor is used in the Old Testament to describe the covenant relation between the Lord and Israel (Hos. 2:20; Jer. 2:2; Ezek. 16:8; 23:3; Isa. 62:4 f.). It is a symbol of joy when the relation is faithful (Jer. 7:34; 16:9; 25:10), and that is its meaning in John. Christ as bridegroom is introduced early in Mark (ch. 2:19 f.), but it is even earlier in John. The final testimony of John to Jesus appears before John is imprisoned. A narrative pericope (John 3:22-30) exalts Jesus above John by the testimony that John is only the Hebrew *shoshebin,* the friend of the bridegroom who acts as his agent in the marriage arrangements. After that he fades away into the background. That is why John the Baptist is fulfilled (*kelal* in Aramaic) by his decrease (*qelal*) in importance.

The joy of the new age of the Spirit is suggested in the wedding feast in Cana. B. F. Westcott thought the water that was turned into wine came not from the six waterpots for purification, an odd source for new wine to say nothing about the excessive amount, but from the well as the seventh source.[12] The six waterpots represented the old age of Jewish ceremonialism, but the well symbolizes the spiritual source of joy in the new age inaugurated by Jesus. The good wine was drawn (John 2:8, *antlēsate*), and ch. 4:11 indicates that an *antlēma,* a bucket on the end of a pole or rope, was used to draw. One would need only to "dip" water from pots. Many reject this symbolism, but it is illuminating as background to the parable of the groomsman who prepares the way for the presentation of Jesus as the new source of joy inspired by the Spirit.

The commentary that follows (John 3:31-36), perhaps by the author of the Gospel, compares Jesus and John in powerful poetry. The true and only God sends his true and only Son. He who receives the testimony of Jesus sets his seal that this is so, and the Son gives the Spirit to him. The reference to the Spirit reads:

> For he whom God has sent
>   utters the words of God,
>   for it is not by measure that he gives the Spirit.

Commentaries are divided on who gives the Spirit, God or Jesus. Most look backward and interpret Jesus as the receiver of the Spirit from God. As in ch. 1:32, in the descent of the dove, God gives the Spirit without measure to Jesus, whereas he measured the Spirit to all the prophets, including John the Baptist. It is this abundance of the Spirit that enables Jesus to utter the words of God.

If the interpreter looks forward to chs. 4:23 f.; 6:63; 7:37-39, it is just as logical to think of Jesus as the giver of the Spirit that he has received. This would emphasize Jesus as the true baptizer, as in ch. 1:33. Despite the support of some manuscripts that substitute "God" for "he," as in the AV (ch. 3:34), and the conclusions of most commentaries, it seems more in harmony with other passages in John to speak of Jesus as the fountain out of whom the words of God and the Spirit of God flow. Before the death of Jesus the words of God go forth from him, but after his death the Spirit of God pours forth. The Son of God is the Spirit-giver as the Spirit of God is the life-giver (ch. 6:63). Of course, one can say it is not "crucial to decide whether John means the Father or Jesus gives the Spirit." [13] This is true, but that which follows tends toward Jesus as the giver of the Spirit. God gave the Spirit to him, but he gives the Spirit to others. This is more in harmony with John's strong Trinitarianism.

The fourth passage portrays Jesus as the source of the Spirit and the teacher of true worship in the Spirit. After presenting himself as the giver of eternal life, "the spring of water leaping up to eternal life" (John 4:14), Jesus teaches the Samaritan woman true worship in these words (vs. 23 f.):

But the hour is coming, and now is,
    when the true worshipers will worship the Father in
        Spirit and truth,
        for such the Father seeks to worship him.
God is Spirit,
    and those who worship him
        must worship in Spirit and truth.

It will not be long before the worship of God will cease both on Mt. Gerizim and Mt. Zion (vs. 21 f.), but the true worship of God has already arrived with Jesus.

The contrast between temporal worship in the temples of the Samaritans and the Jews does not exalt pietistic individualism above corporate worship, as the quotation of these words often implies. The Spirit incorporates himself in a fellowship, not in isolated individuals, but the fellowship had been disrupted by the Samaritan schism. The Samaritans justified their place by appeal to "the old-time religion." Shechem was an "older" shrine than Jerusalem, and the Pentateuch was truly "the old book" of temple worship. This is the hardest tradition to dislodge before truth.

The manner of worship should be guided by the meaning of God. If "God is Spirit," then true worship must be "in Spirit and in truth." Biblical thought speaks more of the "name" of God, his personal and self-communicating reality, but Johannine theology approaches a definition of his nature in three affirmations. The First Letter of John says that "God is light" (ch. 1:5) and that "God is love" (ch. 4:8), but John 4:24 is almost a creed: *pneuma ho theos*. There is no verb. This is not an abstract metaphysical definition of God as in Greek philosophy, for God works through matter and in history in the Hebrew thought expressed in John. Spirit is the boundary between the created and the Creator, but the Creator works in his creation. Perhaps the nearest Old Testament statement to the Johannine view of God is found in Isa. 31:3:

> The Egyptians are men, and not God;
> and their horses are flesh, and not spirit.

"God" and "spirit" are synonyms, but the context is one in which God works in human history.

Truth in this text is as often distorted as Spirit. It is not unusual to hear it used to describe "sound doctrine," so that schism is justified as "contending for the faith." Sound doctrine, healthy teaching, is not to be disparaged, but *alētheia* in John means much more than correct teaching. The clue

158

to its meaning appears in a comment in the Prologue: "Grace and truth came through Jesus Christ" (John 1:17). *Alētheia* is that which is no longer hidden, but man does not discover it. God gives it to man in his grace. It is given in the event of history by which the Son of God became man. "Grace and truth came." They came "through Jesus Christ," the supreme disclosure of ultimate reality. In this light, man must worship God. "Only in the Church, where the redemptive work of Jesus is an historical fact, can man, under the guidance of the Holy Spirit, come to the whole truth." [14] This union of "Spirit and truth" is the most distinctive teaching about the Spirit in Johannine thought: "The Spirit is the truth" (I John 5:7).

The fifth passage speaks of the Spirit in the context of the true bread from heaven. The discourse on the bread of life spoke seven times about Jesus' "descending" from heaven into the realm of flesh below (John 6:33, 38, 41, 42, 50, 51, 58). The Jews murmured (v. 41), as did the wilderness generation (Ex. 16:2, 7, 8; I Cor. 10:10), and disputed among themselves (John 6:52), and even the disciples were scandalized (v. 60) either by the "bread of life" interpretation of the Old Testament example (vs. 25-51) or the Eucharistic application (vs. 52-59) or both. Then comes the "ascending" (v. 62), followed by the giving of life through the Spirit.

> It is the Spirit that gives life,
>   the flesh is of no avail;
>   the words that I have spoken to you
>   they are Spirit and they are life.

The first two lines appear to be a citation, and the other two lines are perhaps comment.

The reference to the Spirit as the life-giver is rooted in the Old Testament. Many passages speak of earthly life being given through the Spirit (Gen. 2:7; 6:3, 17; 7:15, 22; Ps. 104:29 f.; Job 34:14), but the nearest to this New Testament saying is Ezek. 37:5 ("I will cause *ruach* to enter you, and you shall live"). Paul approaches the idea in his teaching about the two Adams (I Cor. 15:45), but the contrast between the two covenants is nearest: "The written code kills, but the Spirit gives life" (II Cor. 3:6). This indicates a saying of this type in the Ephesian tradition. The Pauline form appears later when the Nicene Creed speaks of "the Holy Spirit, the Lord and Life-giver."

The statement that "the flesh is of no avail" was used by Zwingli to support his spiritual view of the Eucharist against the theory of transubstantiation, but this is not true to the two-story theology of John. A theology that says "the Word became flesh" (John 1:14) does not deny the flesh. Denial of the flesh is Gnosticism (I John 4:2 f.), and there is no manuscript evidence that this is a Gnostic gloss. It means the flesh below is not the source of eternal life. It may become the means by which eternal life is mediated, as in the incarnation and the Eucharist, but it is not the source. Eternal life has its source "above" and not "below," from the Spirit and not from the flesh. This is the same as in John 3:6.

The comment on the citation interprets the words of Jesus as the medium by which both the Spirit and eternal life are communicated. When this is compared with the Eucharistic words of John 6:52-58, it seems clear that the two media of word and sacrament have been together from the beginning. Severing the two into a Catholic versus Protestant either/or has greatly weakened the New Testament view of the means of grace. Sign and sound, down "below," may be used by the Spirit who comes down from "above." The lower in the service of the higher is the right order.

The power of the word has Old Testament roots too. The Spirit broods over the waters as the word of God is spoken in the very first chapter of the Bible (Gen. 1:2 f.). The power of the word to communicate earthly life (John 4:50) and eternal life (ch. 5:21-29) comes out in Peter's confession in John: "Lord, to whom shall we go? You have the words of eternal life" (ch. 6:68).

As the contrast between Spirit and flesh has already appeared in ch. 3:6, so the combination of words and Spirit has appeared in v. 34. All of these are brought together in the

160

saying about the true bread. Eternal life is mediated by the incarnate flesh (ch. 6:27, 32 f.) and in the Eucharistic flesh (vs. 57, 68), through the bread and the blood, but only when there is faith and the action of the Spirit. Eduard Schweizer has well said: "The force of 6:63 is then that this *sarx* is only profitable when the *pneuma* gives the knowledge that it is precisely in this *sarx* that *zōē* is to be found." [15] There is an "eternal sphere" that is not the source of eternal life, as there is a "spirit sphere" that is.[16]

Aileen Guilding has pointed out the use of the Paradise story in the Passover lectionary and suggests a return to Paradise in the references that speak of not being driven out (v. 37) and eating bread to receive eternal life (vs. 50 f.). This has been received by some with reservations, but others have subjected it to criticism.

The sixth passage on the Spirit is the great invitation by Jesus at the Feast of Tabernacles. Second only to the Feast of Pentecost in importance, Tabernacles was the occasion for the dedication of Solomon's Temple (I Kings 8:2). During the time of the exile Ezekiel had a vision of the water that would flow from beneath the restored Temple (Ezek. 47:1), a vision finally to be fulfilled in the new heaven and the new earth (Rev. 7:17; 22:1). After the exile it took on added significance as the Jews remembered the time of the exodus when their fathers dwelt in tents in the wilderness generation. It was widely believed that the Messiah, who was hidden, would suddenly manifest himself at this feast, held around the first of October. For seven days at first, then eight, the wilderness wandering was remembered in a dramatic way.

Each day a golden pitcher was filled with water from the spring of Gihon that furnished water for the pool of Siloam in the southeastern corner of the city. On the seventh day expectation ran high as a priest filled the pitcher, as the choir sang Isa. 12:3 ("With joy you will draw water from the wells of salvation"), then the throng followed in procession, with bunches of myrtle and willow twigs tied together with a palm (the *lulab*) in the right hand and a lemon or small citron in

161

the left (the *ethrog*). The procession joined in the singing of Psalms 113 to 118, the Hallel, with the many reminders of the wilderness days, as they moved down the street to the northeast corner of the city, through the Water Gate, until they reached the altar. Seven times they marched around the altar of sacrifice, then a priest went up the ramp to pour the water into a silver funnel from which it flowed into the ground as a symbolic prayer for rain. An oracle in Zech., chs. 9 to 14, indicates the hopes that hovered about this dramatic action, and several of the psalms other than the Hallel express this imagery (e.g., Ps. 42:1 f.; 78:15 f., 24; 105:40 f.).

On the occasion described in detail in John, chs. 7 to 9, at the most dramatic moment, the cry of a prophet was heard (ch. 7:37):

> If any one thirst, let him come to me [*pros me*];
> and let him drink who believes in me [*eis me*].

This punctuation (no period after "drink" as in AV) got only as far as the margin in the Revised Standard Version, but it was finally adopted in *The New English Bible*. This is known as the Western punctuation, since most fathers in the Western church from Justin Martyr onward follow it.[17] Strangely, Greek texts and English translations until *The New English Bible* followed Origen and the Eastern punctuation influenced by him. The punctuation adopted above can claim the support of Boismard, Braun and Mollat, Bultmann and Jeremias, Stanley, Hoskyns, MacGregor, Dodd, and Brown.[18]

The Eastern punctuation, followed in the West by Cortes Quirant, by Zahn, Schlatter, Rengstorf, Behm, Michaelis and Schweizer, Lightfoot, Bernard and Barrett, argues that the water flows out of the believer, as in the Authorized Version, American Standard Version, Revised Standard Version, etc., but this disturbs the poetic structure.[19] Most of all there is no text in the Old Testament to support this, and John's comment says: "As the scripture has said" (ch. 7:38). In the New Testament, John 4:14 speaks of "a spring of water leaping up to eternal life," but nothing is said about it flowing out to

162

others. Where does one find the statement: "Out of his belly shall flow rivers of living water"? Almost these exact words are found as the Lord instructs Moses to strike the rock in the wilderness:

Behold, I will stand before you there on the rock at Horeb; and you shall strike the rock, and *water shall come out of it*, that the people may drink. (Ex. 17:6, italics added.)

This became a type of Messiah that would be stricken in order to inaugurate the new age of the Spirit. This typology was highly developed in the Ephesian tradition by the time Paul wrote I Cor. 10:1-13, and this seems to be the meaning in John 7:37-39. First Corinthians 10:4 says, "The Rock was Christ." The whole context of John, chs. 7 to 9, favors this typological interpretation.

If there is any doubt left after the examination of the above passages, then the interpretation in John 7:39 should settle the issue: "Now this he said about the Spirit, which those who believed in him were to receive; for as yet the Spirit had not been given, because Jesus was not yet glorified." Language could hardly be plainer, yet scholars with the erudition of Barrett still follow Origen. The whole theme of the Spirit in John is centered around the view that the true baptizer (ch. 1:32 f.) will give the Spirit without measure (ch. 3:34). Three of the passages (chs. 1:32; 3:34; 6:63) speak of Jesus as bearer of the Spirit, but the other three (chs. 3:3-8; 4:23 f.; 7:37) speak of the Spirit as available for others. The water of ch. 7:37 f. is the same as "the living water" offered to the Samaritan woman (ch. 4:10). The Spirit was given in some measure before Jesus was lifted up and glorified by crucifixion-resurrection-ascension, but a new age of the Spirit was to follow. It was to be in such great measure that the Greek says, "The Spirit was not" before Jesus was glorified. The interpretation "not yet given" softens the shock of the text.

Up to this point, up to the great invitation, the teachings have centered on the Holy Spirit as power manifested before Jesus is glorified. The other six passages portray the Holy

Spirit as person and look beyond his crucifixion-resurrection-ascension to the bestowal of the Spirit on the first Easter evening (ch. 20:22). The great invitation is the climax of the first six passages, while the great insufflation of v. 22 is the climax of the last six and the whole of the Gospel of John.

THE PARACLETE (JOHN, CHS. 14 TO 16; 20)

Five sayings about the Holy Spirit as Paraclete assign personal attributes to the supernatural power that Jesus promised his disciples. Both Acts (chs. 13:2; 16:6 f.) and Paul (Rom. 8:26 f.; Eph. 4:30) give clear indication that the Holy Spirit was personality, but most of the time he indicates the supernatural power by which God acts in creation and history. It is in the Paraclete sayings that the personality of the Spirit is most pronounced, and the pattern of a Holy Trinity is highly developed.

Literary structure and theology are again intertwined in the five sayings. Hans Windisch has subjected the sayings to a detailed literary analysis and concluded that they were originally a hymn to the Paraclete now incorporated into the farewell discourses of Jesus to his disciples.[20] C. K. Barrett has searched for the sources of the term "Paraclete," but he leaves the question unsolved.[21] The meaning of the term as applied to the Holy Spirit, for the most part, must be derived from the saying.

The first saying (John 14:15-17): *the Paraclete as Helper.* Translators have rendered the Greek *paraklētos* by a number of words: "Comforter," "Counselor," "Helper," "Intercessor," and "Advocate." None is completely satisfactory, but "Helper" is very near the meaning in the first saying. *Paraklētos* means "one called to our side to help." When John Wycliffe chose the word "Comforter," it was a good choice, for Comforter comes from the Latin word *fortis,* "brave." The Holy Spirit gives strength and enables one to be brave. It is no longer adequate when the meaning is confined to sorrow. The *Paraklētos* puts the spirit back into one and gives one

164

courage. *The New English Bible* chose " Advocate," and it fits well for the English reader. " Helper " is perhaps better for Americans.

The first saying may be translated into English as follows:

> 1. If you love me,
> 2. you will keep my commandments.

> 3. And I will make request of the Father,
> 4. and he will give you another Paraclete,

> 5. that he may be with you forever (even the Spirit of truth),
> 6. whom the world cannot take;

> 7. for it does not see him,
> 8. neither does it know him;

> 9. for he is now abiding beside you
> 10. and shall be inside you.

This first saying has five parallels, and there is a significant teaching in each.

Lines 1 and 2 require obedience as evidence for love. This is basic in Biblical thought, but Johannine thought lifts it to the highest level. In lines 3 and 4, Jesus' prayer is for " another Paraclete " (*allon paraklēton*). If it were *heteron*, as in Gal. 1:6 f., it would mean another of a different kind, but *allon* means a Paraclete of the same kind. Jesus is called a Paraclete with the Father in I John 2:1, but here it is the Paraclete with the disciples. The Paraclete with the Father is Jesus, who was visible when on earth, but the Holy Spirit is the invisible Paraclete with the disciples after Jesus ascended back to the Father.

Lines 5 and 6 indicate a great difference between the visible Paraclete as Jesus and the invisible Paraclete as the Holy Spirit. Jesus would be with the disciples only for a while longer, but the invisible Paraclete, identified by the parenthetical statement as " the Spirit of truth," would be with them " forever." The world could " take " Jesus by arrest and crucifixion. The aorist infinitive *labein* may mean either " to take " or " to

165

receive," but "take" seems better here (note the same use in John 10:18; Acts 15:14; Rev. 6:4). The world will not be able to "take" or arrest the Holy Spirit, for it neither sees nor knows him, as lines 7 and 8 explain. The last lines (9 and 10) indicate the Holy Spirit in Jesus was abiding "beside" *(para)* them until after the ascension, then he would in the future be "inside" *(en)* them after Jesus gave the Holy Spirit to them (John 20:22). Many manuscripts have the present tense in the last line, but the meaning is future in any case.

The second saying (John 14:25 f.): *the Paraclete as Teacher.* The second Paraclete saying advances to the function of the Holy Spirit as teacher. The continuation of the hymn says:

{ 11. These things have I spoken to you
{ 12. while abiding with you.

{ 13. But the Paraclete (even the Holy Spirit),
{ 14. whom the Father will send in my name,

{ 15. he shall teach you all things,
{ 16. and bring to your remembrance all things (which I said to you).

These six lines include a second identification of the Paraclete with the Spirit, the first time "the Spirit of truth" and this time "the Holy Spirit." The first parenthesis helps balance the line, but the second is only explanatory.

The key thought in lines 11 and 12 is the ministry of Jesus while "abiding" in the flesh. *Menein* ("to abide") is a special word in the Johannine vocabulary.[22] Here the word *menōn* has reference to Jesus as teacher while he, the eternal Logos and Son of God, took up the ministry of truth in human flesh down below. While he made his abode in the flesh he was the "truth" (ch. 14:6), the disclosure of God in the human situation. Now this ministry is about to be ended by crucifixion, but "the Spirit of truth" will take up the ministry he began.

The first discourse (John, chs. 13; 14) with the disciples is dominated by this preparation for his departure. His "going away" (ch. 13:31-38) will be followed by his "coming again"

166

(ch. 14:3, 22 f.), but this "coming again" is not the *parousia*, the second coming in glory. His "coming again" has been clarified by the parable (*paroimia*, "dark sayings") of the orphans (vs. 18-24). Plato spoke of the disciples of Socrates as orphans when their great teacher died to leave them forlorn. Now a greater teacher than Socrates, the incarnate Son of God, is about to leave his disciples, but he will not leave them orphans, he will return to take up his abode with them. After a "little while" (*mikron*, ch. 13:33), he will leave, but in a "little while" he will return (ch. 14:19).

This return will be a mystical manifestation, an *emphany* (ch. 14:21 f.) that the world will not see. The Father's house, which has many abodes (*monai*, v. 2), will be established among them in love. That is what Jesus means when he says:

> If a man loves me, he will keep my word, and my Father will love him, and we will come to him and make our abode [*monē*] with him. (V. 23.)

This does not exclude the future eschatology of a glorious manifestation at the Last Day and the resurrection of the dead (chs. 5:28; 6:39 f., 44, 54), but the "realized eschatology" is assigned to the ministry of the Holy Spirit, the other Paraclete. This is why Jesus says: "I go away, and I will come to you" (ch. 14:28; cf. vs. 3, 23).

The ministry of the Paraclete is to be one of representation and remembrance. He is to come as the representative of Jesus, the Paraclete whom the Father will send in the "name" of Jesus. Jesus came in the "name" of the Father (John 5:43), as the personal representative of the Father. Now Jesus will request the Father (ch. 14:16) to send the Paraclete as the personal representative of Jesus, in his "name" (v. 26). The teaching of the invisible Paraclete does not displace the teaching of Jesus, the visible Paraclete. His teaching is a bringing to remembrance of the things Jesus said. Dark sayings (*paroimia*) will become plain sayings (*parrēsia*).

The sayings of Jesus in his earthly ministry were not always plain. An example of this is the saying about the destruction

167

of the Temple. The people thought he had reference to Herod's Temple which was started in 20–19 B.C. and was still unfinished. The ministry of the Spirit brought this to remembrance and taught them that it had reference to the temple of Jesus' body (ch. 2:21). John explains that (v. 22):

> When therefore he was raised from the dead,
> his disciples remembered that he spoke this;
> and they believed the scripture
> and the word which Jesus spoke.

This is an example of the ministry of remembrance, and all of the Gospel of John may be classified as things the Holy Spirit caused to be remembered. The Paraclete interprets the things said and done by Jesus.

The third saying (John 15:26 f.): *the Paraclete as Witness.* The third Paraclete saying, like the second, identifies the Paraclete with "the Spirit of truth," and the phrase is again a parenthetical statement.

{ 17. But when the Paraclete is come,
{ 18. whom I will send to you from the Father (even the Spirit of truth)

{ 19. who proceeds from the Father,
{ 20. he shall bear witness of me;

{ 21. and you also bear witness of me,
{ 22. because you have been with me (from the beginning).

The first three lines add new light on the procession of the Spirit, and the last three introduce the new theme of the witness.

The giving (*dōsei*) of the Spirit by the Father at the request of Jesus was mentioned in the first saying, and the sending (*pempsei*) in the name of Jesus was noted in the second. Now the giving and the sending has been described as a procession (*ekporeuetai*). In ch. 14:16, the Father gives the Paraclete, and in v. 26 the Father sends in the name of Jesus, but ch. 16:7 will later say that Jesus sends him. The unity of

168

these sayings is found in the statement "whom I shall send to you from the Father" (ch. 15:26). The Father gives and sends in the Son's name, so the Son sends from the Father.

Debate over the procession of the Spirit was an issue in the great schism between Eastern and Western Christendom in A.D. 1054. When the West added *filioque* ("and the Son") to the Creed which spoke of the procession of the Spirit "from the Father," there was much controversy. The West did so to protect the doctrine of the Trinity against the advance of Arianism, especially in Spain. Arianism denied the eternal Son, holding that he was the first creature of God, an intermediary between God and man. The Jehovah's Witnesses still teach this creature Christology, and it can be found in the writings of the founder of Southern Baptist Landmarkism, J. R. Graves.[23]

The controversy, like most theological controversy, was colored with ecclesiastical politics, but there was a theological issue. Origen of Alexandria and Caesarea spoke of Jesus as a "second God" (*deuteros theos*) and described the Trinity in terms of Neoplatonic emanation.[24] All the Eastern fathers followed this subordinationism, but Arius went too far. Eastern Orthodoxy finally, at the Second Council of Nicaea in A.D. 787, settled on the procession of the Spirit from the Father "*through* the Son." This is a good solution to the problems raised by the Paraclete sayings.

Western Orthodoxy started with Tertullian's attack on the Sabellianism of Praxeas, perhaps a pseudonym for Calixtus, later pope. Sabellius denied the eternal Trinity, holding that the Father, Son, and Spirit were only three different masks worn by the same actor. Tertullian declared that this "put to flight the Paraclete and crucified the Father" (*Against Praxeas*, 1.30). This great Carthaginian theologian illustrated the Trinity with the root-shoot-fruit symbol at times, at other times the spring-stream-canal one, but his best effort was the sun-beam-light one. The sun illustrated the Father from whom the Son as a beam came, and the illumination of the light was like the Holy Spirit. It is clear that he wanted to defend the

169

belief that the God revealed in history is the same as the God of eternity. The Trinity eternally immanent in God is revealed in the economic Trinity of the Christian dispensation (*oikonomia*). Development of the psychological analogy through Augustine, whose Trinity is often no more than memory, understanding, and will (or love) later led to unitarianism, but the sociological unity of the Lover (the Father), the Beloved (the Son), and Love (the Spirit) in eternal relation, found in classic form in Richard of St.-Victor, preserved the Trinity in the West.

The witness of the Spirit takes the thought out of the schoolroom into the courtroom. Roman court was early in the morning, from 5 to 7 A.M., so that all witnesses could be present before the day's work began. The third saying portrays Jesus on trial before the world, but he is not without witnesses. The great witness is the Paraclete, who comes to make clear that Judas is the instrument of Satan (John 6:70; 13:27), "the son of perdition" (ch. 17:12), and that Jesus is the temple of the Spirit, "the Son of God" (ch. 1:32-34).

His witnesses are both divine and human. The disciples bear witness of him because they had been with him from the beginning of his ministry (ch. 15:27; cf. 3:11; 4:39; I John 1:2; 4:14; 5:7; III John 12; Acts 1:15-26; 13:31). Historical revelation, to which the disciples bear witness, is strengthened by the continuing revelation through the Paraclete. That which was revealed once for all in concreteness and uniqueness is renewed by the ministry of the Holy Spirit. This distance between the historical events and the generations that follow is bridged by the Paraclete. As in Acts, the eyewitnesses can say: "We are witnesses to these things, and so is the Holy Spirit whom God has given to those who obey him" (Acts 5:32). The succession of witnesses is seen in the High-Priestly Prayer of John, ch. 17. Jesus reveals the truth (vs. 1-5), then the disciples become his witnesses (vs. 6-19), and all the future disciples that believe their testimony become witnesses to the world.

Witnessing is a great theme in John. A week of witnessing

was seen in the ministry that began with John the Baptist (chs. 1:19, 29, 35, 43; 2:1). Five witnesses, one of which was John, are brought forth in John, ch. 5. There are John the Baptist himself (vs. 30-35), then the works which Jesus did (v. 36), the Father in heaven (vs. 37 f.), the Scriptures (vs. 39-44), and especially Moses (vs. 45 f.). The five with the Holy Spirit and the disciples make seven witnesses to Jesus in John's Gospel, but the great witness is the Paraclete, the Holy Spirit.

The fourth saying (John 16:4b-11): *the Paraclete as Judge.* The departure of Jesus and the vindication of his ministry by the ministry of the Paraclete are the major themes of the fourth Paraclete saying.

23. I did not say these things to you (from the beginning),
24. because I was with you.

25. But now I am going to him who sent me;
26. yet none of you asks me, "Where are you going?"

27. But because I have said these things to you,
28. sorrow has filled your hearts.

29. Nevertheless I tell you the truth:
30. it is to your advantage that I go away,

31. for if I do not go away,
32. the Paraclete will not come to you;

33. but if I go,
34. I will send him to you.

35. And when he comes,
36. he will convict the world (of sin and of righteousness and of judgment):

37. of sin,
38. because they do not believe in me;

39. of righteousness,
40. because I go to the Father (and you will see me no more);

41. of judgment,
42. because the ruler of this world is judged.

The three parentheses are perhaps explanatory expansions of the Paraclete hymn, but the first twelve lines continue the departure of the farewell discourses, while the last eight voice the new theme of vindication.

The departure of Jesus from the disciples has been the dark background to both farewell discourses, but now it is declared an advantage. It was not until the end of his ministry that this departure was announced. The question of the departure appeared in the first discourse (John 13:36; 14:5), but it appears again in the Paraclete hymn (ch. 16:5), an indication that the hymn had an independent circulation before it was included in the farewell discourses.

Sorrow filled the disciples' hearts when they heard of the departure of the great teacher. They no doubt thought they would be left as orphans, as with the disciples of Socrates, but it was really an advantage. As long as the visible Paraclete was present the ministry of the invisible Paraclete could not begin. This does not mean the Holy Spirit was not active outside of Jesus in the days of the incarnation of the Son of God in human flesh, but it does declare the age of the Son before the age of the Spirit. The force of John 7:39 is seen again: "*Pneuma* was not yet, because Jesus was not yet glorified."

The vindication of Jesus is the threefold conviction of the *kosmos*, the order of darkness and death and hate opposed to light and life and love. The American Standard Version translation of "convict" is better, if a choice must be made, than the Revised Standard Version "convince," for the Greek word *elenchein* means "to cross-examine." The Paraclete will cross-examine the world to bring out the charges against it. This was the work of a good Roman judge. He was supposed to cross-examine three times the one charged, as one sees so vividly in the trial of Jesus (John 18:33; 19:1, 9). Jesus was once on trial before the world, but the world is brought to trial with the Paraclete where Pilate was before.

The world is found guilty on three charges: sin, righteousness, judgment. The great sin is unbelief (chs. 3:19 f.; 18:47;

172

15:22). The world has chosen the murderer, the devil, and rejected the Truth, Jesus (cf. ch. 8:44). After the return of Jesus to the Father and the ministry of the Paraclete begins, Jesus will be vindicated as "the Holy and Righteous One" (cf. Acts 2:36; 3:14; 5:30-32). The world will be found unrighteous and Jesus righteous. The third charge, judgment, will bring to light by cross-examination that the invisible ruler of this fallen *kosmos* is Satan (John 12:31; 14:30; cf. I Cor. 2:8; II Cor. 4:4; Eph. 2:2; 6:11-13).

The fifth saying (John 16:12-15): *the Paraclete as Guide.* The fifth Paraclete saying is a promise that the Paraclete, called for the third time "the Spirit of truth," will guide the disciples into truth (vs. 12 f.) and glorify Jesus (vs. 14 f.).

{ 43. I have many things to say to you,
{ 44. but you cannot bear them now.

{ 45. When the Spirit of truth comes,
{ 46. he will guide you into all the truth;

{ 47. for he will not speak on his own authority,
{ 48. but whatever he hears he will speak.

{ 49. And he will declare to you things to come:
{ 50. he will glorify me,

{ 51. for he will take what is mine
{ 52. and declare it to you.

{ 53. All that the Father has is mine;
{ 54. therefore I said

{ 55. that he will take what is mine
{ 56. and declare it to you.

Six lines are about guiding, and the last eight glorifying, lines 51 f. and 55 f. being the same.

Things are about to happen that would crush the disciples if they did not have help of the Holy Spirit to guide them in their understanding. They are about to pass through a dark tunnel that will lead them into a mammoth cave of meaning. It will take a guide to lead them into the hidden truth of the crucifixion crisis. Before the event the disciples have neither

173

the capacity to receive nor the ability to endure this deep disclosure. The Spirit will guide the disciples, as the Spirit speaks what he hears.

As the Spirit guides the disciples he will glorify Jesus. The "things to come" are disclosed from the very depths of God. The Father discloses them to the Son, the Son to the Spirit, and the Spirit to the disciples. As the Son glorified the Father (John 12:28), revealing his reality and presence, so the Spirit will glorify the Son. The glory of the Son that flashed through the signs (ch. 11:4) and was hidden behind the dark cloud of death (chs. 12:23; 13:31) will be disclosed to the disciples by the Holy Spirit. The event that appeared to be a departure will turn out to be a disclosure of the abiding presence of Christ.

The disclosure situation came in the upper room on the first Easter evening. This became the occasion for the great insufflation (ch. 20:22), the great inbreathing of the Spirit into the disciples. Before breathing upon the disciples, a twofold blessing was bestowed in the form of a Hebrew *shalom:* "Peace be with you" (vs. 19, 21). After the second *shalom* he gave them a commission after the pattern of the Hebrew *shaliach:* "As the Father has sent me, even so I send you." There were no successors to the Hebrew *shaliach,* but the Great *Shaliach* from God, Jesus Christ, transfers his mission to the disciples.

The breathing of the Spirit is the transfer of the commission and the authority. As God breathed upon man to give him the breath of life (Gen. 2:7), so now Jesus breathes upon the disciples to give them authority to forgive sins in his name. The great invitation (John 7:37-39) made it clear that the Spirit would not be poured out in this manner until after the glorification of Jesus (crucifixion-resurrection-ascension). Even an ascension had taken place by the first Easter evening (cf. ch. 20:17), and Jesus is able to appear among the disciples with the door shut (v. 19). Other appearings took place later (chs. 20:26-29; 21), but the first Easter evening stands out as the first bestowal of the Spirit. The public bestowal of

174

the Spirit at Pentecost has been already discussed in Chapter 3.

The claims of the "Chair of Peter" by Rome has made the transfer of authority to forgive sin a controversial issue. Both Peter in particular and all the disciples in general are portrayed with this authority in Matthew (chs. 16:19; 18:18). All the disciples received this authority in the great insufflation (John 20:22 f.). As the Spirit speaks not with his own authority (ch. 16:13), so the disciples act not in their own name but in the name of him who breathed upon them the Spirit. As receiving the Spirit is no Roman monopoly, so the forgiveness of sins may be pronounced in the name of Christ by all who receive the Spirit.

THE KOINŌNIA (FIRST JOHN)

Koinōnia ("fellowship") is the key to all the teachings of The First Letter of John: "That which we have seen and heard we proclaim also to you, so that you may have *koinōnia* with us; and our *koinōnia* is with the Father and with his Son Jesus Christ" (I John 1:3). This comes forth clearly when the passages on the Spirit are considered. The Spirit unites God's children to the Father and the Son in one great fellowship of light, life, and love.

Most commentaries think of the passages that speak of an anointing (*chrisma*, ch. 2:20, 27) as references to the Holy Spirit. This has become the popular interpretation, reflected in the prayer of an earnest deacon for the guest evangelist: "O Lord, unctionize this preacher." The anointing of prophets, priests, and kings in the Old Testament and the anointment of Jesus with the Holy Spirit at his baptism (Acts 10:38) form the background for this belief that this has reference to an anointment with the Holy Spirit of each believer at his baptism (Acts 8:17).

Another interpretation has been urged by C. H. Dodd, and this is reflected in *The New English Bible* translation of which he was chairman. His commentary on the Johannine

175

letters views the *chrisma* against the background of the mystery religions that spoke of a secret anointing at "the third portal" that gave superior knowledge. John is claiming this for all Christians, not just a select few, and this knowledge was given to them at the time that they were initiated into the fellowship. If only I John 2:20 were considered ("anointed by the Holy One"), the older interpretation might go unchallenged, but the later references to the *chrisma* as that which was "received" and "teaches" and was "taught" (ch. 2:27) lends support to Dodd's view.[25] It is a question that needs more light.

Passages that speak of *pneuma* are the primary sources for understanding the function of the Holy Spirit in First John. There are four of these and they may be grouped under the two headings: *koinōnia* with the Father (chs. 3:19-24; 4:13-16) and *koinōnia* with the Son (chs. 4:1-6; 5:6-12). Albert Schweitzer has written of the Christ-mysticism of Paul in contrast to the God-mysticism of John.[26] This in general is helpful, and Schweitzer rightly sees both in the Johannine writings. The God-mysticism is dominant and is surveyed first.

Koinōnia *with the Father.* Fellowship with the Father brings assurance to the believer (ch. 3:19-24). Reassurance is offered to the doubtful in a Trinitarian pattern that begins with boldness (*parrēsia*) before God. When the heart condemns and there is doubt as to how one stands with God, he is to remember that "God is greater than our hearts, and he knows everything" (v. 20). Reassurance comes through the confession of sin with the knowledge that God "is faithful and just, and will forgive our sins and cleanse from all unrighteousness" (ch. 1:9). One must remember that there is a Paraclete with the Father for those who fall into sins and that this Paraclete, "Jesus Christ the righteous," is the atoning sacrifice for our sins and even for the whole world (ch. 2:1).

When one has accepted this forgiveness, there is a holy boldness before God that enables one not only to ask in prayer but to receive an answer. Mortal sin is beyond the reach of prayer, and one is not encouraged to pray for that, but the occasional sins into which a Christian brother may fall are not beyond forgiveness (ch. 5:13-17). *Parrēsia* ("boldness," "confidence," "freedom of speech") in prayer is a great word in John. Those who abide in God may stand before God at his *parousia* with this *parrēsia* (ch. 2:28). "And this is the *parrēsia* which we have in him, that if we ask anything according to his will he hears us" (ch. 5:14). This is reassurance that lifts prayer to the highest level.

Obedience to God requires the right relation to his Son Jesus Christ and to one's Christian brother. Belief, personal trust in Jesus, and the practice of brotherly love are the basic acts of obedience to God (ch. 3:23). They are the two hinges on the door that opens the way to *parrēsia* before God. God is pleased, and prayer is heard and answered.

The gift of the Spirit enables one to have this "fellowship with the Father and with his Son Jesus Christ" (ch. 1:3). Obedience brings the knowledge of this gift. "All who keep his commandments abide in him, and he in them. And by this we know that he abides in us, by the Spirit which he has given us" (ch. 3:24). The gift of the Spirit accomplishes this mutual indwelling, this interpenetration of God and man. This coinherence is communion with God, God-mysticism, the highest of all spirtual knowledge.

> Speak to Him, thou, for He hears, and Spirit with Spirit can meet —
> Closer is He than breathing, and nearer than hands and feet.[27]

This is not absorption of man into God. It is God indwelling man, and man indwelling God. God's Spirit and man's spirit meet, but they do not merge.

The assurance of man before God flowers into the abode of God in man (ch. 4:13-16). The previous passage moved from God to the Son to the Spirit. Now the movement is reversed from the Spirit to the Son to God. The first is the movement of God to man, while the second is the movement of man to God. God moves first, in love. Again the gift of the Spirit is

177

the source of knowledge that "we abide in him and he in us" (ch. 4:13; cf. 3:24).

Reception of the Spirit enables those who have seen the incarnate Word to "testify that the Father has sent his Son as the Savior of the world" (ch. 4:14). Those who believe their testimony receive the witness of the Spirit within themselves that their testimony is true. The whole world may not be saved, but God has made an atoning sacrifice not only for those who have believed but for all the world which may believe (ch. 2:2). The sacrifice has been made by grace, but the benefits must be received by faith. The Augustinian-Calvinist doctrines of limited atonement and irresistible grace have no place in Johannine theology.

Behind the giving of the Spirit and the sending of the Son is the God of love. His love provides the atoning sacrifice, the *hilasmos* for sin (chs. 2:2; 4:10). This is offered to all. "Whoever confesses that Jesus is the Son of God, God abides in him, and he in God. So we know and believe the love God has for us. God is love, and he who abides in love abides in God, and God abides in him." (Ch. 4:15 f.) The giving of the Spirit and the sending of the Son reveal the abiding love of God. This is the Holy Trinity of Christian experience. This is the God of holy love.

Koinōnia *with the Son*. Fellowship with God requires fellowship with the Son. "No one who denies the Son has the Father. He who confesses the Son has the Father also." (Ch. 2:23.) A God-mysticism without Christ-mysticism is impossible for John. Fellowship with the Son is the foundation for fellowship with God. "This is the antichrist, he who denies the Father and the Son." (V. 22.) The belief that *the* Antichrist would appear before the *parousia,* the second coming of Christ, was in the background of Johannine eschatology. This much was assumed, but many had not noted the many antichrists, the forerunners of the Antichrist (v. 18).

The denial of the "flesh" of Jesus Christ was a sure sign that the antichrists had arrived to prepare the way for the Antichrist (ch. 4:1-6). How was one to know which prophets

178

spoke under the inspiration of God's Spirit and which were the messengers of Satan? The criterion of Johannine teaching was the flesh of Jesus Christ. "By this you know the Spirit of God: every spirit which confesses that Jesus Christ has come in the flesh is of God, and every spirit which does not confess Jesus is not of God." (Vs. 2 f.)

Denial of the flesh of Jesus Christ was "the spirit of antichrist" (v. 3), about whom they had heard in the eschatological teachings around Ephesus. Denials of the true humanity, not the true deity of Christ, were the great threat to the faith. The Gnostics, as they were later called, taught that Jesus Christ only "appeared" to be human, so they were often called docetists, from the Greek *dokein*, "to appear." Christ was an *aiōn*, an intermediary between God and man who was neither God nor man. Those who preached such heresy did not speak under the inspiration of the Spirit of God. They were "false prophets" (v. 1).

The "blood" of Jesus Christ brings the humanity of Jesus into fuller focus. John's Gospel saw profound spiritual significance in the water and the blood which flowed from the side of Jesus after he died on the cross (John 19:34). Jesus was no mythological god who ate ambrosia, drank nectar, and had ichor in his veins; he was a real human being with human bones, flesh, and blood. The denial of the human blood of Jesus, as in a popular form of Docetic fundamentalism often heard today, would have been blasted as downright heresy by John.[28]

The Docetism refuted in the Johannine doctrine of incarnation apparently made room for a baptismal incarnation or for the incarnation of the Son of God at the baptism of Jesus, as a form of liberalism teaches today.[29] It is a question as to which misses the message of Johannine theology most, the fundamentalism of M. R. De Haan or the liberalism of Colwell and Titus. Ancient heresy is very much alive today.

The ancient docetist apparently believed in the incarnation at the baptism of Jesus by John, but they claimed that only Jesus of Nazareth died on the cross. The Son of God departed

179

before the crucifixion. This was the Docetism denounced by Irenaeus of Lyon in the second century and it was perhaps popular already around Ephesus when John wrote. Cerinthus was the name of the Ephesian heretic. This is the Christology rejected by John when he says: "This is he who came by water and blood, Jesus Christ, not with the water only but with the water and the blood" (I John 5:6). In other words, Jesus was not only the Son of God at his baptism, but it was the Son of God incarnate in Jesus who shed his blood on the cross.

The descent of the Spirit upon Jesus at his baptism was not an act of incarnation but a testimony. It was the witness of God that brought the Messiah out of hiding into his public ministry as the Son of God (John 1:32-34). "And the Spirit is the witness, because the Spirit is the truth." (I John 5:7.) The Spirit descends to disclose Jesus as the Son of God. Truth is that which is no longer hidden. As the Spirit brings the hidden Messiah out into the open, out of mystery into manifestation in history, this is "the moment of truth."

The historical evidence for the humanity of Jesus is threefold. "There are three witnesses, the Spirit, the water, and the blood; and these three agree." (I John 5:8.) Reference to the three heavenly witnesses in the AV was first quoted by the Spanish heretic called Priscillian in the fourth century. It did not appear in any Greek manuscript before the fourteenth century. It appeared first in the Latin Vulgate in 1514, but Erasmus did not include it in his Greek text of 1516. It was only after a furor and the evidence produced in one Greek manuscript that Erasmus reluctantly put it in the text. Stephanus included it in his *Textus Receptus* of 1550, and from this it got into the Authorized Version. It is not heretical, but there is no doubt that the modern texts and translations, all of which omit it, are correct.

The passage has to do with the testimony of God for the historical incarnation, the flesh and blood reality of Jesus' humanity. In Hebrew testimony, truth was established by two or three witnesses. God has given three witnesses for the humanity of Jesus (water at baptism, blood at crucifixion, and the Spirit from baptism onward). If the testimony of men is received, so should the testimony of God be received. Again, let it be said, the descent of the Spirit was "the moment of truth." And "the Spirit is the truth" (v. 7).

8

THE SPIRIT OF CHRIST
IN OTHER NEW TESTAMENT WRITINGS

THE OTHER New Testament writings that use the Greek word
pneuma have been dated across several decades. The date for
The Letter of James ranges from A.D. 40 to A.D. 150! Hebrews is
dated as early as A.D. 60 and as late as A.D. 95, and First Peter
is usually dated about the same time. The dates of Second Peter
and Jude are also very uncertain, but they have either a direct
or an indirect connection. Parts of the Johannine Apocalypse,
Revelation, may belong to a period before the fall of Jerusalem
in A.D. 70, but the final form is usually dated in the time of
Domitian (A.D. 81—96).

The use of *pneuma* in these writings is a miscellany, but
there is a general coherence when the term indicates the Holy
Spirit. These teachings are far more primitive, nearer to Jewish
Christianity, than those in the Pauline and Johannine writings,
even though they are later than most Pauline writings. In the
most general way the words "Spirit of Christ" express their
point of view, although the phrase is found only in I Peter
1:11.

THE SPIRIT OF WISDOM (JAMES)

The Letter of James uses the Greek word *pneuma* only twice,
and each time it has reference to the human spirit. In James
2:26 the relation between body and spirit is used to illustrate
faith and works: "For as the body apart from the spirit is
dead, so faith apart from works is dead." This is the Biblical
psychology in which the living soul is the unity of body and

182

spirit. When God gives his spirit to the body of dust, it is alive; when he takes spirit away, the body is dead (Gen. 2:7; Job. 33:4; Eccl. 12:7).

The human spirit as the unitive principle in man is the point of contact with the Holy Spirit, the unitive Being of God. The Holy Spirit is not mentioned as such in James 4:5, but the relation between God and the human spirit is expressed in the mystical language of Old Testament covenant theology (Jer. 3:14; Hos. 2:19 f.). There is reference to an unknown scripture which said: "He yearns jealously over the spirit which he has made to dwell in us."

The Greek will allow for the human spirit longing for God ("the spirit he planted within us zealously longs for God") or God longing for the human spirit, accepted in the Revised Standard Version. The Authorized Version, following the first translation, conveys Augustine's famous confession: "Thou hast made us for thyself and our heart is restless until it comes to rest in thee" (*Confessions* I.1). The Revised Standard Version is preferred, for the preceding verses indicate that man is hostile to God and longs for pleasure, and the following verse (James 4:6) confesses God's grace. The human spirit for which God yearns is "the breath of life" which he breathed into us in our creation (Gen. 2:7).

The longing of God stands in powerful contrast to the lust of man. Human lust leads to divisions among men. The source of the divisions is described in terms of the Stoic vices of pleasure (*hēdonē,* James 4:1) and desire (*epithymia,* v. 2). The second has special significance for James' understanding of temptation: "Then desire when it has conceived gives birth to sin; and sin when it is full-grown brings forth death" (ch. 1:15).

Such uncontrolled passion hinders prayer (ch. 4:3 f.). This combination of the best in Stoic morality, in which man is taught to master his passions, and the best in Jewish morality, which made much of prayer and God's mastery over man, is Christian morality for James. When passion takes the place of prayer and the world displaces God, the result is spiritual

183

adultery (v. 4). This is Old Testament theology in which God and Israel are bound by the marriage vows of the covenant (Ex. 34:15 f.; Deut. 31:16; Hos. 9:1; Jer. 3:20; Isa. 54:5; Ps. 73:27).

God's longing for the human spirit is a jealous longing. He is married to man, and he is jealous when the pleasures of the world and the devil take his place. Jealous is even a name for God in the covenant relation of the Old Testament (Ex. 34:14), and there is constant emphasis on God's jealous yearning to have first place in the human spirit (Ex. 20:5; Deut. 32:16, 21; Zech. 8:2). This longing of God for the human spirit is, on the other hand, a gracious longing for the humble who resist the pleasures of the world and put the devil to flight.

Divisions among men and lack of devotion to God develop the habit of duplicity in man, a condition for which James apparently coined the new word *dipsychos* (" double-minded," *duplex animo* in Latin). The double-minded man is "unstable in all his ways" (James 1:8). He acts and talks like a religious man (chs. 1:26; 2:14), but pleasure and riches mean more to him than God (chs. 4:4, 13; 5:1 ff.). He is deceived (ch. 1:22), hollow (v. 26), partial (ch. 2:4), inhuman (vs. 15 f.), hypocritical (ch. 3:17), and worldly (ch. 4:4). Resistance to the devil and submission to God is the only way to establish the right relation between God and the human spirit. "Draw near to God and he will draw near to you. Cleanse your hands, you sinners, and purify your hearts, you men of double mind." (Ch. 4:8.)

In summary, unfaithful wives and double-minded men describe the condition of the human spirit that is turned away from God. The human spirit controls the passions of the body only when the human spirit gives to God first place and unmixed devotion. Even though this is never expressed in the Pauline language of the witness of God's Spirit with man's spirit, the meaning in James is very much the same as seen in Gal. 5:16-25; Rom. 8:1-27.

These teachings are nearest to the concept of wisdom in

184

the Old Testament, and the functions of the right human spirit are very close to the Old Testament concept of "the spirit of wisdom." Wisdom and spirit in James are never joined, but "wisdom" is described very much in terms of "the spirit of wisdom" (James 1:5; 3:17; cf. Eph. 1:17).

The teachings on *pneuma* in the rest of the New Testament writings have occasional references to the human spirit, but most of the time the Holy Spirit of God is meant. The major teachings are to be grouped around three phrases: (1) "the Spirit of grace" (Heb. 10:29), (2) "the spirit of glory" (I Peter 4:14), and (3) "the spirit of the prophecy" (Rev. 19:10).

THE SPIRIT OF GRACE (HEBREWS)

There is general agreement that Hebrews was written either to Rome or from Rome (Heb. 13:24). It seems that most questions are answered if Barnabas wrote the treatise to Hellenistic Jewish Christians in Rome around A.D. 69. This would be forty years after the crucifixion, a full generation of hesitation as to the Messianic claims of Jesus. This fits better the evidence than the date A.D. 60 adopted by William Manson.[1]

The author's attitude toward Scripture is unusual. His quotations are always anonymous from the human side. God, Christ, or the Holy Spirit are always the source of Scripture to him. The Old Testament is viewed always as the voice of God and fully inspired.[2] This view is well illustrated by his references to the Holy Spirit and Scripture.

The Holy Spirit speaks in Scripture (Heb. 3:7). It is evident that the warnings against apostasy (v. 12) have been greatly influenced by Ps. 95:7-11. The warning in Heb. 3:7 to 4:13 is a Christian homily or catechism based on the desert generation that wandered for forty years in the wilderness. The authority of this psalm is indicated by the introduction: "Therefore, as the Holy Spirit says" (Heb. 3:7).

This theology of the exodus typology is first noted in I Cor. 5:7; 10:1-11, but it underlies much of the New Testament teaching on salvation as a journey from Egypt, through the

185

wilderness of the world, to the Promised Land. The danger of turning back at Kadesh-barnea and falling in the wilderness is accepted by the author as the voice of the Spirit in Scripture (Num., ch. 20). The emphasis on the forty years in the wilderness may indicate forty years between the death of Christ and the date of the letter, A.D. 69.

The analysis of sin in Hebrews is similar to that seen in The Letter of James (James 1:15). When man no longer hears the voice of God, he passes through five steps to apostasy: yielding to sin, self-deception, hardness of heart, unbelief or disobedience, and finally falling away from the living God (Heb. 3:12-14). Salvation is more than leaving Egypt, even more than passing by Sinai and getting to Kadesh-barnea. It is the whole journey from Egypt to the Promised Land. Confidence (*parrēsia,* "freedom of speech" before God, "boldness" in worship) must be held fast from the first to the finish, from *archē* to *telos* (vs. 6, 14). This is the interpretation in Hebrews of what "the Holy Spirit says" in Ps. 95:7-11.

The Holy Spirit also signifies priesthood in Scripture (Heb. 9:8). Only Psalm 110 is more important for the author than Psalm 95. The reference to Melchizedek in Ps. 110:4 becomes the basis for his comparison of the Levitical priesthood and the priesthood of Melchizedek (Heb., ch. 7), the former being earthly and temporal and the latter heavenly and eternal (ch. 8). The earthly must come to an end before the heavenly can begin. With the death of Christ this transition took place (chs. 9 to 10:18).

In this contrast between the earthly and temporal and the heavenly and eternal, in the midst of this comparison between the religion of shadows and the faith based on spiritual substance, the striking statement is made: "By this the Holy Spirit signifies that the way into the sanctuary is not yet opened as long as the outer tabernacle is still standing (which is symbolic for the present age)" (ch. 9:8 f.). This *parabolē* ("figure," "symbol") of the present age has been used as proof that the Temple was still standing when the latter was

186

written.[3] This may well be, but it is not the main point of the *parabolē*.

The main point is that the Day of Atonement and the prescriptions of priesthood indicated that there was no direct access to God as long as the service of the first Tabernacle stood. With the death of Christ every believer could come boldly into the Holy of Holies and have direct access to God. The whole discussion is a Christian midrash or homily on the Day of Atonement in Lev., ch. 16. All was signified by the Holy Spirit.

Thirdly, the Holy Spirit witnesses in Scripture (Heb. 10:15). Appeal in the first two references has been primarily to the Psalms and the Pentateuch, but now attention turns to the Prophets. Jeremiah's famous prophecy on the new covenant is unmistakable evidence for two covenants; the old and the new, the first and the second (Heb. 8:6 f., 13).

The new and second covenant brings to an end the old and first covenant by the *ephapax* ("once for all time") death of Jesus Christ (ch. 10:10). "For by a single offering" he has perfected for all time those who are "sanctified" (v. 14). In the prophecy of Jeremiah "the Holy Spirit also bears witness to us" at two main points: the new covenant is inward ("on the hearts," "on their hearts," "on their minds"), and the forgiveness of sins is complete. The outward and temporal is no longer when the inward and the eternal has come.

The Holy Spirit and salvation touches on three of the five warnings against apostasy in Hebrews (chs. 2:1-4; 3:7 to 4:13; 6:1-20; 10:19-39; 12:1-29). The aorist infinitive *apostēnai* ("to fall away"), from which the noun "apostasy" ("falling away") is derived, is found only in Heb. 3:12, but several synonyms will be noted. Salvation in Hebrews is never complete until the Promised Land is reached (chs. 1:14; 2:3, 10; 5:9; 6:9; 9:28; 11:7). Confusion is compounded when a punctiliar fallacy, a salvation at one point all in the past, is substituted for this exodus typology of the pilgrim's journey from Egypt to the Promised Land. Note especially Heb. 1:14 and 9:28.

The distribution of spiritual gifts by the Holy Spirit (ch. 2:4) is the climax of the first warning against apostasy. Those who have heard the gospel have a greater opportunity than those who had heard only the law mediated by angels, but their dangers are greater too. They may drift away from what they have heard (v. 1), and neglect the great salvation (v. 3). "Drift" translates *pararruōmen*, from *pararreō* ("flow past"), and the passive of "flow" is "drift."

The ingenious exegesis that has God drifting by man rather than man drifting away from God, simply on the basis of the passive, tortures the text more than it illuminates the meaning.[4] God is no more the drifter than he is the one who neglects the great salvation ("we drift," v. 1; "we neglect," v. 3). The witnesses to this salvation, which is so much greater than the law, are more important than Moses and the angels who mediated the law. Therefore drift and neglect of the great salvation is a serious matter.

It was declared at first by the Lord, and it was attested to us by those who heard him, while God also bore witness by signs and wonders and various miracles and by gifts of the Holy Spirit distributed according to his own will. (Vs. 3 f.)

Participation in the Holy Spirit, followed by falling away, is a spiritual tragedy beyond remedy. There are few passages in the New Testament more discussed than the following:

For it is impossible to restore again to repentance those who have once been enlightened, who have tasted the heavenly gift, and have become partakers of the Holy Spirit, and have tasted the goodness of the word of God and the powers of the age to come, if they then commit apostasy, since they crucify the Son of God on their own account and hold him up to contempt. (Heb. 6:4-6.)

The "partakers of the Holy Spirit" (v. 4) have had the same experience as the "holy brethren, partakers of a heavenly calling" (ch. 3:1, ASV) and the "partakers of Christ" (v. 14, ASV). They are all called *metochoi*. Immediately before this third warning the readers have been described as immature, as babes in need of "milk, not solid food" (ch. 5:12). The "solid food is for the mature, for those who have their faculties trained by practice to distinguish good from evil" (v. 14). It is the slowness of these babes to reach maturity that calls forth the warning.

The context identifies those who are "partakers of the Holy Spirit" with "those who have once been enlightened." The aorist participle with only a change from "those" to "you" is used in ch. 10:32 to describe entrance into the Christian life (vs. 32-39). The noun (*phōtismos*) is a technical term in Paul for entrance into the new creation (II Cor. 4:4, 6), so the term became a synonym for "baptism" in the second century (Justin Martyr, *I Apology*, 61).

The "partakers of the Holy Spirit" are also those "who have tasted the heavenly gift." Those who dismiss this statement by saying these are "mere tasters" should note that the same word is used of our Lord Jesus, who suffered death, "so that by the grace of God he might taste death for every one" (Heb. 2:9). He was no "mere taster." The term is perhaps an echo of Ps. 34:8 ("O taste and see that the LORD is good!"), and it is used in another writing of Hellenistic Jewish Christianity to describe "newborn babes" (I Peter 2:2 f.). It means the same in Heb. 6:4. The same aorist participle is used again when they are said to "have tasted the goodness of the word of God and the powers of the age to come" (v. 5).

The Greek has five aorist participles, the last of which is *parapesontas,* from *parapiptō,* "to fall beside" or "aside," and means "having fallen aside" or "commit apostasy" (cf. ch. 3:12 where *apostēnai,* "to fall away" is actually used). A. T. Robertson sees a parallel between the falling away in Hebrews and falling from grace in Gal. 5:4 ("Ye fell out of grace"). "*Adunaton* ["impossible"]," he says, "bluntly denies the possibility of renewal for apostates from Christ (cf. Heb. 3:12 to 4:2). It is a terrible picture and cannot be toned down. The one ray of light comes in vs. 8-12, not here." [5] This "one ray of hope" is found in the persuasion that the spiritual tragedy of apostasy will not overtake the readers. Clarence S.

Roddy well summarized the theme of this passage as "Immaturity may lead to apostasy" and called it "A Bolt of Lightning." [6]

. Most of the exegetical commentaries in French, German, and English agree with the briefer statements by Robertson and Roddy. Only a few commentaries by extreme dispensational fundamentalists, such as Arthur W. Pink and Kenneth Wuest, have tried to force the passage into the straitjacket of the doctrine of perseverance, first found in Augustine and modified by Calvinism.

Herschel H. Hobbs says the teaching of the first four aorist participles in Greek "assumes they have been regenerated," but he argues that the aorist participle *parapesontas* about falling away means that these "Hebrew Christians" face only "the peril of arrested Christian growth" and "are in peril of falling short of their ultimate destiny in Christian behavior and service." [7] R. E. Glaze follows Hobbs on the first two warnings, but here he takes the very opposite view from Hobbs. He repeatedly argues that the first four participles represent experiences that "could accrue to unconverted Jews who share in the worship experiences of a Christian congregation." [8] One of the two is bound to be wrong, and the most careful studies of Hebrews indicate that both are. Let those who think otherwise examine carefully the whole of the message of Hebrews. [9]

The despite (*enubrisas*, "having insulted," "outraged") to "the Spirit of grace" (Heb. 10:29) advances the understanding of apostasy another step forward. This is part of the fourth warning (vs. 19-39). This other aorist participle (*enubrisas*) is from *enubrizō*, found only here in the New Testament, but the concept of apostasy as willful sin is rooted in the Old Testament teachings on sinning "with a high hand" (Num. 15:30). Apostasy in all five warnings in Hebrews is far more serious than a normal lapse. It is renouncing all faith in Christ, "falling away from the living God" (Heb. 3:12). A. T. Robertson has again stated the point clearly when he says that "one has renounced the one and only sacrifice for sin that does and can remove sin." [10]

The failure to distinguish between the one unforgivable sin of apostasy and the many occasional sins that may lead to apostasy was an error of early Christianity that has not been completely corrected until this day.[11] This willful sin of apostasy is stated in the thundering question:

> How much worse punishment do you think will be deserved by the man who has spurned the Son of God, and profaned the blood of the covenant by which he was sanctified, and outraged the Spirit of grace? (Ch. 10:29.)

The last of the five warnings on apostasy in Hebrews (ch. 12:1-29) does not mention the Holy Spirit, but it presents the same awesome picture of apostasy.

The seventh and last topic on the Holy Spirit in Hebrews to be considered is almost the heart of the letter. It has reference to "the blood of Christ, who through the eternal Spirit offered himself without blemish to God" (ch. 9:14). The comment by Alexander C. Purdy explains why this has been left for the climax of the author's thought.

> *The blood of Christ* offered *through the eternal Spirit* is a vivid juxtaposition of phrases and indeed realms of thinking. Here we are close to the very genius of the author. He means both phrases to be understood literally, yet not mechanically or magically. The offering Christ made was in the realm of reality, as tangible and real as blood, as central and decisive as life (blood). Yet it was not an offering on the plane of animal existence; it was transmuted into an eternal redemption because it was made *through the eternal Spirit.* At the point of human sin and its consequences in suffering and death, at that point God through his eternal Spirit entered by his Son to rob death of its sting and its victory.[12]

To the "eternal redemption" (Heb. 9:12) and "the eternal Spirit" (v. 14), the "eternal inheritance" (v. 15) should be added. The Mt. Everest of the Spirit and of the atonement has been reached. God and man have met in the perfect meeting.

191

The Spirit of Glory (I, II Peter, Jude)

References to the Spirit of God in the Petrine writings are generally connected with the glory of God. First Peter 4:14 unites the two ideas with the unique expression *to tēs doxēs kai to tou theou pneuma* ("the of glory and the of God Spirit"), so the translation "the spirit of glory and of God" is perhaps correct. Jude is so closely related to II Peter that it is best discussed after the two Petrine letters. Five topics are found in this collection of texts: the Holy Spirit in sanctification (I Peter 1:2), salvation (vs. 10-12), suffering (ch. 4:14), Scripture (II Peter 1:20), and sensuality (Jude 19 f.).

The reference to the sanctification of the Spirit appears in a rudimentary Trinitarian formula. Parts of a baptismal hymn appear in chs. 1:20; 3:18 f., 22; 4:6, and the following may be a baptismal formula (ch. 1:2):

> According to the foreknowledge of God the Father,
>> in sanctification of the Spirit,
>>> unto obedience and sprinkling of the blood of Jesus Christ.

Trinitarian formulas may change the order of Father-Son-Spirit. The important point is whether the historical functions are assigned eternal relations.

Trinitarian patterns that offer materials for a formula are definitely found prior to I Peter in the New Testament (II Thess. 2:13 f.; Gal. 3:11-14; 4:6; II Cor. 1:21 f.; 3:3; Rom. 14:17 f.; 15:16, 30). First Corinthians 12:4-6 and II Cor. 13:14 have already achieved the status of Trinitarian formulas, and it is likely that I Peter 1:2 has reached that stage too. Arthur W. Wainwright is too hasty in his conclusion when he declares: "I Peter 1:2 carries no implication of a doctrine of the Trinity. Nothing is said about the relationship between Father, Son, and Spirit." [13]

The reference to the sanctification of the Spirit between "the foreknowledge of God" and "obedience and sprinkling

192

of the blood of Jesus Christ" has a Christological purpose. The sufferings of Christ, mentioned seven times in the letter (I Peter 1:11; 2:21, 23 f.; 3:18; 4:1, 13; 5:1), are brought to the fore in order to discuss the sufferings of Christians, found also seven times in the letter (chs. 2:19; 3:14, 17; 4:1, 15 f., 19; 5:9 f.). The blood of Christ comes last for much the same reason "the grace of the Lord Jesus Christ" comes first in II Cor. 13:14 (cf. II Cor. 8:9). The formula in I Peter is followed by a long Trinitarian passage on the Father (ch. 1:3-5), Son (vs. 6-9), and Spirit (vs. 10-12) that indicates the normal order. The Trinitarianism here is not far behind that found in Eph. 1:3-14.[14]

Those foreknown by God the Father and sprinkled with the blood of Christ have also been "sanctified by the Spirit" who takes up his abode in them as "a spiritual house" (I Peter 2:5). It is clear that "the Spirit of Christ" (ch. 1:11) is the same as the Spirit of the Lord who spoke through the prophets, but there is also clear indication that Jesus Christ himself had a preexistent relation to God (v. 20):

Having been foreknown on the one hand from the foundation of the world,
having been manifested on the other at the end of the times.

The possibility that this parallel is part of the great hymn that continues at ch. 3:18 f., 22, and ch. 4:6 makes it even more likely that the Trinity is here viewed as eternal Being in relation as well as historical manifestation and function.[15]

Salvation in I Peter is even more eschatological than in Hebrews. It is always future, "a salvation ready to be revealed in the last time" (I Peter 1:5), "the outcome" (*telos*) of faith (v. 9) at the revelation of Jesus Christ in glory (vs. 8, 13). All Christian growth is toward this goal (ch. 2:2). There is one passage that suggests that the way of salvation, passage through the waters of destruction, began at baptism (ch. 3:21), but even this is to be understood in the same way as the passage through the Red Sea at the beginning of the long pilgrim journey to the Promised Land. There is a history of salvation as there is a history of revelation, but both remain hidden until the days of final visitation when the glory of God is made manifest.

The Holy Spirit is the hidden work of God in salvation. He was at work in the Old Covenant.

> The prophets who prophesied of the grace that was to be yours searched and inquired about this salvation; they inquired what person or time was indicated by the Spirit of Christ within them when predicting the sufferings of Christ and the subsequent glory. It was revealed to them that they were serving not themselves but you, in the things which have now been announced to you by those who preached the good news to you through the Holy Spirit sent from heaven, things into which angels long to look. (I Peter 1:10-12.)

These were the Old Testament prophets with messages such as Isaiah in ch. 53, not New Testament prophets.

The Old Testament prophets saw the sufferings and glory of Christ without any clear distinction as to an age of the Holy Spirit in between. It is this interim between the first and the second coming of Christ, this interim when the gospel is preached "through the Holy Spirit sent forth from heaven," that makes the major difference between Judaism and Christianity. Both hope for the time when the manifestation of the glorious presence of God will bring in an age of peace, but Christians believe this Messianic Age will be ushered in by the revelation of a Messiah who has already suffered and died among men, then raised from the dead to return in glory (I Peter 5:1).

Sufferings may become a blessing when the Holy Spirit is present. The Jewish rabbis believed the Spirit rested on men only in times of joy (*Berakoth* 31A), but First Peter teaches that even suffering can be transformed into joy by the Holy Spirit (ch. 4:13). Contemporary Judaism taught that this joy of the Spirit was granted only to martyrs, but First Peter has modified this idea.[16] It is the purpose of the suffering and

194

the presence of the Spirit that shapes its quality. "If you are reproached for the name of Christ, you are blessed, because the Spirit of glory and of God rests upon you." (V. 14.)

The first readers of First Peter were living between a "fiery ordeal" (vs. 12-16) and the future judgment (vs. 17-19). It is possible that the fiery ordeal has reference to the burning of Rome and the persecution that followed the rumor that these Christians had set the fire. A vivid account of this Neronian persecution indicates the severity of this inhuman attack. Christians, charged with arson and as haters of humanity, were "set on fire to serve to illuminate the night when daylight failed" (Tacitus, *Annals*, XV, 44).

If Nero is the roaring lion (ch. 5:8) in whom Satan prowls, then the letter would be dated sometime between July 18-24, 64, when Rome burned, and June 9, 68, when Nero committed suicide. Those who assign the letter to a later date will find other sufferings, but the date adopted by *The Oxford Annotated Bible* seems to be the right setting.[17] Their faith was truly "tested by fire" (ch. 1:7).

The resting of the Spirit of God upon the persecuted Christians recalls the resting of the Spirit upon the Davidic Messiah (Isa. 11:2) and upon the seventy elders selected to assist Moses (Num. 11:25 f.). The verb in the LXX is the same as that in I Peter 4:14.

The reference to "the spirit of glory" indicates the Shekinah glory, the pillar of fire by night and the pillar of cloud by day, which rested upon the persecuted people of God in the Old Testament in their wilderness journey (Ex. 13:21 f.; 40:34-38, etc.). The Targum on Ps. 82:1 says "the divine Presence [Shekinah] resteth upon the congregation of the godly."[18] Usually this is related to Jesus (James 2:1; I Cor. 2:8; II Cor. 3:17 f.; John 1:14),[19] so the concept of "the spirit of glory" is distinct. "The spirit of glory" and "the Spirit of God" are identical with "the Spirit of Christ" (I Peter 1:11). Cf. "the Spirit of his Son" (Gal. 4:6), "the Spirit of Christ" (Rom. 8:9), "the Spirit of Jesus Christ" (Phil. 1:19), and "the Spirit of Jesus" (Acts 16:7).

Three other references to *pneuma* are found in I Peter, but all of them have reference to the human spirit. The "gentle and quiet spirit" of a Christian woman is precious in the sight of God. In his human spirit, separated from his body between death and resurrection, Jesus "preached to the spirits in prison" (I Peter 3:18 f.), i.e., to the fallen angels.[20] The gospel was preached to the dead that "they might live in the spirit like God" (ch. 4:6).[21]

The glory of God and the Spirit of God have a special connection in II Peter, ch. 1. The chapter begins with the reminder of the "divine power" by which God "has granted to us all things that pertain to life and godliness, through the knowledge of him who called us to his own glory and excellence" (ch. 1:3). Growth in grace will take believers to the point of no return, where they "will never fall" (v. 10), and assure them of a rich "entrance into the eternal kingdom of our Lord and Savior Jesus Christ" (v. 11). Entrance into this future Kingdom is entrance into glory.

The departure (*exodos*) of Peter from his earthly body, his tent (*skēnōma*), into glory is assured by the transfiguration, interpreted by II Peter as a vision (cf. Matt. 17:9) of the *parousia*, the second coming. The two Greek words suggest knowledge even of the Lucan version of the transfiguration, and the reference to the Majestic Glory, the Shekinah, out of which God spoke is also the vocabulary of Luke (ch. 9:43).

It is only a step from this manifestation of the glory of God as assurance for the *parousia* to the further assurance of the prophetic word, the Scriptures inspired by the Holy Spirit. Prophecy is related to the *parousia* like a light in the darkness is related to the day dawn. Firm conviction in the inspiration of the Scriptures is the ground of this guarantee. "First of all you must understand this, that no prophecy of scripture is a matter of one's own interpretation, because no prophecy ever came by the impulse of man, but men moved by the Holy Spirit spoke from God." (II Peter 1:20 f.) This exclusion of the human will or impulse takes the view of inspiration beyond the more general statement "the Spirit of

196

Christ within them" (I Peter 1:11). Scripture is indeed God-breathed (II Tim. 3:16). True prophets spoke as they were "borne along [*pheromenoi*] by the Holy Spirit." The word used to describe their inspiration is used of a ship borne along by the wind (Acts 27:15, 17).

Inspiration and correct interpretation are the very anchors of the apostolic faith. Ignorance of the apostolic tradition and fantastic interpretations distorted both the Old Testament Scriptures and the letters of Paul (II Peter 3:15 f.). False teachers follow the way of the false prophets of the Old Testament who spoke according to their own will and desires. They predicted what they and their rulers wanted to happen rather than what God revealed. True prophets stood in the very *sod* ("counsel") of God, so that the things they saw and heard came to pass (Jer. 23:18-22).

The clearest example of true inspiration is that of Micaiah in the days of Ahab (I Kings, ch. 22). His only promise was: "As the LORD lives, what the LORD says to me, that I will speak" (v. 14). The apostles, following the way of true prophets, "did not follow cleverly devised myths" (II Peter 1:16). They spoke the word of the Lord, things seen and heard, and transmitted this word to the next generation. Second Peter confronts in an acute way the dangers of distortion as the period of apostolic faith is fading and the perils of post-apostolic faith arise.[22]

The new age of *idia epilusis* ("private interpretation") was a threat to apostolic doctrine and morals. The *parousia* in particular was mocked as a myth never to be fulfilled, and a morality that called for holiness in body and spirit was attacked by the apostate form of Christianity, later called Gnosticism.

The apostolic counterattack withered the Gnostics:

These are waterless springs and mists driven by a storm; for them the nether gloom of darkness has been reserved. For, uttering loud boasts of folly, they entice with licentious passions of the flesh men who have barely escaped from those who live in error. They promise them freedom, but they themselves are slaves of corruption; for whatever overcomes a man, to that he is enslaved. (II Peter 2:17-19.)

The whole of this chapter hurls illustrations from history, animals, and nature at these apostates who tempt the immature to follow them. The last chapter is a defense of the *parousia*, denied by these false prophets. Second Peter is a classic critique of false prophecy, and its application to the present is difficult to resist.

The little letter of Jude, following in the same apostolic tradition, perhaps later, has sharpened the distinction between false and true prophecy even more. The introduction urges the readers "to contend for the faith which was once for all delivered to the saints" (v. 3) and warns them of certain "ungodly persons" who had gained secret admission into the Christian fellowship (v. 4). Their faith and morals are such that they "pervert the grace of our God into licentiousness and deny our only Master and Lord, Jesus Christ" (v. 4; cf. II Peter 2:1).

The body of the letter compares apostate Christianity (Jude 5-16) with apostolic Christianity (vs. 17-23) advocated and defended by Jude. The scoffers classified humanity into three classes: the somatic who are material and wholly animalistic, the psychic or sensuous, and the spiritual. There was no hope offered for the somatic, but the psychic could attain salvation by subordinating the sensual to the spiritual. The spiritual claimed a natural affinity for the unseen world and immunity from immorality. Indulgence in the sensual was amoral for them as it was not for the psychic.

This divorce of spirituality from moral standards demonstrated to Jude that these schismatic scoffers were not spiritual at all. "It is these who set up divisions, worldly people, devoid of the Spirit." (V. 19.) The Greek for these "worldly people" is *psychikoi* ("soulish," "natural"). The adjective *psychikē* ("natural") is united by James with the earthly and devilish to describe the wisdom which is not from above (ch. 3:15) and Paul spoke of the natural man as *psychikos*. With all of them the sure sign of the Spirit was morality.

Jude seeks to secure the saints against this ungodly sensuality by calling them back to apostolic faith, "the faith which was once for all delivered" (v. 3), the "most holy faith" (v. 20). On this foundation of the apostolic doctrine the structure of sound morals is to be built. The steps in the building suggest the Trinity:

> Pray in the Holy Spirit;
> > keep yourselves in the love of God;
> > > wait for the mercy of our Lord Jesus Christ
> > > (unto eternal life).

This Trinitarian building is their bulwark against the second-generation revolt.

Prayer in the Spirit is prayer under the Spirit's guidance and in the Spirit's power. This is not a natural possession that permitted sensuality, as the scoffers boasted, but an endowment from God through the grace of Jesus Christ. These ungodly sensualists "pervert the grace of our God into licentiousness and deny our only Master and Lord, Jesus Christ" (v. 4). Jude agrees with Paul that God's love conquers all visible and invisible powers against the soul (Rom. 8:31-39), but they must keep themselves "in the love of God." The fortress of Christ is sufficient, but the fortress must not be abandoned. God's Spirit and God's love are always together, and those "devoid of the Spirit" are not "in the love of God."

As in Hebrews and Second Peter growth in grace from immaturity to maturity is the true security against falling away. All who hold the apostolic faith will find God's power sufficient when those who substitute sensuality for true spirituality tempt unsteadfast souls to follow them (Jude 22 f.). This is the meaning of the great binitarian benediction with which the letter of Jude closes:

Now to him who is able to keep you from falling and to present you without blemish before the presence of his glory with rejoicing, to the only God, our Savior through

199

Jesus Christ our Lord, be glory, majesty, dominion, and authority, before all time and now and for ever. Amen. (Vs. 24 f.)

If II Cor. 13:14 may be called the apostolic benediction, then this is the postapostolic benediction.

THE SPIRIT OF PROPHECY (REVELATION)

The Johannine Apocalypse was not discussed with the Johannine Gospel and The First Letter of John. All the previous writings in this chapter, with the possible exception of James, are connected with Rome. The Johannine Apocalypse originated in Asia Minor but it is focused on the relationship between Rome and Asia Minor very much as noted in I Peter. It seems almost certain that both writings belong to the same period in time, whether this is the seventh or the tenth decade. Much of Revelation reflects the struggle with Nero even if the writings took final form in the time of Domitian.[23]

The concept of the Spirit in the Apocalypse is pre-Gnostic and prophetic. "Without the Apocalypse," says Eduard Schweizer, "we would not know how primitive the conceptions of the Spirit were in the Christian community." [24] These primitive concepts, however, are introduced in a Trinitarian setting (Rev. 1:4):

> Grace to you and peace
> from him who is and who was and who is to come,
> and from the seven spirits which are before the throne,
> and from Jesus Christ the faithful witness, the first-born from the dead, and the ruler of the kings of the earth.

The salutation at the first unites that which is basic in Christian grace and Hebrew peace and then blends the most elementary with the most advanced concepts of the God of history.

The seven spirits standing between God and Christ have

200

been variously interpreted. Martin Rist's mythological approach, following Ernst Lohmeyer, identifies them with "the seven angels of Jewish speculation." [25] Others recognize the mythological background, but they see a transformation of astral speculation by historical revelation. Jewish-Christian apocalyptic thinking roots the manifold energies of the Spirit in the sevenfold manifestation of Isa. 11:2, LXX. "Thus they represent," says Schweizer, "the Spirit of God in its fulness and completeness, while at the same time they represent the angels of the throne and correspond to the angels of the churches." [26]

The seven spirits burn like torches before the throne of God (Rev. 4:5), but they belong to Jesus Christ (ch. 3:1) and are sent out as the seven eyes of the Lamb into the whole earth (ch. 5:6). The omnipresence of Christ in his churches and in the world is thus dramatically portrayed. This high symbolism of the sevenfold energies of the Holy Spirit may be compared to the seven colors of light when passed through a prism. The sevenfold Spirit in the Trinitarian formula belongs to the same pattern of thought as the sevenfold pronouncement to the seven churches: "He who has an ear, let him hear what the Spirit says to the churches" (chs. 2:7, 11, 17, 29; 3:6, 13, 22).

Seven remaining passages express the spirit of prophecy in the Apocalypse. These may be grouped in three pairs with a glorious invitation at the end. In the first pair of references revelation is the main function of the Spirit. Much of the time the Jewish-Christian writings confine revelation to the consummation, but this future revelation has been disclosed in the present in the Apocalypse. This belongs to the nature of apocalyptic thinking.[27] The writing is indeed "the revelation of Jesus Christ, which God gave him to show to his servants what must soon take place; and he made it known by sending his angel to his servant John, who bore witness to the word of God and to the testimony of Jesus Christ, even to all that he saw" (ch. 1:1 f.). The prophetic revelations of the Old Testament belonged more to this age (Amos 3:7).

The first revelation is a vision of Jesus Christ walking among the seven churches in Asia. This came to John while he was in a state of mystical ecstasy. "I was in the Spirit on the Lord's day" he said, "and I heard behind me a loud voice like a trumpet." (Rev. 1:10.) Background to this type of experience may be seen in Ezekiel (chs. 2:2; 3:12, 14) and in the revelations through trance and vision in other New Testament writings (Acts 10:3, 10 f., 17, 19; 11:5; 22:17; II Cor. 12:1-10). John's vision of the risen Lord came while he was "in the Spirit" (Rev. 1:10, *en pneumati*), and this was a state of trance and vision too.

The time of this mystical ecstasy was "on the Lord's day." Some interpreters have understood this to be a state in which "John was projected forward to the future day of the Lord." [28] This would indeed be apocalyptic, but most interpreter's think the day to be the first day of the week when Christians were most mindful of the risen Lord.[29] Ignatius of Antioch, writing a few years later, spoke of Christians as those "no longer living for the Sabbath, but for the Lord's Day, on which also our life sprang up through him and his death" (*To the Magnesians* ix.i, Loeb Classical Library). The feminine adjective *kyriakēn* ("Lord's") is the same as in Rev. 1:10 (*kyrikēi*), and *kyrikon*, the masculine, is used of the Lord's Supper in I Cor. 11:20. It is not necessary to assume that all the visions took place on this one Lord's day. Ezekiel's visions covered four Sabbaths (Ezek. 1:1; 3:16, 23; 8:1; 40:1).

The second revelation "in the Spirit" (Rev. 4:2) was a two-fold vision in which adoration of God and the Lamb is seen in heaven (chs. 4:1 to 5:14). Visions are seen and voices are heard much as in the prophetic utterances in Amos and other classical prophets. The first scene in this vision reveals God as Creator (ch. 4:1-11), the second as Redeemer (ch. 5:1-14). The first vision (chs. 1:9 to 3:22) does not go beyond "the things which are" (ch. 1:19, KJV), but this second vision is the beginning of "the things which shall be hereafter" (cf. ch. 1:19 with ch. 4:1, KJV). Of the four schools of thought (allegorical, preterist, historical, futurist) the futurist seems

202

nearest to the truth, although there are surely elements of truth in the other three.

The futurist interpretation does not require the dispensational theory of a pretribulation rapture. The pretribulation rapture has been popularized by the note on Rev. 4:1 in the Scofield Reference Bible: "This call seems clearly to indicate the fulfilment of I Thess. 4:14-17." George E. Ladd has all but demolished this theory by showing that it does not belong to original premillennialism and that it is exegetically unsound.[30] John F. Walvoord, who represents those who have vigorously opposed Ladd, is forced to admit that "the rapture as a doctrine is not a part of the prophetic foreview of the book of Revelation."[31] Even so, he hangs on with the claim that "the rapture may be viewed as having already occurred in the scheme of God before the events of chapter 4 and following chapters of Revelation unfold."[32] There is not a passage in the New Testament to support Scofield. The call to John to "come up hither" has reference to mystical ecstasy, not to a pretribulation rapture.

The call to John implies that he was translated or transported through the open door into heaven itself. Paul "was caught up to the third heaven . . . into Paradise" (II Cor. 12:2 f.), and the rapture of John seems much the same. Two other passages in Revelation describe the translation or transportation of John to earthly places.

On another occasion John was transported into a desert place. This time one of the seven angels called him to "come" (Rev. 17:1) and carried him "away in the Spirit into a wilderness" (v. 3). To be carried away (*apēnenken*, from *apopherō*, "to bear away") means to be caught up in a mystical ecstasy. The verb is used of the angels who bore Lazarus away to the bosom of Abraham (Luke 16:22), and the translation again recalls the experiences of Ezekiel (chs. 2:2; 3:14 f.; 8:3; 11:24).

The vision was of the great harlot. The imagery may be suggested by Isa. 21:1, which speaks of Babylon as "the wilderness of the sea." Tyre is also described with the song of a harlot: "Take a harp, go about the city, O forgotten harlot" (ch. 23:16). In Revelation it is the city of Rome that is personified as "the great harlot who is seated upon many waters" (Rev. 17:1). Jeremiah described old Babylon as sitting on many waters (ch. 51:13), so now the imagery is transferred to the new Babylon, the city of Rome ruled by the beast (Nero or Domitian).

The second translation of John into an earthly place took him to a mountain (Rev. 21:10). This time he saw the Bride of the Lamb, the counterpart to the great harlot and the beast. The Bride was another city, "the holy city Jerusalem coming down out of heaven from God" (v. 10). The contrast between the wilderness and the mountain corresponds to the contrast between the two cities, Rome and Jerusalem. Rome symbolizes things ungodly, while Jerusalem symbolizes the dwelling of God himself with his people. It was again one of the seven angels who called John to "come" and carried him away "in the Spirit" (vs. 9 f.).

Revelations and translations "in the Spirit" are found with the more common claims of inspiration through the Spirit. A blessing for the dead is attributed to the Spirit (ch. 14:13). This is the second of the seven blessings in the Apocalypse (chs. 1:3; 14:13; 16:15; 19:9; 20:6; 22:7; 22:14). The Voice says:

> Write this:
> Blessed are the dead who die in the Lord henceforth . . .
>   that they may rest from their labors,
>   for their deeds follow them!

This Christian *baraca*, after the pattern of a Hebrew *Berakah*, promises rewards in the life to come for the deeds done in this life. This belongs to the main purpose for the writing of the Apocalypse (chs. 2:23; 20:12 f.; 22:12). Faith in the Lamb of God assures his followers of a blessed immortality, after the death of the body, but the extent of this blessedness is measured by good works.[33]

The nature of these rewards is clearly presented in the

204

seven promises made by the Spirit to the seven churches (chs. 2:7, 11, 17, 29; 3:6, 13, 22). They are:

> To him who conquers I will grant to eat of the tree of life, which is in the paradise of God (ch. 2:7);

> He who conquers shall not be hurt by the second death (v. 11);

> To him who conquers I will give some of the hidden manna, and I will give him a white stone, with a new name written on the stone, which no one knows except him who receives it (v. 17);

> He who conquers and who keeps my works until the end, I will give him power over the nations, and he shall rule them with a rod of iron, as when earthen pots are broken in pieces, even as I myself have received power from my Father; and I will give him the morning star (vs. 26-28);

> He who conquers shall be clad thus in white garments, and I will not blot his name out of the book of life; I will confess his name before my Father and before his angels (ch. 3:5);

> He who conquers I will make him a pillar in the temple of my God; never shall he go out of it, and I will write on him the name of my God, and the name of the city of my God, the New Jerusalem which comes down from my God out of heaven, and my own new name (v. 12);

> He who conquers, I will grant him to sit with me on my throne, as I myself conquered and sat down with my Father on his throne (v. 21).

After the fourth (ch. 19:9) of the seven blessings, the testimony of Jesus is attributed to the inspiration of the Spirit: "For the testimony of Jesus is the Spirit of prophecy" (v. 10). Eduard Schweizer has declared this the dominant concept of the Apocalypse.[34] This was John's commission at the very beginning when he said:

> I John, your brother, who share with you in Jesus the tribulation and the kingdom and the patient endurance,

was on the island called Patmos on account of the word of God and the testimony of Jesus. (Ch. 1:9.)

The whole of the Apocalypse was inspired by the Spirit, and the first of the seven blessings is promised to those who read and give heed to its contents (chs. 1:3; 22:7). Those who reject are warned with these words:

> I warn every one who hears the words of the prophecy of this book: if any one adds to them, God will add to him the plagues described in this book, and if any one takes away from the words of the book of this prophecy, God will take away his share in the tree of life and in the holy city, which are described in this book. (Ch. 22:18 f.)

The final passage on the Spirit in the Apocalypse is the great invitation (v. 17):

> The Spirit and the Bride say, " Come."
> And let him who hears say, " Come."
> And let him who is thirsty come,
>   let him who desires take the water of life
>   without price.

A Trinitarian formula introduced the Apocalypse (ch. 1:4), and now the epilogue elaborates this pattern: God (ch. 22:8 f.), Christ (vs. 12 f., 16), and the Spirit (v. 17).

The Bride is the church, the Lamb's wife (ch. 21:9), through which the Spirit acts to invite all to come to the fountain of life. Many commentaries interpret the words as a petition for Christ to come, as in ch. 22:20, but the following words indicate an invitation to men, as in Isa. 55:1. Until the Lord Jesus does come in glory the Spirit manifests himself in the Bride. The apocalyptic hope of glory and the invitation of a spiritual church are blended. Long ago, in a most unusual way this was seen by Joachim de Fiori (ca. 1145–1202). His *Commentary on the Apocalypse* (1:5) saw three ages of mankind: that of the Father(the Law), that of the Son (the Gospel), and that of the Holy Spirit that he believed was about to dawn.[35]

206

Actually, the dawn came in the first century, but centuries of dead ceremony and tradition have put the Spirit in eclipse at noonday. It is the task of our time to let the age of the Spirit prepare the way for the age of glory. Reunion has become the theme of the twentieth century, but ecumenical discussions have accomplished very few results. Rigid tradition, dead dogmas, and useless institutions have often been more of a hindrance than a help. Power structures too often react against renewal and reforms necessary for any Christian unity worthy of the name. Resistance must yield to that "third force" of charismatic renewal if orderly structure and orthodox doctrine survive. Structure and doctrine are not despised, as in much recent polemic, but neither should the Spirit be quenched.[36]

NOTES

Chapter 1. THE SPIRIT OF THE LORD IN THE OLD TESTAMENT

1. This brief survey may be supplemented by a detailed study by Daniel Lys, *Ruach* (Paris: Presses Universitaires de France, 1962). A. M. Henry, *The Holy Spirit*, tr. by J. Lundberg and M. Bell (Hawthorn Books, Inc., Publishers, 1960), pp. 7-61. Lloyd Neve, *The Spirit of God in the Old Testament* (Tokyo: Seibunsha, 1972).

2. J. Lindblom, *Prophecy in Ancient Israel* (Muhlenberg Press, 1963).

3. Marghanita Laski, *Ecstasy: A Study of Some Secular and Religious Experiences* (Indiana University Press, 1962). Laski's empirical study is too skeptical about the supernatural reference, but it is the most detailed study of the phenomenon thus far. William G. MacDonald called my attention to the arguments against ecstasy in Old Testament prophecy in the *Bulletin of the Evangelical Theological Society* (Summer, 1966), but these articles give little space for stages in Hebrew prophetism.

4. Lindblom, *op. cit.*, p. 33.

5. *Ibid.*, p. 65, n. 32.

6. O. Eissfeldt, "The Prophetic Literature," *The Old Testament and Modern Study*, ed. by H. H. Rowley (Oxford: Clarendon Press, 1951), pp. 119–126.

7. H. Neil Richardson, in *Journal of Biblical Literature* (March, 1966), p. 89.

8. H. H. Rowley, *The Servant of the Lord and Other Essays on the Old Testament* (London: Lutterworth Press, 1952), p. 114. In the Basil Blackwell & Mott, Ltd., Oxford, edition, pp. 120 f.

9. *The Interpreter's Bible*, 12 vols., ed. by George A. Buttrick *et al.* (Abingdon Press, 1951–1957), Vol. 6, p. 913.

10. Rowley, *The Servant of the Lord*, p. 110

11. Paul Volz, *Der Geist Gottes* (Tübingen: J. C. B. Mohr,

1910), p. 9; Gustav Hölscher, *Die Propheten* (Leipzig: J. C. Hindrische Verlag, 1941), p. 35; Henry, *The Holy Spirit*, pp. 7–61.

12. A brief note and bibliography is in *The Oxford Dictionary of the Christian Church*, ed. by F. L. Cross (London: Oxford University Press, 1961), p. 1245.

13. Detailed studies have been done by G. W. H. Lampe, *The Seal of the Spirit* (London: Longmans, Green & Co., Inc., 1951), and Burkhard Neunheuser, *Baptism and Confirmation*, tr. by John Jay Hughes (Freiburg: Herder & Co.; London: Burns & Oates, 1964).

14. *The Oxford Dictionary of the Christian Church*, pp. 1411 f.

15. Rowley, *The Servant of the Lord*, pp. 54 f.

16. Alexander Heidel, *The Babylonian Genesis* (The University of Chicago Press, 1951).

17. J. E. Fison, *The Blessing of the Holy Spirit* (London: Longmans, Green & Co., Inc., 1956), p. 70.

Chapter 2. THE DESCENT OF THE DOVE
IN THE SYNOPTIC GOSPELS

1. C. K. Barrett, *The Holy Spirit in the Gospel Tradition* (London: S.P.C.K., 1947).

2. *Ibid.*, p. 39.

3. Vincent Taylor, *The Gospel According to St. Mark* (London: Macmillan & Co., Ltd., 1952), p. 161.

4. Jean Steinmann, *Saint John the Baptist and the Desert Tradition* (Harper & Brothers, 1958), pp. 58–71.

5. J. E. Yates, *The Spirit and the Kingdom* (London: S.P.C.K., 1963), pp. 22–46.

6. David Daube, *The New Testament and Rabbinic Judaism* (London: Athlone Press, 1956), p. 112.

7. In G. Kittel (ed.), *Theological Dictionary of the New Testament* (Wm. B. Eerdmans Publishing Company, 1964), Vol. I, p. 141. Ernest Best, *The Temptations and the Passion* (Cambridge: Cambridge University Press, 1965), pp. 3–10, has argued against Jeremias.

8. Jean Daniélou, *From Shadows to Reality: Studies in the Biblical Typology of the Fathers*, tr. by Wulstan Hibberd (London: Burns & Oates, 1960), pp. 11–65.

9. Ulrich W. Mauser, *Christ in the Wilderness* (London: SCM Press, Ltd., 1963), pp. 77–102.

10. J. M. Robinson, *The Problem of History in Mark* (London: SCM Press, Ltd., 1957).

11. Best, *op. cit.*, p. 20.

12. Details are in *The Interpreter's Dictionary of the Bible*,

4 vols., ed. by George A. Buttrick *et al.* (Abingdon Press, 1962), Vol. I, pp. 817–824.

13. Barrett, *The Holy Spirit in the Gospel Tradition*, pp. 131 f.

14. *Ibid.*

15. G. R. Beasley-Murray, *A Commentary on Mark Thirteen* (London: Macmillan & Co., Ltd., 1957), p. 46.

16. A. Dupont-Sommer, *The Essene Writings from Qumran*, tr. by G. Vermes (Oxford: Basil Blackwell & Mott, Ltd., 1961), p. 210.

17. The question was first discussed by F. C. Conybeare in *Zeitschrift für neutestamentliche Wissenschaft* (1901), pp. 275–288. See also, David Bosch, *Die Heidenmission in der Zukunftschau Jesu* (Zurich: Zwingli Verlag, 1959), p. 188.

18. Karl Barth, *Dogmatics in Outline*, tr. by G. T. Thomson (Philosophical Library, Inc., 1949), p. 95. See also *Church Dogmatics*, Vol. I, Part 2, tr. by G. T. Thomson and Harold Knight (Charles Scribner's Sons, 1956), pp. 172–202. Detailed history of the virgin birth in Christian theology may be found in Thomas Boslooper, *The Virgin Birth* (The Westminster Press, 1962). A critical study of the early period has been done by Hans von Campenhausen, *The Virgin Birth in the Theology of the Ancient Church*, tr. by Frank Clarke (London: SCM Press, Ltd., 1964).

19. The following six paragraphs are from my article on the " Virgin Birth " in *The Interpreter's Dictionary of the Bible.*

19a. Ludwig Koehler and Walter Baumgartner (eds.), *Lexicon in Veteris Testamenti Libros* (Wm. B. Eerdmans Publishing Company, 1951–1953), p. 709.

20. Günther Bornkamm, in *Tradition and Interpretation in Matthew,* by Günther Bornkamm, Gerhard Barth, and Heinz Joachim Held, tr. by Percy Scott (The New Testament Library; The Westminster Press, 1963), p. 84.

21. Steinmann, *op. cit.*, pp. 19–61.

22. This is the first of ten hymns in Luke, chs. 1; 2. For details see R. A. Aytoun, " The Ten Lucan Hymns of the Nativity in Their Original Language," *Journal of Theological Studies*, 1917, pp. 274–288.

23. Joachim Jeremias, *The Central Message of the New Testament* (Charles Scribner's Sons, 1965), pp. 9–30.

24. A. R. C. Leaney, *The Gospel According to St. Luke* (Harper & Brothers, 1958), pp. 59–68.

Chapter 3. THE GIFT OF THE HOLY SPIRIT IN ACTS

1. Arthur T. Pierson, *The Acts of the Holy Spirit* (Fleming H. Revell Company, 1896); William Barclay, *The Promise of the*

Spirit (The Westminster Press, 1960), p. 46.

2. W. O. Carver, *The Acts of the Apostles* (Sunday School Board, Southern Baptist Convention, 1916), pp. 3, 10.

3. Hans Conzelmann, *The Theology of Saint Luke*, tr. by Geoffrey Buswell (Harper & Brothers, 1960), pp. 16 f. This is rejected in the typological criticism of M. D. Goulder, *Type and History in Acts* (London: S.P.C.K., 1964), pp. 142–144.

4. Ernst Käsemann, *Essays on New Testament Themes*, tr. by W. J. Montague (London: SCM Press, Ltd., 1964), pp. 85–94.

5. Leander E. Keck and J. Louis Martyn (eds.), *Studies in Luke-Acts* (Abingdon Press, 1966), especially the chapter by Ulrich Wilckens.

6. A. Q. Morton and G. H. C. MacGregor, *The Structure of Luke and Acts* (London: Hodder & Stoughton, Ltd., 1964), p. 106.

7. The five points were suggested by William Barclay, *The Promise of the Spirit*, pp. 46–49.

8. W. D. Davies, *Paul and Rabbinic Judaism* (London: S.P.C.K., 1948), p. 184.

9. *The Interpreter's Bible*, Vol. IX, pp. 69–72.

10. J. G. Davies, in *Journal of Theological Studies*, 1952, p. 228.

11. J. N. D. Kelly, *Early Christian Creeds* (London: Longmans, Green & Co., Inc., 1950), pp. 1 f.

12. *Encyclopedia Biblica* (Macmillan Co., 1903), Vol. IV, p. 4768.

13. Barclay, *The Promise of the Spirit*, p. 55.

14. *International Standard Bible Encyclopedia* (The Howard Severance Co., 1915), p. 2996.

15. Wilhelm Michaelis, as quoted in Maurice Barnett, *The Living Flame* (London: The Epworth Press, Publishers, 1953), pp. 85 ff.

16. Barnett, *op. cit.*, pp. 86 ff.

17. Goulder, *op. cit.*, pp. 184–187.

18. More sources on the various views discussed above may be found in J. R. Estes, "A Biblical Concept of Spiritual Gifts," thesis in Southern Baptist Theological Seminary (1957), pp. 30–75. Abundant evidence is produced in this study to discount the "foreign language" theory of Acts 2:6b-11. Languages they were, but this was due to the gift of interpretation. If foreign languages were ever spoken under inspiration, the New Testament does not record it. Ecstatic utterances were abundant in the Bible and in history, but the ability to speak a foreign language in ecstasy has not been demonstrated. For representative views and recent bibliography, see Watson Mills, ed., *Speaking in Tongues: Let's Talk About It* (Waco: Word Books, 1973).

19. In *The Beginnings of Christianity*, 5 vols., ed. by F. J.

Foakes-Jackson and Kirsopp Lake (London: Macmillan & Co., Ltd., 1920–1933), Vol. V, p. 118. Cf. Abraham Kuyper, *The Work of the Holy Spirit*, tr. by Henry De Vries (Funk and Wagnalls Co., 1900), pp. 134-136; Barnett, *op. cit.*, pp. 82-86. R. F. Zehnle, *Peter's Pentecost Discourse* (Nashville: Abingdon Press, 1971).

20. Lewis Sperry Chafer, *Systematic Theology* (Dallas Theological Seminary, 1948), Vol. VII, pp. 32–43.

21. *The Beginnings of Christianity*, Vol. I, p. 340.

22. Lampe, *op. cit.*, pp. 51 f.

23. Joachim Jeremias, *Infant Baptism in the First Four Centuries*, tr. by David Cairns (The Library of History and Doctrine; The Westminster Press, 1962), pp. 40 f.

24. G. R. Beasley-Murray, *Baptism in the New Testament* (London: Macmillan & Co., Ltd., 1962), pp. 342 f.

25. W. C. van Unnik, *The Christian's Freedom of Speech in the New Testament* (Manchester: The John Rylands Library, 1962), pp. 477–479.

26. The most controversial and complete study is Lampe's *The Seal of the Spirit*. J. D. C. Fisher, *Christian Initiation* (London: S.P.C.K., 1965), and G. W. Bromiley, *Baptism and the Anglican Reformers* (London: Lutterworth Press, 1953) supplement Lampe. James D. G. Dunn, *Baptism in the Holy Spirit* (London: SCM, 1970), pp. 55-72, argues that the delay in receiving the Holy Spirit was due to a defective faith, as in the case of Simon the Magician, but this is not obvious.

27. G. W. H. Lampe in *Peake's Commentary on the Bible*, ed. by Matthew Black and H. H. Rowley (London: Thomas Nelson & Sons, 1962), p. 897.

28. Hugo Mantel, *Studies in the History of the Sanhedrin* (Harvard University Press, 1961), pp. 190–198.

29. Frank Stagg, *The Book of Acts* (Broadman Press, 1955), pp. 90 f., 135–137.

30. Ernst Haenchen, *Die Apostlegeschichte* (Göttingen: Vanderhoeck & Ruprecht, 1961), p. 486. James D. G. Dunn, *op. cit.*, pp. 88 f.

31. Käsemann, *op. cit.*, p. 148.

32. *Ibid.*, pp. 144, 148.

33. *The Interpreter's Bible*, Vol. 9, p. 249.

34. Rudolf Bultmann, *History of the Synoptic Tradition*, tr. by John Marsh (Harper & Row, Publishers, Inc., 1963), p. 247, n. 1.

35. See my essay on "Charismatic and Official Ministries," *Interpretation*, Vol. XIX, No. 2 (April, 1964), pp. 168-181. The studies by J. H. E. Hull, *The Holy Spirit in the Acts of the Apostles* Cleveland: The World Publishing Company, 1968); F. D. Bruner,

213

A *Theology of the Holy Spirit* (Grand Rapids: Wm. B. Eerdmans Publishing Co., 1970); D. G. Dunn, *op. cit.*, and Michael Green, *I Believe in the Holy Spirit* (Grand Rapids: Wm. B. Eerdmans Publishing Co., 1975) do not require revisions of this chapter.

Chapter 4. THE SPIRIT OF LIFE
IN THE EARLY PAULINE WRITINGS (I)

1. Eduard Schweizer, *The Spirit of God*, tr. by A. E. Harvey (London: Adam & Charles Black, Ltd., 1960), pp. 54 ff.

2. Heinrich Greeven, *Geistesgaben bei Paulus* (Bielefeld: E. Gieseking, 1959).

3. See my book on *The Hope of Glory* (Wm. B. Eerdmans Publishing Company, 1964), pp. 180–184.

4. A Heidelberg dissertation by Philipp Vielhauer, "*Oiko-domē*" (1941), has explored the rich meaning of this word from the New Testament to Clement of Alexandria.

5. Werner Kramer, *Christ, Lord, Son of God*, tr. by Brian Hardy (London: SCM Press, Ltd., 1966), pp. 65–71; Reginald Fuller, *The Foundations of New Testament Christology* (Charles Scribner's Sons, 1965), pp. 204–214.

6. Agreeing in part with Heinrich Greeven against Wilhelm Michaelis in a lively debate in *Wort und Dienst*, 1959, pp. 111–120.

6a. *Interpretation*, XIII. 4 (Oct., 1959), pp. 402 f.

7. Literature on tongues and their modern resurgence is abundant. The following critiques are helpful as introductions to the wider literature: Nils Block-Hoell, *The Pentecostal Movement* (London: George Allen & Unwin, 1964); Anthony A. Hoekema, *What About Tongue-Speaking?* (Wm. B. Eerdmans Publishing Company, 1966); John Thomas Nichol, *Pentecostalism* (Harper & Row, Publishers, Inc., 1966). An exposition of I Cor., chs. 12 to 14, by Ekkehard Krajewski, *Geistesgaben* (Kassel: Oncken, 1963), is concerned with the Biblical basis of this modern movement.

8. George Duncan, *St. Paul's Ephesian Ministry* (London: Hodder & Stoughton, Ltd., 1929).

9. *The Interpreter's Dictionary of the Bible*, Vol. I, p. 105.

10. See my book on *The Hope of Glory*, p. 86.

11. The theology of II Cor., chs. 1 to 7, has been studied in great detail by Karl Prümm, *Diakonia Pneumatos* (Rome: Herder & Co., 1960). An investigation of II Cor. 3:16-18 and related ideas has been done by Ingo Hermann, *Kyrios und Pneuma* (Munich: Kösel Verlag, 1961). The translations are at variance with some commentaries on the meaning of "the spirit of faith" in 2 Cor.

214

4:13. G. R. Beasley-Murray says that this is "almost certainly" a reference to "the Holy Spirit, who enables man to step out in faith." I am not so sure. See *The Broadman Bible Commentary* (Nashville: Broadman Press, 1971), Vol. 11, p. 32. Cf. Jean Hering, *The Second Epistle of Saint Paul to the Corinthians*, tr. A. W. Heathcote and P. J. Allcock (London: Epworth Press, 1967), p. 33; C. K. Barrett, *The Second Epistle to the Corinthians* (New York: Harper & Row, 1973), p. 142; Fred Fisher, *Commentary on 1 & 2 Corinthians* (Waco: Word Books, 1975), p. 324. C. K. Barrett credits this to Rudolf Bultmann, but he misread Bultmann. Cf. Dunn, *op. cit.*, p. 94.

12. See again *The Hope of Glory*, pp. 88–94. Eduard Schweizer, *op. cit.*, p. 62, has rightly pointed out that "the idea of a spiritual body underneath the physical body" shucked off at death is a Gnostic notion, not Pauline.

Chapter 5. THE SPIRIT OF LIFE
IN THE EARLY PAULINE WRITINGS (II)

1. Ragnar Bring, *Commentary on Galatians*, tr. by Eric Wahlstrom (Muhlenberg Press, 1961), p. 107.

2. William Barclay, *The Letters to Galatians and Ephesians* (The Daily Study Bible; The Westminster Press, 1958), p. 26.

3. Joseph Fletcher, *Situation Ethics: The New Morality* (The Westminster Press, 1966).

4. W. D. Davies, *Paul and Rabbinic Judaism*, 2d ed. (London: S.P.C.K., 1955), pp. 21–27.

5. There is a little classic on the works of the flesh and the fruit of the Spirit by William Barclay, *Flesh and Spirit* (London: SCM Press, Ltd., 1962).

6. Fuller, *The Foundations of New Testament Christology*, pp. 165–167. Fuller challenges the claim that this is adoptionism, a view advocated from Johannes Weiss to Werner Kramer, *Christ, Lord, Son of God*, pp. 108–111. He became (*genomenou*) the Son of David, but he was designated (*horisthentos*) the eschatological Son of God.

7. Some of the historical ramifications of this have been traced by Bernard Ramm, *The Witness of the Spirit* (Wm. B. Eerdmans Publishing Company, 1960).

8. William Barclay, *The Letter to the Romans* (The Daily Study Bible; The Westminster Press, 1957), p. 176; Franz J. Leenhardt, *The Epistle to the Romans*, tr. by Harold Knight (London: Lutterworth Press, 1961), p. 315.

9. For details see my book on *The Hope of Glory*, pp. 143–192.

Chapter 6. THE SPIRIT OF UNITY
IN THE LATER PAULINE WRITINGS

1. Schweizer, *op. cit.*, pp. 97-99, assigns Ephesians and the Pastorals to this "school." Günther Bornkamm, *Paul*, tr. M. G. Stalker (New York: Harper & Row, 1971) represents how presuppositions can be piled up without sufficient justification until six of Paul's thirteen letters have been declared "inauthentic" (pp. 242 f.). After due consideration has been given to the role of the amanuenses in the composition of Paul's letters and to recent evidence in archaeology, I am inclined to agree with those who date all the prison letters of Paul during the Caesarean imprisonment, A.D. 55-57, and to defend the Pauline authorship of the Pastoral Letters of Titus, 1, 2 Timothy. It is not that the extreme views of Bornkamm, Lohse, etc. have not been examined, but that their assumptions now appear precarious.

2. J. Hugh Michael, *The Epistle of Paul to the Philippians* (Harper & Brothers, 1927), pp. xii–xxi.

3. Gustaf Wingren, *Man and the Incarnation*, tr. by Ross Mackenzie (Edinburgh: Oliver & Boyd, Ltd., 1959), has written a profound exposition of Irenaeus' theology.

4. My exposition of Ephesians as a whole may be seen in *Christ and the Church* (Wm. B. Eerdmans Publishing Company, 1963). Passages are discussed in more detail there.

5. Lampe, *op. cit.*

6. *The Interpreter's Bible*, Vol. 10, pp. 660 f.

7. Michael B. Foster, *Mystery and Philosophy* (London: SCM Press, Ltd., 1957), pp. 41 f.

8. The KJV changes corporate worship into individual worship with the incorrect translation " speaking to yourselves . . . in your heart."

9. Schweizer, *op. cit.*, p. 99.

10. John Calvin, *Commentaries on the Epistles to Timothy, Titus, and Philemon*, tr. by William Pringle (Wm. B. Eerdmans Publishing Company, 1948), p. 249.

11. *Annual*, Southern Baptist Convention, 1963, p. 270.

12. Max Thurian, *Consecration of the Layman,* tr. by W. J. Kerrigan (Helicon Press, Inc., 1963).

13. The standard work by Eduard Lohse, *Die Ordination im Spätjudentum und im Neuen Testament* (Göttingen: Vandenhoeck & Ruprecht, 1951), p. 101, comes to this conclusion.

14. Mantel, *op. cit.*, pp. 191–195.

15. Daube, *op. cit.*, pp. 224–246.

16. *The Apostolic Tradition of St. Hippolytus of Rome,* ed. by Gregory Dix (London: S.P.C.K., 1937), pp. 13 f.

17. Robert S. Paul, *Ministry* (Wm. B. Eerdmans Publishing Company, 1965), p. 132.

18. But see *The Interpreter's Bible*, Vol. 11, pp. 444 f.

19. J. Ysebaert, *Greek Baptismal Terminology* (Nijmegen: Dekker & Van De Vegt N.V., 1962), p. 62.

20. Lampe, *op. cit.*, pp. 59 f., 136 f.

21. Alec Gilmore, *Baptism and Christian Unity* (Judson Press, 1966).

22. George S. Hendry, *The Holy Spirit in Christian Theology*, Revised and Enlarged Edition (The Westminster Press, 1965), pp. 132–135.

Chapter 7. THE SPIRIT OF TRUTH
IN THE JOHANNINE GOSPEL AND FIRST LETTER

1. Eusebius, *Historia Ecclesiastica* VI. xiv. 7.

2. T. Barrosse, "The Seven Days of the New Creation in St. John's Gospel," *Catholic Biblical Quarterly*, Vol. 21 (1959), pp. 507–516.

3. C. K. Barrett, *The Gospel According to St. John* (London: S.P.C.K., 1955), p. 148.

4. Raymond E. Brown, *The Gospel According to John I–XII* (Doubleday & Company, Inc., 1966), pp. XLIV–XLVII.

5. E. C. Hoskyns, *The Fourth Gospel* (London: Faber & Faber, Ltd., 1947), p. 177.

6. *Ibid.*, p. 196.

7. E. C. Colwell and Eric L. Titus, *The Gospel of the Spirit* (Harper & Brothers, 1953), p. 111. See also Eric L. Titus, *The Message of the Fourth Gospel* (Abingdon Press, 1957), pp. 51–62.

8. Brown, *op. cit.*, p. 142.

9. *Ibid.*

10. Dwight Moody Smith, *The Composition and Order of the Fourth Gospel* (Yale University Press, 1964), pp. 182, 216, 232.

11. See my article in *Journal of Biblical Literature*, Vol. 72 (1953), pp. 213–219.

12. B. F. Westcott, *The Gospel According to St. John* (Wm. B. Eerdmans Publishing Company, 1951), p. 38.

13. Brown, *op. cit.*, pp. 161 f. George Johnston, *The Spirit Paraclete in the Gospel of John* (Cambridge University Press, 1970), p. 40.

14. Alf Corell, *Consummatum Est: Eschatology and Church in The Gospel of St. John* (The Macmillan Company, 1958), p. 161.

15. Schweizer, *op. cit.*, p. 93.

16. Cf. Peder Borgen, *Bread from Heaven* (Leiden: E. J. Brill, 1965), pp. 182 f.

17. Brown, *op. cit.*, pp. 278–280.

18. *Ibid.*, p. 320.

19. *Ibid.*

20. Hans Windisch, " Die fünf johanneischen Parakletsprüche," in *Festgabe für Adolf Jülicher zum 70. Geburtstag* (Tübingen: Verlag von J. C. B. Mohr, 1927), pp. 110-137. Windisch is now in English translation by James W. Cox (Philadelphia: The Fortress Press, 1968). Otto Betz, *Der Paraklet* (Leiden/Köln: E. J. Brill, 1963), pp. 147-149, attempts to establish a connection between "the Spirit of Truth" in Qumran and the Paraclete in John's Gospel.

21. C. K. Barrett, "The Holy Spirit in the Fourth Gospel," *Journal of Theological Studies*, N. S., Vol. I, Part I (April, 1950), pp. 7–15.

22. Brown, *op. cit.*, pp. 510–512.

23. J. R. Graves, *Seven Dispensations* (Baptist Sunday School Committee, 1928), pp. 61 f.

24. Jean Daniélou, *Origen,* tr. by Walter Mitchell (Sheed & Ward, Inc., 1955), p. 257.

25. C. H. Dodd, *The Johannine Epistles* (Harper & Brothers, 1946), pp. 58–63.

26. Albert Schweitzer, *The Mysticism of Paul the Apostle,* tr. by William Montgomery (Henry Holt and Company, 1931), p. 5.

27. Alfred Tennyson, " The Higher Pantheism."

28. Martin R. De Haan, *The Chemistry of the Blood, and Other Stirring Messages* (Zondervan Publishing House, 1943), pp. 9, 35.

29. Colwell and Titus, *op. cit.*, pp. 107–141.

Chapter 8. THE SPIRIT OF CHRIST
IN OTHER NEW TESTAMENT WRITINGS

1. Cf. William Manson, *The Epistle to the Hebrews* (London: Hodder & Stoughton, Ltd., 1951), pp. 159–184.

2. B. F. Westcott, *The Epistle to the Hebrews*, 2d ed. (Wm. B. Eerdmans Publishing Company, 1892), pp. 474–476.

3. Westcott, *op. cit.*, pp. XLII f.

4. Herschel H. Hobbs, *Studies in Hebrews* (Sunday School Board, Southern Baptist Convention, 1954), p. 19; R. E. Glaze, Jr., *No Easy Salvation* (Broadman Press, 1966), p. 29.

5. A. T. Robertson, *Word Pictures in the New Testament* (Broadman Press, 1933), Vol. V, p. 375. Although H. H. Hobbs now agrees that my views are supported by most translators and commentators, including A. T. Robertson and W. H. Davis, his *How to Follow Jesus* (Nashville: Broadman Press, 1971) elaborates

the improbable theory that falling away in Hebrews means no more than a loss of opportunity in God's world mission with no reference to salvation (p. 16-18, 36-39, 58-62, 106, 128).

For a more reliable discussion on both the biblical and historical problems involved, see I. Howard Marshall, *Kept By the Power of God* (Minneapolis: Bethany Fellowship, 1974). The fact that Marshall's study was accepted as a thesis in the University of Aberdeen, 1963, and that he is now lecturer in New Testament in that once citadel of Calvinism indicates how biblical exegesis is now triumphing over traditions that go back to Augustine. However, Scripture twisting will no doubt continue among those who believe that Calvinistic confessions must be defended at all cost.

6. Clarence S. Roddy, *The Epistle to the Hebrews* (Baker Book House, 1962), pp. 66, 68.

7. Hobbs, *op. cit.*, pp. 53, 55.

8. Glaze, *op. cit.*, p. 22. Cf. pp. 38–46, 52 f.

9. A good guide is the recent work by F. F. Bruce, *The Epistle to the Hebrews* (Wm. B. Eerdmans Publishing Company, 1964).

10. Robertson, *op. cit.*, Vol. V, p. 413.

11. A splendid survey is found in Bruce, *op. cit.*, pp. 258–262.

12. *The Interpreter's Bible*, Vol. 11, p. 692.

13. Arthur W. Wainwright, *The Trinity in the New Testament* (London: S.P.C.K., 1962), p. 244.

14. See my book on *Christ and the Church*, pp. 16–28.

15. Fuller, *op. cit.*, pp. 218 f.

16. Cf. Schweizer, *op. cit.*, p. 101.

17. Bo Reicke, *The Epistles of James, Peter, and Jude* (Doubleday & Company, Inc., 1964), p. 72.

18. E. G. Selwyn, *The First Epistle of St. Peter* (London: Macmillan & Co., Ltd., 1949), p. 223.

19. See my article on " *Shekinah* " in *The Interpreter's Dictionary of the Bible.*

20. See my book on *The Hope of Glory*, pp. 61 f.

21. *Ibid.*, p. 61.

22. Bo Reicke, *op. cit.*, pp. XIV–XXIX.

23. T. F. Glasson, *The Revelation of John* (Cambridge: Cambridge University Press, 1965), p. 13.

24. Schweizer, *op. cit.*, p. 104, n. 1.

25. Martin Rist in *The Interpreter's Bible*, Vol. 12, p. 369.

26. Schweizer, *op. cit.*, p. 106.

27. Rist, *loc. cit.*, p. 347.

28. John F. Walvoord, *The Revelation of Jesus Christ* (Moody Press, 1966), p. 42.

29. *The Interpreter's Bible*, Vol. 12, pp. 373 f.
30. George E. Ladd, *The Blessed Hope* (Wm. B. Eerdmans Publishing Company, 1956). Cf. my book on *The Hope of Glory*, p. 181. See also Dave MacPherson, *The Late Great Pre-Trib Rapture* (Kansas City: Heart of America Bible Society, 1974).
31. Walvoord, *op. cit.*, p. 103.
32. *Ibid.*
33. *The Interpreter's Dictionary of the Bible*, Vol. IV, pp. 71-74.
34. Schweizer, *op. cit.*, p. 104. J. M. Ford, *Revelation, The Anchor Bible*, Vol. 38 (Garden City, N.Y.: Doubleday and Co., 1975) pp. 19 f. fails to see the importance of the Spirit in Revelation.
35. Rufus M. Jones, *The Flowering of Mysticism* (The Macmillan Company, 1939), pp. 53-55.
36. Some useful studies have been done on the importance of the biblical teachings on the Holy Spirit in the history of Christianity. A brief description is offered for the following:

R. A. Knox, *Enthusiasm*. Oxford University Press, 1950. A Roman Catholic review through the eighteenth century that was begun in scorn but completed in appreciation.

Regin Prenter, *Spiritus Creator*, tr. John M. Jensen. Philadelphia: Muhlenberg Press, 1953. A Lutheran study of Luther's views both before and after his encounter with charismatic Anabaptists.

Lindsay Dewar, *The Holy Spirit and Modern Thought*. New York: Harper & Row, 1959. An Anglican study through George Fox and the Quakers that applies psychological theory in a constructive way.

Lycurgus M. Starkey, Jr., *The Work of the Holy Spirit*. (Nashville: Abingdon Press, 1962); *The Holy Spirit at Work in the Church* (Nashville: Abingdon Press, 1964). The historical meaning and practical value of Wesleyan revivalism.

Nils Bloch-Hoell, *The Pentecostal Movement: Its Origin, Development and Distinctive Character*. London: Allen and Unwin, 1964. A definitive history done with insight, sympathy, and balance.

John Thomas Nichol, *Pentecostalism*. New York: Harper and Row, 1966. A readable survey of twentieth-century Pentecostalism by one with spiritual roots in the movement.

Frederick Dale Bruner, *A Theology of the Holy Spirit*. Grand Rapids: Wm. B. Eerdmans Publishing Co., 1970. Scholarly and detailed in both topics and bibliography, but the author's confessional Calvinism lacks appreciation for the charismatic.

Walter J. Hallenweger, *The Pentecostals*. Minneapolis: Augsburg, 1972. A history that goes beyond Bloch-Hoell.

John P. Kildahl, *The Psychology of Speaking in Tongues*. New

York: Harper and Row, 1972. A careful study that confuses description and explanation.

Michael P. Hamilton, ed., *The Charismatic Movement*. Grand Rapids: Wm. B. Eerdmans Publishing Co., 1975. Essays representing current reactions edited by the Canon of Washington Cathedral.

No effort has been made to add a systematic statement, but the following are helpful:

Hendrikus Berkhof, *The Doctrine of the Holy Spirit*. Richmond, Va.: John Knox Press, 1964.

George S. Hendry, *The Holy Spirit in Modern Theology*. Revised and Enlarged Edition. Philadelphia: The Westminster Press, 1965.

Michael Green, *I Believe in the Holy Spirit*. Grand Rapids: Wm. B. Eerdmans Publishing Co., 1975. Practical and useful where the charismatic movement is divisive despite some mistakes in composition.

221

INDEX

OF SCRIPTURE REFERENCES

OLD TESTAMENT
Genesis
1:1 34
1:2 .... 28, 34, 151
1:2 f. 160
2:7 ... 11, 159, 174, 183
2:19 12
6:1–4 13
6:3 14
6:3, 17 159
7:15, 22 159
7:22 12
8:8–12 36
11:1–9 63
11:7 61
16:11 47
17:19 47
24:43 47
26:35 14
34:3 47
34:12 48
38:24 47
41:8 14
41:38 29
45:27 14
48:14–17 142

Exodus
2:2 47
2:8 47
4:15 42
8:19 ...... 43, 56
10:13, 19 13
13:21 f. 195

14:21 13
16:2, 7, 8 159
17:6 163
19 63
19:1–25 61
20:5 184
20:18–21 61
22:16 f. 48
24:18 37
31:1–11 67
31:3 29
34:14 184
34:15 f. 184
34:28 37
34:29–35 103
34:29 ff. 69
34:34 105
35:30 ff. 67
35:31 29
40:34–38 195

Leviticus
16 186
19:18 112
23:9–21 61
25:10 26

Numbers
11:16–30 142
11:25 .... 61, 68
11:25 f. 195
11:29 32
11:29 f. 31
15:30 190
20 186

24:2 .... 26, 29
24:3 f. 29
27:18 ...... 68, 143
27:18, 23 142
27:20 68
27:23 ...... 68, 142

Deuteronomy
9:9 37
10:10 37
20:7 48
21:17 18
22:23–24 48
22:25–27 48
31:16 184
32:16, 21 184
34:9 ..... 132, 142, 143

Joshua
4:14 ff. 36

Judges
3:10 .... 15, 53
6:34 .... 15, 61
9:23 16
13:3, 5, 7 47
13:6 19
13:25 15
14:6, 19 15
15:14 15

Ruth
4:5, 10 48

223

I Samuel
1:20 47
9:6–10 19
10 18
10:6, 9 16
10:9 21
10:26 16
16:14 17
16:14–23 .... 17, 26
18:10 f. 17
18:25 48
19:18–24 16

II Samuel
6:16–23 16
11:5 47
22:16 12
23:1–7 ...... 23, 26

I Kings
8:2 161
13 19
18:12 .... 18, 72
19:8 37
19:11 f. 13
19:16 26
22 .... 18, 197
22:14 197
22:19–23 17

II Kings
2:6–18 34
2:9 18
2:12 18
2:16 .... 18, 72
3:15 19
4 to 6 19
9:11 20
10:10 53

I Chronicles
12:18 .... 15, 29
16:36 99

II Chronicles
15:1 29
20:14 29
24:20 .... 15, 29

Nehemiah
8:6 99
9:20, 26, 30 30
9:26 30
9:30 30

Job
1:8 86
2:3 86
33:4 183
34:14 ...... 14, 159
41:1 27

Psalms
2:7 36
18:15 12
33:6 28
34:8 189
42:1 f. 162
51:10 f., 17 30
51:11 31
68:25 47
69:25 60
73:27 184
74:9 33
74:14 27
78:15 f., 24 162
82:1 195
89 115
91:11–14 43
95 186
95:7–11 ... 185, 186
95:7b–11 30
104:26 27
104:29 f. 159
104:30 28
105:40 f. 162
106:33 14
106:48 99
109:8 60
110 186
110:4 186
113 to 118 162
139:7 f. 31

Proverbs
1 to 9 93
20:27 29
30:19 47

Ecclesiastes
12:7 183

The Song of Solomon
1:3 47
6:8 47

Isaiah
4:4 23
5:7 47
7:14 .... 24, 47
7:14–24 47
8:3, 18 47
8:18 47
9:2–7 24
11 24
11:2 ... 24, 53, 132,
          195, 201
11:4 138
11:6–8 37
11:6–11 38
12:2 47
12:3 161
20:6 47
21:1 203
21:9 47
23:16 204
27:1 27
28:7 20
28:11 f. 99
30:33 12
31:3 158
32:15 23
37:36 47
40:1 53
40:3 34
40:9 f. 47
42:1 .... 25, 36, 152
42:1–4 25
44:3 23
47:14 47
48:10 47
48:16 23
49:1–6 25
49:13 53
49:25 39
50:4–11 25
51:9–11 38
51:22 47

52:13 to 53:12 . 25
53 .... 32, 194
54:5 184
55:1 206
58:6 53
59:9 47
59:21 23
61:1 53
61:1–3 26
42:4 f. 156
62:11 47
63 to 66 38
63:10 ... 30, 70, 137
63:11–14 30
65:6 47
65:15 37
66:14 f. 43

Jeremiah
2:2 156
3:14 183
3:20 184
5:13 20
7:34 156
16:9 156
23:18–22 197
23:21 21
25:10 156
31:33 21
51:13 204

Ezekiel
1:1 202
1:4 21
1:12, 20 f. 21
2:2 .... 21, 202, 203
3:12 21
3:12, 14 202
3:14 f. 203
3:16, 23 202
8:1 202
8:3 203
8:3 f. 21
11:1, 24 21
11:5 21
11:19 21
11:21 21
11:24 203
16:8 156

18:31 22
23:6 156
36:26–28 22
37:1–14 22
37:5 159
37:9–14 61
40:1 202
43:5 21
47:1 161

Daniel
4:8, 9, 18 29
5:11, 14 29
5:12 29
6:3 29

Hosea
2:19 f. 183
2:20 156
9:1 184
9:7 20

Joel
2:28 f. 32
2:28–32 64

Amos
1:1 20
3:7 201
3:7 f. 20
7:12–14 19

Jonah
1:4 14
4:8 14

Micah
2:7 20
2:11 20
3:8 20

Haggai
2:5 31

Zechariah
4:6 31
6:8 31
8:2 184
9 to 14 162

12:10 32
13:4 f. 33

Malachi
3:1 .... 34, 151
3:1 f. 43
4:5 f. 51

NEW TESTAMENT
Matthew
1:18, 20 ..... 45, 48
1:18, 25 48
1:19 48
1:19 f. 48
1:20 48
1:23 ..... 46, 47, 49
2:6, 15, 18, 23 . 47
3:11 .... 35, 42
4:1 .... 43, 54
4:1–11 37
4:10 43
4:11 43
7:15 95
10:20 42
11:20 95
11:29 115
12:18–21 25
12:28 ...... 43, 56
12:32 43
16:19 175
17:9 196
18:18 175
18:20 49
22:43 43
24:11, 24 95
25:1–13 48
27:66 133
28:16–20 44
28:20 49

Mark
1:1–13 34
1:3, 4, 12 37
1:4, 8 34
1:5 34
1:8 35
1:9–11 36
1:10 36
1:12 54

1:12 f. 37
1:13 37
1:22 39
1:23 f. 40
1:34 40
1:39, 43 40
2:19 f. 156
3:11 40
3:14 f. 40
3:15 39
3:15, 22 40
3:20–30 .... 34, 38
3:27 .... 39, 41
3:28–30 39
3:30 40
5:2, 7 f., 13 40
5:30 39
5:34 94
6:5 142
6:7 40
6:13 40
6:14 39
7:26 40
9:13 51
9:18, 28 40
9:23 95
9:38–41 40
10:16 142
10:20 41
10:52 94
11:22 95
11:27 39
11:28 f., 33 39
12:11 f. 41
12:36 41
13:11 41
13:22 95
14:56–58 69
16:9–20 44

Luke
1:1–4 50
1:14 f. 51
1:14–17 50
1:16 f. 51
1:32 51
1:35 .... 49, 62
1:41 52
1:41–44 50

1:42–55 52
1:67 52
1:76 50
1:80 50
1; 2 .... 73, 211n 22
2:22–38 53
2:26 53
2:27 53
2:29–35 53
2:36–38 53
2:40 52
2:40, 52 50
2:52 52
3:1 to 4:30 50
3:15 78
3:16 .... 35, 42
3:21 .... 53, 70
4:1 .... 27, 54
4:1–13 37
4:13 54
4:18 f. 26
5:16 53
5:17 95
6:12 53
8:46 18
9:18, 28 53
9:29 69
9:43 196
9:51 79
9:51 to ....
    18:14 ..... 50, 54
10:7 146
10:17–22 54
10:18 54
10:19 f. 54
10:21 f. 55
10; 11 50
11:2 56
11:9–13 54
11:14–23 54
11:20 ...... 43, 56
16:22 203
17:6 95
20:41 43
21:15 .... 42, 69
22:3 54
22:40, 46 54
22:44 53
22:66 146

23:34 70
23:46 70
24:47 58
24:49 ... 15, 57, 58,
        59, 61

John
1:1 150
1:3–5 150
1:5 158
1:6–8, 15–17,
    19–42 78
1:10 f., 14, 18 .. 150
1:12 ...... 122, 155
1:13 155
1:14 ...... 160, 195
1:17 159
1:19, 29, 35,
    43 171
1:21 50
1:25, 31, 33 151
1:26, 31, 33 151
1:29, 35, 43 ... 151
1:32 157
1:32 f. 151, 163
1:32–34 ... 151, 170
1:33 157
2:1 .... 151, 171
2:1–11 48
2:8 156
2:19 ff. 69
2:21 ...... 152, 168
2:22 168
3:1–8 153
3:3 ... 153, 154, 155
3:3, 5 153
3:3–8 163
3:5 .... 154, 155
3:6 .... 154, 160
3:6–8 155
3:8 .... 13, 154
3:11 170
3:19 f. 172
3:22 151
3:22–30 ... 155, 156
3:22–36 78
3:31 153
3:31–36 156
3:33 f. 155

3:34 ..... 157, 160, 163
4:1–3 78
4:2 151
4:8 158
4:10 163
4:11 156
4:14 ...... 157, 162
4:21 f. 158
4:23 f. ... 131, 157, 163
4:24 158
4:39 170
4:50 160
5 171
5:21–29 160
5:28 167
5:30–35 171
5:35 f. 78
5:36 171
5:37 f. 171
5:39–44 171
5:43 167
5:45 f. 171
6:25–51 159
6:27, 32 f. 161
6:33, 38, 41, 42, 50, 51, 58 ... 159
6:37 161
6:39 f., 44, 54 167
6:50 161
6:52 159
6:52–58 160
6:52–59 159
6:57, 68 161
6:62 159
6:63 ..... 157, 161, 163
6:68 160
6:70 170
7:37 ...... 15, 163
7:37–39 .. 157, 163, 174
7:38 162
7:39 ...... 35, 163, 172
7 to 9 163
8:44 173

10:18 166
11:4 174
12:23 174
12:28 174
12:31 173
13:27 170
13:31 174
13:31–38 166
13:33 167
13:36 172
13; 14 166
14:3, 22 f. 167
14:3, 23 167
14:5 172
14:6 166
14:15–17 .... 164 f.
14:16 ..... 167, 168
14:18–24 167
14:19 167
14:21 f. 167
14:23 167
14:25 f. 166
14:26 ..... 167, 168
14:28 167
14:30 173
15:3 155
15:22 173
15:26 169
15:26 f. 168
15:27 170
16:4b–11 171
16:5 172
16:7 168
16:12–15 173
16:13 175
17 170
17:1–5 170
17:6–19 170
17:12 170
18:33 172
18:36 153
18:47 172
19:1, 9 172
19:11, 23 153
19:34 179
19:37 32
20:17 174
20:19 174
20:19, 21 174

20:22 ..... 13, 164, 166, 174
20:22 f. 175
20:26–29 174
21 174

Acts
1:1–5 60
1:1 to 6:7 59
1:2 59
1:4 60
1:6–11 60
1:8 ..... 58, 59, 61, 62, 66
1:12–14 60
1:14 .... 54, 60
1:15–26 170
1:17 60
1:20 60
1 to 12 ...... 58, 59
2 61
2:1 60
2:4 62
2:6 61
2:6b–11 .... 62, 63, 212n18
2:13 138
2:14–21 64
2:16 32
2:17, 33 147
2:17, 39 65
2:22–36 64
2:32 67
2:33 64
2:36 173
2:37–42 64
2:38 .... 44, 79
2:39 65
2:42 .... 54, 66
2:43–47 .... 65, 66
2:44 66
2:46 72
3:1 to 4:31 65
3:14 173
3:15 67
3:20 116
4:8 65
4:13 65
4:18 67

227

4:29 65
4:31 ..... 54, 61, 65
4:32–35 ..... 65, 66
4:36 to 5:11 ... 65
4:37 66
5:1–11 66
5:3 66
5:9 66
5:11 75
5:12 71
5:12–15 ..... 65, 66
5:17 67
5:17–32 ..... 65, 67
5:30–32 173
5:32 ...... 67, 170
5:42 65
6:1–6 .... 67, 68, 81
6:3 68
6:3, 5 74
6:3, 10 132
6:4, 6 54
6:5 ..... 68, 69, 138
6:6 ..... 68, 71, 75,
                143
6:7 .... 58, 65
6:8 69
6:8 to 8:3 69
6:8 to 9:31 69
6:8 to 12:24 ... 59
6:10 .... 42, 69
6:15 69
7:51 70
7:55 70
7:56 70
7:59 70
8:1, 3 75
8:4–25 ...... 69, 70
8:4–40 70
8:8 70
8:14 ff. 79
8:14–17 71
8:15 f. 64, 175
8:15, 17 54
8:16 .... 44, 72, 73
8:17 142
8:18 72
8:26 72
8:29 f. 72
8:39 .... 18, 72

9:11–40 54
9:17 ..... 71, 72, 74
9:17–19 .... 79, 142
9:18 72
9:19 72
9:20–22 73
9:31 .... 58, 75
9:32 to 12:24 .. 73
10:3 73
10:3, 10 f., 17,
    19 202
10:3, 17, 19 73
10:4 54
10:19 73
10:38 ..... 37, 73,
            103, 152
10:42 116
10:44 72
10:44–48 ... 64, 72,
            73, 79
10:46 .... 62, 63, 73
10:46, 47 73
10:48 44
11:5 202
11:13 73
11:15 ...... 72, 73
11:21 75
11:22, 26 75
11:24 ... 66, 74, 138
11:27 ...... 74, 95
11:27 f. 80
11:28 74
11:30 ......85, 146
12:1, 5 75
12:5 54
12:24 58
12:25 to 16:5 .. 74
13:1 ... 74, 75, 80,
                95
13:1 f. 74
13:1–3 147
13:2 .... 74, 164
13:3 ..... 54, 68, 69
13:6 95
13:9 76
13:31 170
13:52 ...... 72, 76
13; 14 107
13 to 28 .. 58, 59, 74

14:3 71
14:14 ..... 75, 143
14:23 ...... 54, 85,
            143, 146
14:23, 27 75
15:2, 4, 6,
    22 f. 146
15:3, 4, 22, 41 . 75
15:8 f. 76
15:14 166
15:28 76
15:32 ...... 80, 95
16:1, 14 f. 100
16:4 146
16:5 .... 58, 75
16:6 f. 76
16:6 f. 164
16:6 to 19:20 .. 76
16:7 ...... 76, 195
16:9 76
16:34 72
17:1 85
17:4, 12, 34 100
17:6 84
17:31 116
18:5 93
18:8 65
18:22 75
18:24 f. 77
18:24 to 19:7 .. 76
18:25 ...... 77, 124
18:26 77
18:28 78
19:1 78
19:1–6 ..... 64, 79
19:2 78
19:3 78
19:5 .... 44, 78
19:6 .... 62, 63, 71,
            78, 142
19:11 71
19:12 18
19:20 58
19:21 79
19:21 to 28:31 . 79
20:17 ... 75, 80, 146
20:17–35 79
20:22 f. 80
20:22–24 79

20:28 ...... 75, 80
20:30 80
21:8 f. 53
21:9 .... 74, 80, 95
21:10 ...... 74, 95
21:11 79
21:12 79
21:13 79
21:18 146
22:5 146
22:16 44
22:17 202
23:11 ...... 53, 76
26:32 53
27:15, 17 197
28:8 71
28:30 f. 58

Romans
1:3 116
1:9 131
1:11 92
1:18–32 119
1:28 123
2:28 f. 118, 131
2:29 ...... 116, 117
3:31 118
5:1–5 117
5:2 f. 122
5:5 ... 114, 126, 131
5:12–21 118
5:15 92
6:4 .... 121, 148
6:14 118
6:23 ...... 92, 118
7:6 ... 116, 117, 118
7:7–13 118
7:7–25 118
7:14–25 118
7:22 135
7:24 118
8:1–27 .... 118, 184
8:2 105
8:4 118
8:5–8 118
8:6 119
8:9 120
8:9–11 119
8:10 120

8:11 120
8:12 f. 120
8:13 121
8:14 f. 121
8:15 f. 110
8:15–17 122
8:17 122
8:18–21 122
8:18–25 122
8:22–25 122
8:24 118
8:26 f. 123, 131, 164
8:31–34 199
9:22 114
10:9a 92
11:12, 25 125
11:29 92
11:33 ...... 90, 94
12:1 f. 126
12:2 ...... 119, 123
12:3 94
12:6 92
12:6–8 97
12:8 ..... 85, 95, 97
12:11 .... 77, 123, 124
12:12 124
13:8–10 110
13:11 117
14:2 124
14:5 f. 125
14:13 125
14:15 125
14:17 .... 113, 123, 124
14:17 f. ... 125, 192
14:19 ...... 87, 125
14:20 125
14:20 f. 125
14:21 125
15:2 87
15:4 140
15:13 ..... 114, 125
15:13, 18 f. 123
15:16 ..... 124, 126
15:16, 30 192
15:18 f. 95, 126
15:19 109

15:25–27 107
15:30 .... 124, 126, 131
15:30–32 129
16:1 f., 3, 6, 12 f., 15 100
16:5 75

I Corinthians
1:5 94
1:7 92
1:9 106
1:9, 18 115
1:13–17 148
1:16 65
1:18 to 2:16 ... 93
2:4 f. 89
2:6–9 90
2:8 195
2:10–13 90
2:11 90
2:12, 16 93
2:13 90
2:14 .... 90, 91
2:15 91
3:1 91
3:5–9 88
3:5–17 121
3:9 87
3:10–15 88
3:16 119
3:16 f. 88
4:20 90
5:5 88
5:7 185
5:9 106
6:11 88
6:19 119
6:19 f. 89
7 115
7:7 92
7:17 75
7:40 .... 92, 140
8:1 ...... 87, 89, 94
8:7 94
8:7–13 94
9:24–27 115
10:1–11 185
10:1–13 163

229

10:2–4 96
10:4 163
10:10 159
10:13 115
10:16 f. 106
10:23 87
11:4 95
11:5 100
11:7–12 95
11:16 75
11:20 202
11:29 f. 88
12:1 92
12:1–11 92
12:3 93
12:4–6 .... 104, 192
12:4, 9, 28,
   30 f. 92
12:7 93
12:8–10 96
12:12 97
12:12 f. 96
12:12–31 96
12:14–26 97
12:18 97
12:24 f. 97
12:27 97
12:27–31 97
12:28 97
12:28, 30 .... 95, 97
12:31 .... 101, 131
13:1–13 131
13:2 94
13:8–13 89
14 ... 62, 63, 74, 98,
       101, 139
14:1–12 98
14:1–19 98
14:2 98
14:2, 14, 18 119
14:3 95
14:3, 4, 5, 12,
   17 87
14:4 f. 98
14:5 101
14:6 .... 94, 99
14:9 98
14:10–12 98
14:13–15 98

14:13–19 98
14:16 102
14:16 f. 98
14:18 ... 86, 99, 101
14:20–22 99
14:20–25 99
14:21 20
14:21 f. 99
14:22 99
14:23 100
14:23–25 99
14:26 ..... 87, 100,
             101
14:26–32 86
14:26–40 100
14:27 f. 100
14:28 100
14:30 100
14:33 100
14:33 f. 75
14:34 100
14:39 ..... 86, 101
14:40 ..... 80, 98
15:20, 23 61
15:22 118
15:26 101
15:30–32 101
15:45 ..... 104, 159
15:45–49 105
15:51–57 106
15:53 120
16:1, 19 75
16:8 103
16:15 85
16:16, 18 85
16:19 75

II Corinthians
1:8 f. 101
1:11 129
1:18–22 102
1:21 f. 192
1:22 ...... 105, 133
1 to 5 104
1 to 9 102
2:1–11 102
2:14 94
3 103
3:1–3 104

3:3 192
3:4–11 104
3:6 ..... 104, 116,
       117, 118, 160
3:12–18 104
3:16 105
3:17 ...... 76, 110
3:17 f. 105, 195
3:18 104
4:4–6 189
4:6 94
4:16 135
5:1 105
5:1–5 105
5:4 106
5:5 103
5:8 105
6:6 94
6:14 106
6:14 to 7:1 ... 88,
             106
8:1, 18 f., 23 f. . 75
8:7 94
8:9 193
10:5 94
10:8 87
10 to 13 ... 102, 107
11:6 94
11:8, 28 75
12:1–4 14
12:1–10 202
12:2 f. 203
12:13 75
12:19 87
13:10 87
13:14 ..... 93, 104,
       106, 130, 192, 193,
             200

Galatians
1:2, 22 75
1:6 165
1:6 f. 108
3:1–5 108
3:3 95
3:6–29 110
3:11–14 192
3:14 110
3:27 ..... 120, 148

4:1-7 110
4:1-11 110
4:4 f. 110
4:4-6 152
4:6 ... 110, 192, 195
4:7 110
4:8 111
4:21-31 111
4:29 111
4; 5 121
5:1 111
5:4 ...... 111, 189
5:5 111
5:7 111
5:13 112
5:14 112
5:16, 25 112
5:16-25 184
5:16-26 117
5:17 112
5:19-21 112
5:19-24 120
5:21 113
5:22 131
5:22 f. 113
6.1 115
6:2 118
6:7 f. 118
6:8 115
6:15 f 112

Ephesians
1:3-14 .... 133, 193
1:9, 17 94
1:10 131
1:13 ...... 103, 133
1:14 ..... 103, 133,
                 137
1:17 ...... 132, 185
1:18 135
2:2 ...... 121, 132
2:4-10 114
2:7 114
2:18 ...... 114, 134
2:20 95
2:20 f. 134
2:22 119,
           133, 134

3:4 134
3:4-16 135
3:5 .... 95, 134
3:5, 16 133
3:6 135
3:8 135
3:10 ..... 94, 135
3:16 135
3:20 f. 136
4:2 f. 136
4:3 f. 136
4:3 f., 30 133
4:4 96
4:4-6 136
4:5 138
4:11 97
4:12, 16, 29 87
4:13 136
4:14 136
4:17-31 121
4:17 to 5:14 ... 148
4:18 119
4:23 ..... 121, 132
4:30 ..... 30, 103,
           137, 164
5:16 124
5:18 ..... 133, 137
5:18-20 137
6:11-13 132
6:17 138
6:17, 18 133
6:18 139

Philippians
1:1 85
1:9 114
1:19 195
1:19, 27 129
1:27 130
2:1 ...... 129, 130
2:11 92
3:2 130
3:3 ...... 129, 130
3:8 94
3:20 130
4.2 100
4:4-20 114
4:7 114

Colossians
1:4 131
1:8 131
1:9, 28 94
2:3 94
2:3, 23 94
2:11-15 148
3:1-17 148
3:15 114
4:5 94

I Thessalonians
4:15 75
1:3 84
1:5 83
1:6 .... 84, 113
1:6 f. 83
1:9 f. 84
3:13 85
4:3 .... 84, 85
4:3-8 84
4:6a 84
4:6b 84
4:7 84
4:8 84
4:13 to 5:11 ... 87
4:14-17 203
5:11 87
5:12, 14 86
5:12-20 98
5:12-22 80
5:19 f. 86
5:23 85
5:23 f. 115
5:25 129

II Thessalonians
1:4 75
2:1 f. 87
2:1-12 87
2:2 87
2:9 f. 140
2:13 85
2:13 f. 192
3:1, 2 129

I Timothy
1:17 145
1:18 ...... 140, 146

1:19 f. 145
2:1–15 145
2:5 f. 145
2:11–15 100
2:12 100
3:1 145
3:4 f., 15 85
3:8 145
3:8–13 68
3:15 146
3:16 145
4:1 140
4:1–3 140
4:3, 7 146
4:14 .. 69, 92, 140,
          143, 146
5:12 145
5:17 85
5:17, 19 146
5:17–22 ... 145, 146
5:18 146
5:22 ...... 69, 146
6:15b f. 145
6:20 ... 94, 144, 146

II Timothy
1:6 .... 92, 143, 146
1:6 f. 144
1:7, 14 143
1:9 f. 144, 145
1:9 f., 18 145
1:12–14 144
2:1–6 69
2:11–13 145
2:16–18 145
3:15 141
3:16 197
3:16 f. 142
4:1–8 145

Titus
1:5 .... 85, 146
2:11–14 145
3:4–7 .... 103, 114,
             145
3:5 ... 147, 148, 149
3:6 f. 147

Philemon
2 75
22 129

Hebrews
1:14 187
2:1 188
2:1–4 187
2:3 188
2:3, 10 187
2:4 .... 95, 188
2:9 189
3:1 188
3:1 to 4:13 30
3:6, 14 186
3:7 185
3:7 to 4:13 ... 185,
              187
3:8–12 189
3:12 ..... 140, 185,
     187, 189, 190
3:12–14 186
3:14 188
4:15 37
5:12 189
5:14 189
6:1–20 187
6:2 142
6:4 188
6:4–6 188
6:5 189
6:9 187
7 186
8 186
8:6 f., 13 187
9:8 186
9:8 f. 186
9:12 191
9:14 191
9:15 191
9:28 187
9 to 10:18 186
10:10 187
10:14 187
10:15 187
10:19–39 187,
              190
10:28 f. 137

10:29 ..... 70, 185,
          190, 191
10:32 189
10:32–39 189
11:7 187
12:1–29 ... 187, 191
13:7, 17, 24 ... 80,
              85
13:24 185

James
1:5 185
1:8 184
1:15 ...... 183, 186
1:22 184
1:26 184
2:1 195
2:4 184
2:14 184
2:15 184
2:26 182
3:13–18 89
3:15 198
3:17 185
4:1 183
4:2 183
4:3 f. 183
4:4 184
4:4, 13 184
4:5 183
4:6 183
4:8 184
5:1 ff. 184
5:14 ...... 95, 146

I Peter
1:2 192
1:3–5 193
1:5 193
1:6–9 193
1:7 195
1:8, 13 193
1:9 193
1:10–12 192,
          193, 194
1:11 ..... 182, 193,
          195, 196
1:20 ...... 192, 193
2:2 193

2:2 f. 189
2:5 193
2:19 193
2:21, 23 f. 193
3:14, 17 193
3:18 193
3:18 f. 196
3:18 f., 22 192,
                193
3:18–22 36
3:21 193
4:1, 13 193
4:1, 15 f., 19 ... 193
4:6 ... 192, 193, 196
4:10 92
4:12–16 195
4:13 194
4:14 ..... 185, 192,
                195
4:17–19 195
5:1 ... 85, 193, 194
5:1–5 146
5:1–11 80
5:3 60
5:8 195
5:9 f. 193

II Peter
1 196
1:3 196
1:10 196
1:11 196
1:16 197
1:20 ..... 192, 196
2:1 198
2:17–19 198
3:15 f. 141, 197

I John
1:2 170
1:3 ...... 175, 177
1:9 176
2:1 176
2:2 178
2:18 178
2:20 176
2:20, 27 175
2:22 178
2:23 178

2:27 176
2:28 177
2:29 155
3:1, 2 155
3:9 155
3:19–24 176
3:20 176
3:23 177
3:24 ...... 177, 178
4:1 179
4:1–6 ..... 95, 176,
                178
4:2 179
4:2 f. 160
4:3 179
4:7 155
4:10 178
4:13 178
4:13–16 ... 176, 177
4:14 ..... 170, 178
4:15 f. 178
5:1, 4, 18 155
5:2 155
5:6 180
5:6–12 176
5:7 ...... 159, 170,
              180, 181
5:8 180
5:13–17 177
5:14 177

II John
1 147

III John
1 147
12 170

Jude
3–4 ...... 198, 199
5–16 ..... 198, 199
17–23 198
19 198
19 f. 192
20 199
22 f. 199
24 f. 200

Revelation
1:1 201
1:3 ...... 204, 206
1:4 .... 24, 200, 206
1:4, 11, 20 75
1:5 206
1:7 32
1:9 206
1:9 to 3:22 202
1:10 202
1:19 202
2:7 .... 201, 205
2:7, 11, 17,
   29 .. 75, 201, 205
2:11 205
2:12 205
2:17 205
2:21 205
2:23 204
2:24 90
2:26–29 205
3:1 24
3:5 205
3:6, 13, 22 ... 201,
                205
4:1 ...... 202, 203
4:1 to 5:14 202
4:2 202
4:4, 10 147
4:5 .... 24, 201
5:1–14 202
5:2, 5, 9 133
5:6 .... 24, 201
5:11, 14 147
6:1, 3, 5, 7,
   9, 12 133
6:4 166
7:13 147
7:17 161
8:1 133
11:6 51
14:13 204
16:13 95
16:15 204
17:1 ...... 203, 204
17:3 203
19:9 ...... 204, 205
19:10 ..... 185, 205
19:20 95

20:6	204	22:1	161	22:16	75
20:10	95	22:7	204	22:17	206
20:12 f.	204	22:8 f.	206	22:18 f.	206
21:9	206	22:12	204	22:20	206
21:9 f.	204	22:12 f., 16	206		
21:10	204	22:14	204		

INDEX

OF NAMES

ANCIENT AND MEDIEVAL

Apostles' Creed, 62, 71
Arius, 169
Augustine, 62, 90, 134, 170, 178, 183

Barnabas, 185

Calixtus, 169
Cerinthus, 180
Charlemagne, 25
Charles the Bald, 25
Chrysostom, 62
Clement of Alexandria, 150
Cyril of Alexandria, 62

Damas of Magnesia, 147
Didache, 95
Domitian, 182, 200

Eshnunna Law Code, 48
Eusebius, 44, 216n1

Gregory Nazianzus, 62
Gregory of Nyssa, 56, 62

Harleianus, 154
Helvidius, 45

Ignatius, 147, 202
Irenaeus, 47, 62, 132

Jerome, 45, 47, 62
Justin Martyr, 47, 148, 154, 162 f., 189

Melchizedek, 186
Midrash, 37, 61

Nero, 195, 200
Nicene Creed, 104, 160, 169

Onesimus of Ephesus, 147
Origen, 47, 62, 154 f., 162, 163, 169

Paul of Alexandria, 62 f.
Philo Judaeus, 45, 92
Plato, 46, 152, 167
Plutarch, 46
Polybius of Tralles, 147
Polycarp of Smyrna, 130, 147
Praxeas, 169
Priscillian, 180

Rabanus Maurus, 25
Ras Shamra (Ugarit), 46
Richard of St.-Victor, 170
Rufinus, 62
Rule of Qumran, 35 f.

Sabellius, 169
Samson, 15, 50
Septuagint, 47
Socrates, 167, 172

Tacitus, 195
Talmud, 34 f.
Tertullian, 71, 169

Wycliffe, John, 164

REFORMATION AND MODERN

Aytoun, R. A., 211n22

Baillie, John, 13
Barclay, William, 62, 124, 212n7, 214 f.nn2, 5, 8
Barnett, Maurice, 212nn15, 16
Barrett, C. K., 33, 34, 41 f., 151 f., 162 f., 164, 210n1, 211n13, 216n3, 217n21
Barrosse, Thomas, 216n2
Barth, Karl, 46, 211n18
Barth, Gerhard, 211n20
Beasley-Murray, G. R., 211n15, 213n24
Behm, J., 162
Berkhof, H., 219n36
Bernard, J. H., 162
Best, Ernest, 38, 210n7
Betz, Otto, 217n20
Beyschlag, W., 62
Block-Hoell, Nils, 214n7
Boismard, M.-E., 162
Borgen, Peder, 217n16
Bornkamm, Günther, 211n20
Bosch, David, 211n17
Boslooper, Thomas, 211n18
Braun, F.-M., 162
Bring, Ragnar, 214n1
Bromiley, G. W., 213n26
Brown, Raymond E., 162, 216n4, 217nn17, 18, 19, 22
Bruce, F. F., 218nn9, 11
Bultmann, Rudolf, 162
Büchsel, Friedrich, 9

Calvin, John, 141, 178, 190, 215n10
Campenhausen, Hans von, 211n18
Carver, W. O., 212n2
Chafer, Lewis Sperry, 213n20
Colwell, E. C., 152, 179, 216n7, 217n29
Conybeare, F. C., 211n17
Conzelmann, Hans, 54, 212n3
Corell, Alf, 217n14
Cullmann, Oscar, 38

Daniélou, Jean, 210n8, 217n24

236

Daube, David, 36, 143, 210n6, 216n15
Davies, J. G., 212n10
Davies, W. D., 212n8, 214n4
De Fiori, Joachim, 206
De Haan, Martin R., 179, 217n28
Delitzsch, F., 47
Dibelius, M., 139
Dix, Gregory, 216n16
Dodd, C. H., 35, 63 f., 162, 175 f., 217n25
Duncan, George, 214n8
Dupont-Sommer, A., 211n16

Easton, Burton Scott, 62
Eissfeldt, Otto, 209n6
Erasmus, 180
Estes, J. R., 212n18

Fisher, J. D. C., 213n26
Fison, J. E., 31, 210n17
Fletcher, Joseph, 214n3
Foakes-Jackson, F. J., 212n19
Foster, Michael B., 215n7
Fuller, Reginald, 214n5, 215n6

Gealy, F. D., 139
Gilmore, Alec, 216n21
Glasson, T. F., 218n23
Glaze, R. E., Jr., 190, 217n4
Goulder, M. D., 63, 212nn3, 17
Graves, J. R., 169, 217n23
Greeven, Heinrich, 213n2
Guilding, Aileen, 161
Guthrie, Donald, 139

Haenchen, Ernst, 59, 213n30
Harkness, Georgia, 218n36
Harnack, Adolf von, 61, 65 f.
Harrison, E. F., 139
Heidel, Alexander, 210n16
Held, Heinz Joachim, 211n20
Hendry, George S., 216n22, 219n36
Henry, A. M., 209 f.nn1, 11
Hermann, Ingo, 214n11
Higgins, A. J. B., 139
Hobbs, Herschel H., 190, 217n4
Hoekema, Anthony A., 214n7

Hölscher, Gustav, 210n11
Hoskyns, E. C., 151 f., 162, 216n5

Jeremias, Joachim, 37 f., 55 f., 65, 139, 162, 211n23, 213n23
Jones, Rufus M., 218n35

Käsemann, Ernst, 59, 77, 212n4, 213n31
Keck, Leander E., 212n5
Kelly, J. N. D., 139, 212n11
Kittel, G., 9, 210n7
Koehler, Ludwig, and Baumgartner, Walter, 211n19a
Krajewski, Ekkehard, 214n7
Kramer, Werner, 214n5, 215n6
Kuyper, Abraham, 212 f.n19

Ladd, George E., 203, 218n30
Lake, Kirsopp, 63, 212n19
Lampe, G. W. H., 148, 210n13, 213nn22, 26, 27, 215n5, 216n20
Laski, Marghanita, 209n3
Leaney, A. R. C., 211n24
Leenhardt, Franz J., 124, 215n8
Lightfoot, R. H., 162
Lindblom, J., 209nn2, 4, 5
Lock, W., 139
Lohmeyer, Ernst, 41, 201
Lohse, Eduard, 216n13
Luther, Martin, 45
Lys, Daniel, 209n1

MacGregor, G. H. C., 49, 77, 162, 212n6, 213n33
Machen, J. Gresham, 47
Manson, William, 185, 217n1
Mantel, Hugo, 213n28
Martyn, J. Louis, 212n5
Mauser, Ulrich W., 37, 210n9
Meinertz, M., 139
Michael, J. Hugh, 215n2
Michaelis, Wilhelm, 162, 212n15, 214n6
Mollat, G., 162
Moody, Dale, 211n19, 213nn35, 3, 214nn10, 12, 215nn9, 4, 216n11, 218nn14, 19, 20, 21
Morton, A. Q., 49, 212n6

Nestle, Eberhard, 154
Neunheuser, Burkhard, 210n13
Nichol, John Thomas, 214n7

Parry, J., 139
Paul, Robert S., 216n17
Pierson, Arthur T., 211n1
Pink, Arthur W., 190
Prümm, Karl, 214n11
Purdy, Alexander C., 191

" Q," 49 f., 53 ff.
Quirant, Cortes, 162

Rackham, R. B., 59
Ramm, Bernard, 215n7
Ramsay, W. M., 107
Reicke, Bo, 218n17
Rengstorf, Karl, 162
Richardson, H. Neil, 209n7
Rist, Martin, 201, 218n25
Robertson, A. T., 111, 189 ff., 217n5
Robinson, J. M., 38, 40, 210n10
Roddy, Clarence S., 189 f., 218n6
Rowley, H. H., 19 f., 209 f.nn8, 10, 15

Schlatter, A., 162
Schweitzer, Albert, 176, 217n26
Schweizer, Eduard, 9, 100, 140, 161, 162, 200 f., 205, 213n1, 215n1
Scott, E. F., 139
Selwyn, E. G., 218n18
Simpson, E. K., 139
Smith, Dwight Moody, 216n10
Spicq, C., 139
Stagg, Frank, 213n29
Stanley, D. M., 162
Starkey, Lycurgus M., Jr., 219n36
Steinmann, Jean, 210n4
Stephanus, 180
Strack, H. L., and Billerbeck, P., 48
Streeter, B. H., 49 f., 53, 56
Swete, H. B., 9

Taylor, Vincent, 34, 37 f., 210n3
Tennyson, Alfred, 217n27

237

Thurian, Max, 215n12
Titus, Eric L., 152, 179, 216n7, 217n29

Unnik, W. C. van, 213n25

Vielhauer, Philipp, 213 f.n4
Volz, Paul, 209n11

Wainwright, Arthur W., 192, 218n13
Walvoord, John F., 203, 218n28
Weiss, Johannes, 215n6
Westcott, B. F., 156, 216n12, 217n3

Wilckens, Ulrich, 212n5
Williams, Charles B., 114, 130
Windisch, Hans, 164, 217n20
Wingren, Gustaf, 215n3
Wordsworth, William, 13
Wuest, Kenneth, 190

Yates, J. E., 35 f., 210n5
Ysebaert, J., 216n19

Zahn, Theodor, 162
Zwingli, Ulrich, 160

INDEX

OF SUBJECTS

Abba, 42, 55 ff., 110, 121 f.
" Amen," 102 f.
Apostasy, 140, 186 ff., 198 ff.
Arrabōn, 105 f., 133 f.

Baptism, 34 f., 58 f., 71 ff., 121,
    147 ff.
    blessings of Spirit at, 65 ff.
    infant, 148
    initiation into church, 147 ff.
    of John the Baptist, 34 f., 150 ff.,
        laying on of hands at, 64, 68,
        71 ff., 79, 142 f., 148 f.
    with the Spirit, 34 f., 58 f., 64 f.,
        83, 96 f., 138, 150 f.
    in the Trinity, 44 f., 71 ff.
    with water, 34 f., 58, 64, 154 f.
Benedictus, the, 52

Charisma, charismata, 80, 97 f.,
    143 ff.
Church
    body of Christ, 97 f., 134, 136
    bride of Christ, 206 f.
    God's militia, 138 f.
    ministries, 60, 67 ff., 79 f., 85 ff.,
        97, 145 f.
    worship, 86 f., 98 ff., 145 f.

Dabar, 20, 23 f., 27
Diakonia, 67 f.

Ecstasy, 14 ff.
    ecstatic power, 15 ff.
    prophetic, 17 ff.

Eschatology, 23 f., 117, 124 f.,
    145, 147, 167, 200 ff. *See also
    Parousia*
    " realized eschatology," 35, 87,
        167
Eucharist, Lord's Supper, 60, 72,
    83, 99, 160 f.

Filioque, 168 ff.
Frühkatholizismus, 59 f.

Glossolalia, speaking in tongues,
    20, 71 ff., 78 f., 86
    Corinth, 86 f.
    Pentecost, 61 ff., 71 ff., 95 ff.
    regulation, 100 f.
    significance, 99 f.
Great Commission, the, 44, 49

Inspiration, 23 f., 95 f., 139 ff.,
    185 f.
    and interpretation, 197 f.
    prophetic, 23 f., 52 f., 95 f.
    and revelation, 135
    of Scripture, 139 ff., 185 f.,
        196 f.
    of Spirit, 20, 23 f., 135

Jesus Christ, 45 ff., 55 f., 178 ff.
    baptism, 36, 53 f., 150 f., 180
    birth, 47 ff., 50 ff.
    humanity, 45 ff., 175, 178 ff.
    incarnation, 151 ff., 179 f.
    Spirit-giver, the, 157

239

Stronger One, the, 39 f.
temptation, 37 ff., 43 ff.

Koinōnia, 66 f., 106, 150 f., 175 ff.
  with the Father, 176 ff.
  with the Son, 176, 178 f.

Laying on of hands, 74 f., 79,
  142 ff., 148 f.

Martyria, 66 f.

Nebhi'im, 15 ff., 50, 53
Neshamah, 11 f., 29 f.
  of living creatures, 11 f., 29 f.
  of the living God, 11 f.
Nunc Dimittis, the, 52 f.

Ordination, 25, 142 ff.
  congregational, 68 f., 75 f.
  laying on of hands at, 142 ff.,
    146

Paraclete, 164 ff.
  as guide, 173 ff.
  as helper, 164 ff.
  as judge, 171 ff.
  as teacher, 166 f.
  as witness, 168 ff.
Paradise, 11 ff., 24, 37 f., 161
Parousia, 61, 87, 117, 145, 166 f.,
  196 f.
Parrēsia, 65, 176 ff., 186
Pentecost, 32, 60 ff., 65 f., 138
  " Baptist," 76
  Gentile, 72 ff.
  Samaritan, 69 ff.
Pneuma, 13, 35, 45 ff., 98 f.,
  116 f., 129 ff., 153 ff., 172 f.,
  176, 182 ff., 196

Ruach, 13 ff., 142 f.
  ecstatic, 14 ff.
  evil, 17 f., 20
  God's power, 13
  God's presence, 13, 30 f.
  holy, 30 f.
  in: Amos, 20 ff.; Balaam, 26,
    29 f.; Bezalel, 29; Daniel,

29; Elijah and Elisha, 17 ff.,
  50 f.; Ezekiel, 21 ff.; Gideon, 15; Isaiah, 30; Jacob,
  14; Jepthah, 15; Joel, 32;
  Joseph, 29; Othniel, 15;
  Rebekah, 14; Samson, 15,
  50 f.; Saul and David,
  15 ff., 26 f., 41; Zechariah,
  31 f.; Zedekiah and Mi-
  caiah, 17, 197
  messianic, 19 ff., 22, 25 ff.
  vital force in man, 14

Salvation history, 81, 85
Sanctification, 84 f.
  consecration to Christ, 88 f.
  separation from sin, 88 f.
  of the Spirit, 126
Satan, 27, 38 ff., 54, 140, 170
  Beelzebul controversy, 36 f., 43,
    54 ff.
  Strong One, the, 39 f.
Shophetim, 15 ff., 29, 50, 53
Spirit of God, Holy Spirit, the.
  See also Paraclete, Pneuma,
  Ruach, and Trinity
  age of, 156 f.
  and apostasy, 188 ff.
  baptism with, 34 ff.
  begetting of, 153 ff.
  blasphemy against, 34, 41
  blessings of, 65 ff.
  as creator, 27 ff., 159
  descent upon Jesus, 53 f., 150 f.
  dwelling of, 119 ff.
  and edification, 87 ff.
  fellowship of, 130
  filling of, 65, 76, 137
  firstfruits of, 122 f.
  freedom and, 110 f., 125
  fruit of, 112 f.
  gifts of, 24 f., 93 ff.
  of glory, 192 ff.
  of grace, 185 ff.
  grief of, 137
  intercession of, 123 f.
  and justification, 108 ff.
  law of, 118
  leading of, 121

life in, 120 f.
love of, 126
mind of, 118 f.
and organization, 139 ff.
outpouring of, 64, 81
partaking of, 188
as power, 34 ff., 42, 57, 83, 163
power of, 125 f., 135
as presence, 42 ff.
and proclamation, 83 ff.
as promise, 57
of prophecy, 200 ff.
and recapitulation, 131 ff.
and salvation, 116 ff., 194 f.
seal of, 133, 155 f.
supply of, 109, 129
sword of, 138

as truth, 158 f.
as unitive Being, 183
unity of, 136
of wisdom, 182 ff.
witness of, 121 f.

Trinity, Trinitarian, 44 ff., 76 f.,
   104, 106, 126 f., 157, 169,
   192 f., 198 ff., 206
economic, 170
psychological, 90
temple of, 134
unity in, 93

Virgin birth, the, 47 ff., 211n19

Wonder births, 47 f.